ADVANCES in RESEARCH and PRACTICE in SELF-DIRECTED LEARNING

Huey B. Long and Associates

Manufactured in the United State of America.

International Standard Book Number ISBN 0-9622488-2-7
Library of Congress Catalog Card Number #89-69871

CONTENTS

TABLES AND FIGURES

Tables

Figures

PREFACE

Advances in Research and Practice in Self-Directed Learning is based on selected papers presented at the Third North American Symposium on Adult Self-Directed Learning held at the University of Oklahoma February 26-28, 1989. Since its inception in 1986 the symposium has enlarged its audience and participation beyond North America. Papers presented at the most recent symposium were delivered by scholars from Australia, Nigeria and the United Kingdom as well as the United States.

Interest in self-direction in learning, as a topic of research and practice, has continued to increase since the late 1960s. As discussed in the first chapter of this publication it appears that some conceptual barriers are gradually giving way to additional ways of thinking about self-directed learning. Evidence is revealed in the papers presented at the past three symposia. At the first symposium, consensus on the vagueness of the term was evident. Also, papers eventually published in Self-Directed Learning: Application & Theory (Long and Associates, 1988) emphasized the non-linear nature of learning. Cavaliere's chapter in this volume provides additional support for the premise. In Self-Directed Learning: Emerging Theory & Practice (Long and Associates, 1989) many of the authors discussed various concepts of learner power or control as it relates to self-direction in learning. A progression is observable in this volume as additional explication of various elements (including learner control) may be manifested in self-directed learning. While progress in conceptualizing self-direction in learning is noticeable it is also apparent that we continue to have a great distance to go in developing sound theoretical foundations for self-directed learning.

This volume also illustrates increasing interest in application. Three of the eleven chapters in Self-Directed Learning: Application & Theory deal with application. Also, three of the ten chapters in Self-Directed Learning: Emerging Theory & Practice relate to application. Five of the fifteen chapters included here have practice dimensions. Thus, the papers and the chapters eventually selected for publication reveal dynamic research and theory bases of self-direction in adult learning.

Huey B. Long
January, 1990

REFERENCES

H. Long and Associates (1988). Self-directed learning: Application & theory. Athens, GA: Adult Education Dept., University of Georgia.

H. Long and Associates (1989). Self-directed learning: Emerging theory & practice. Norman, OK: Oklahoma Research center for Continuing Professional and Higher Education, University of Oklahoma.

Chapter One

CHANGING CONCEPTS OF SELF-DIRECTION IN LEARNING

Huey B. Long

Those familiar with the literature concerning self-direction in adult learning will observe that the concept of self-directed learning is gradually changing. The chapters in this book indicate the nature of the change. But, the change is a timid one; boldness and courage in addressing some of the basic differences among ideas is limited. The change increasingly challenges the idea that self-direction in learning must be simplistically conceptually limited to (a) complete independence of the learner from a teacher or institution, (b) an all-or-nothing condition, (c) self-directed learning as an educational method, technique or delivery procedure and (d) self-directed learning as a personality characteristic, hence the label self-directed learners (Long, 1988). For example, the first conceptualization restricts the use of the self-directed learning label to the Robinson Crusoe type of learning activities and to individuals in solitary learning conditions. Proponents of the second idea insists on describing and defining self-directed learning as an absolute quantity. Accordingly, for them, to suggest the possibility of degrees of self-direction is inappropriate. Third, self-direction as an educational method, technique or delivery procedure limits discussion of the idea to correspondence study, computer assisted instruction, educational radio and television or similar methods. Finally, the fourth idea equates self-directed learning with a personality characteristic. More and more writers on self-directed learning are revealing dissatisfaction with the above simplistic concepts.

The increasing varieties of conceptualizations of self-directed learning have both positive and negative consequences. The positive aspects are found in a kind of progressive trend. The trend is from Allen Tough's (1971) useful, but restrictive learning projects ideas to Malcolm Knowles (1970) productive, but also limiting andragogical concepts. Each of the earlier positions as introduced by Tough and Knowles were singular or exclusive. According to the learning projects formulation the kind of learning of interest was the self-teaching that occurred beyond institutional provision. While the andragogical approach esponsed by Knowles focused on what has been referred to as self-teaching within an institutional provision. The obvious critical difference between the positions were never addressed by enthusiasts for self-directed learning. We blindly proceeded as if Knowles and Tough were writing about the same thing. But were they? There is at least one thing common to their positions, but there is also at least one significant difference. They agreed on a relatively consistent set of procedures, such as goal setting, identification of resources and evaluation, to be followed by the learner. Yet they disagreed on the location or sponsorship of the activity. The difference may be described as personally sponsored learning versus institutionally sponsored activity. The idea of locus of sponsorship is potentially an important one that generally is generally neglected in the literature. Personal sponsorship connotes not only personal control, but personal ownership also. Institutional sponsorship connotes a social ownership of the instructional activity. Thus, even in those institutionally based situations where great freedom of choice, e.g. high personal control, is available the question of ownership is likely to have an impact on the learning-teaching transaction. Implications of these differences have not been adequately addressed. Thomas (1967) is one writer who has come close to discussing the problem in his article on studentship versus membership.

The positive aspects of recent trends as revealed in several of the following chapters is the recognition that both Knowles' and Toughs' concepts inadequately define a robust concept of self-directed learning. Hence, at least two additional formulations that include self-directed learning as a personality characteristic and consideration of the possibility that we should discuss self-directed learning in terms of degrees are joining the two older concepts.

The negative aspect of the above developments is a general timidity of recasting self-directed learning in a broader, more comprehensive and inclusive framework. Commendable efforts in that direction are found in the following chapters by Candy, Gerstner, Jarvis and Sgroi. However, we must go beyond their ideas and search for a means of expressing self-direction in learning in its most robust form rather than in its most anemic concept. We need a conceptualization that sufficiently provides for each of the four variables of (a) institutional relationship, (b) personal responsibility/choice, (c) personality and (d) instructional methods, techniques and delivery procedures. We need to reject out-of-hand two frequently appearing positions: (a) the opinion that self-direction in learning is only an absolute entity, e.g. it is an all-or-nothing phenomena; and (b) the suggestion that self-direction in learning is only an extra-institutional phenomena, e.g. it occurs only when learners are unaffiliated with institutionally sponsored activities.

Finally, it would be beneficial if we agreed that self-directed learning is a verb. It is a process and to imply that it is a noun or consequence only muddles the concept. Recognition of self-directed learning as a verb implies action and also provides for representation of the activity at some intersection with personality, instructional method or technique and other variables. To restrict learning to a verb may also help us to differentiate between self-directed learning and the self-directed learner. The one refers to an activity whereas the other refers to a person. Such an observation may be so obvious as to appear to be an unnecessary comment. Yet, the distinction between what Tough's learning projects research was all about and Knowles' ideas about self-directed learning is equally apparent, nevertheless we proceeded as if they were one and the same. So, perhaps it is necessary for us to note that the terms self-directed learning and self-directed learner refer to different things.

If we could agree to discard the earlier simplistic ideas and accept a more complex concept for self-directed learning that integrates several important variables we would address many criticisms. For example, as long as we tend to think of self-directed learning solely as a procedure characterized by certain pedagogically constructed activities as discussed by Jarvis in chapter three we may arrive at questionable conclusions, e.g. that self-direction in learning is a unitary and absolute phenomena. As long as we think of self-direction in learning only as a solitary non-institutionally sponsored activity as the Wright brothers' activity discussed by Cavaliere in chapter nine we cannot write about self-direction in settings such as noted by Sgroi in chapter eleven. To limit the concept to the learner's personality keeps us from investigating instructional principles that might be used to stimulate learner activity and choice as discussed by Long and Agyekum in chapter 13.

A robust theory of self-directed learning would provide for the contingent characteristic of the phenomena. In other words, such a theory would address the relative contributions of environmental, personal and social variables to the learning process and the degree to which that learning activity would be characterized as self-directed. Consequently, we should theorize about the conditions necessary to overcome an extremely passive orientation to learning as well as those conditions that inhibit even those with the most active orientation. One way of representing the major components of theory of self-directed learning is suggested in Figure 1.1.

Figure 1.1: A Graphic Illustration of Suggested Major Components in Self-Directed Learning.

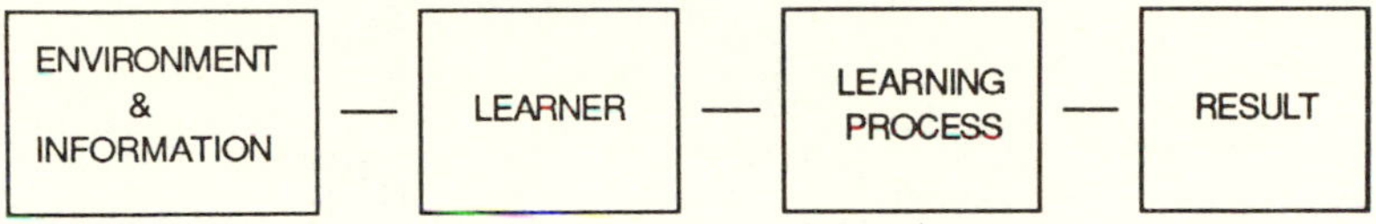

It is obvious that the same components may be equally appropriate to other-directed learning. However, Figure 1.2 illustrates an abstract way of differentiating between the two kinds of learning.

Figure 1.2: A Graphic Illustration of Areas of Influence, Equally Depicted, in Major Components in Learning. (The shaded area indicates variables that may contribute to other-directed learning while the unshaded area represents contribution to self-directed learning.)

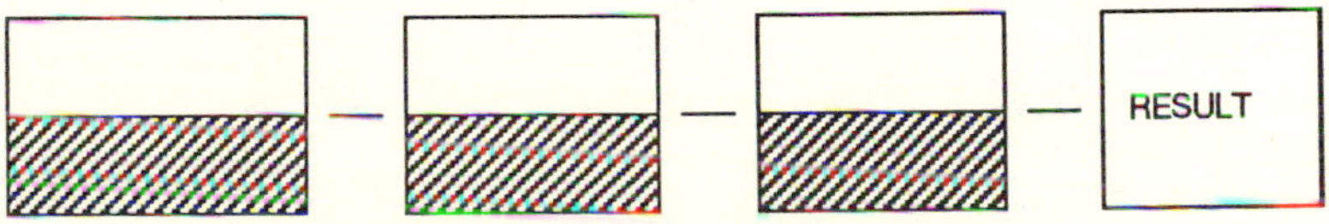

Finally, Figure 1.3 illustrates how a variation among the major components for two different individuals or the same individual at different times may have differential impact. As a result learner X may be self-directing in condition A and other-directed in condition B, while learner Y is other-directed in his or her learning as shown.

FIGURE 1.3: A Graphic Illustration of Different Combinations of Major Components in Learning.

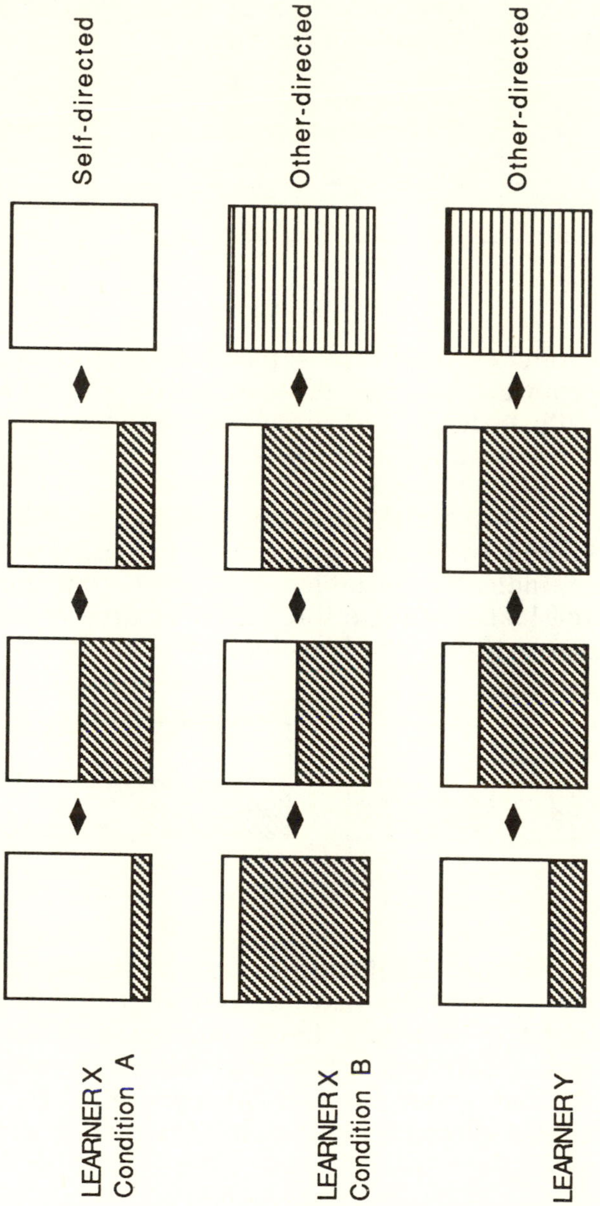

Figure 1.3 illustrates how a major variation in environmental conditions and a major change in learning processes may result in an other-directed learning episode for Learner X. This illustration for Learner Y suggests that environmental conditions favorable to self-directed learning may not be sufficient to off-set the other-directed impacts of learner variables and learning process variables.

CONCLUSIONS

The trend toward multiple concepts of self-directed learning has both positive and negative aspects. Most importantly it reflects a dissatisfaction with efforts to define self-directed learning by a selected simplistic condition or variable. Unfortunately, we yet need to develop an inclusive concept that recognizes that self-direction in learning is a relative behavior that may be contingent upon the interaction of several variables. Some of those variables, broadly defined, have been discussed in this chapter. They include environment (which may be broadly conceived to include pedagogical activities), personal characteristics of the learner other than metacognitive elements, and metacognition or learning process.

REFERENCES

Knowles, M. (1970). The modern practice of adult education: Andragogy versus pedagogy. New York: Association Press.

Long, H. (1988). Self-directed learning: Emerging theory and practice. In H. Long and Associates, Self-directed learning: Emerging theory and practice. Norman, Oklahoma: Oklahoma Research Center for Continuing Professional and Higher Education, University of Oklahoma, 1-12.

Thomas, A. (1967). Studentship and membership: A study of roles in learning. The Journal of Educational Thought, 1 (1), 65-76.

Tough, A. (1971). The adult's learning projects: A fresh approach to theory and practice in adult learning. Toronto: The Ontario Institute for Studies in Education.

Chapter Two

THE TRANSITION FROM LEARNER-CONTROL TO AUTODIDAXY: MORE THAN MEETS THE EYE*

Philip C. Candy

Since the mid 1960s, the notion of self-direction has attained something of a cult status in the literature of adult education. It has been (and is) claimed as central in both the theory and practice of almost every imaginable form of educational endeavor. For instance, self-direction has been advocated both because it contributes to the development of the whole person, and on the instrumental grounds that it allows people to be more responsive to the rapidly changing demands of a market-oriented workplace. Similarly, it is supported by those who espouse the "rugged individualism" of the United States, and the more conservative and conformist social system of the USSR. It is envisaged by some as a useful adjunct to the traditional education system, and by others as a radical alternative to school-based learning. Overall, it is clear that self-direction is indeed a versatile concept. However it seems likely that any term that can be used by such a diverse range of authors might also mask a certain conceptual confusion. It is the purpose of this paper firstly to identify and distinguish some of the various uses and meanings of the phrase self-direction, and secondly to explore the implications for research of distinguishing some of these various meanings from one another.

---

*A portion of this chapter has been published in Studies in Continuing Education, 10, (2), 1988 under the title "Key Issues for Research in Self-Directed Learning". Permission to reprint is gratefully acknowledged.

GOAL AND PROCESS

The first major distinction to be examined is that between self-direction as a goal, and as a process. For many authors, self-direction is seen simply as a method of organizing instruction. For others, self-direction is not so much a method of teaching as a characteristic of learners. Thus, Skager (1984) and Cheren (1983) are clearly referring to a personal quality or characteristic of learners.

In fact, self-direction is increasingly viewed not simply as an attribute which people either have, or do not, but as a quality which may be present in varying degrees. Kasworm (1983) presents a model of increasing self-directedness and, since the appearance of Guglielmino's Self-Directed Learning Readiness Scale (1977), there has been a succession of studies based on the notion that self-direction is a measurable attribute, distributed throughout the adult population.

In itself, the use of the same term for these two phenomena is not particularly problematic; it is usually possible to tell from the context whether the author has in mind self-directedness as an activity or as an outcome. It does have less desirable consequences however, where it is implicitly assumed that there is a necessary connection between one concept and the other. In other words, many people seem to believe that participation in self-directed learning will inevitably lead to the development of self-directedness in some wider sense. Mezirow states explicitly what many adult education theorists seem to believe tacitly:

> It is almost universally recognized, at least in theory, that central to the adult educator's function is a goal and method of self-directed learning. Enhancing the learner's ability for self-direction in learning as a foundation for a distinctive philosophy of adult education has breadth and power. It represents the mode of learning characteristic of adulthood. (1981, p. 21)

It seems to me that this quote embodies an error in thinking to which Hamm alluded, namely that "of mistaking the means for the end ... making no distinction between the characteristics of an ideal end product and the characteristics of the process that is supposed to lead to such a product" (Hamm, 1982, p. 102).

It may well prove to be the case that self-direction as a philosophical ideal is actually promoted by self-directed methods of learning. This is a plausible assumption, but it is little more than that, and until empirical evidence is available to establish a connection between these two ideas, I will draw a distinction between the "method" and the "goal".

The Method of Self-Directed Learning

Having separated self-direction as a goal from self-direction as a method of education, the question which presents itself is this: Is there only one type of self-direction in learning, or does the method itself subdivide? Many people think and write about self-directed learning as if it were a single entity. It is presented as an alternative to other modes of conducting education and, as such, is viewed as a method like other methods: An educational experience is either self-directed, or it is directed by someone else, called a teacher.

Although some authors write as if the teacher's responsibilities and those of the learner are mutually exclusive domains that can be distinguished from one another on the basis of objective criteria, others acknowledge that control over the teaching/learning situation is more like a continuum than a dichotomy. It is perhaps useful to think of teachers and learners as occupying different positions on a continuum extending from teacher-control at one extreme to learner-control at the other, where the deliberate surrendering of certain prerogatives by the teacher is accompanied by the concomitant acceptance of responsibility by the learner or learners. In the sense that there can be a dynamically changing equilibrium in this arrangement, it is reminiscent of Mark Hopkins' famous image of the teacher on one end of a log, with the learner on the other end.

Diagrammatically, the situation may be portrayed as a continuum, where each diminution in the teacher's control may be compensated for by a corresponding increase in the learner's, so that it resembles a sliding scale from complete teacher-control at one extreme to total learner-control at the other. Both Gibbons and Phillips (1982, p. 76) and Millar et al. (1986, p. 437) utilize such diagrams to express the gradual shift in control from one party to the other. To describe this continuum, the term learner-controlled instruction will be used.

Figure 2.1: A Hypothetical Learner-Control Continuum (adapted from Millar et al., 1986, p. 437.

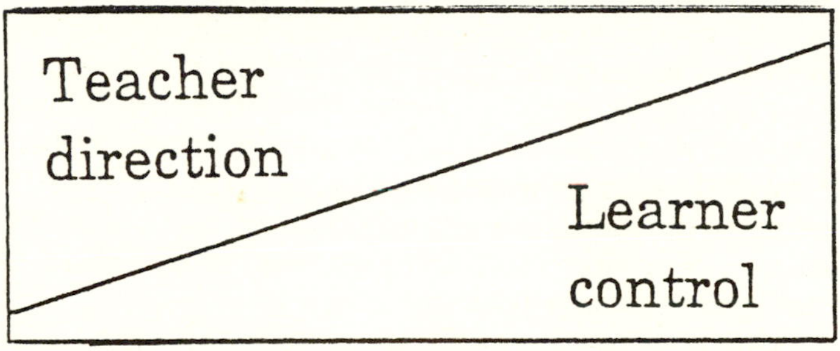

Although the term learner-control was reasonably commonplace in the 1960s (Campbell & Chapman, 1967; Mager & McCann, 1961), it suffered a decline in usage, presumably because of its unfashionable behavioristic connotations. However, it was rehabilitated by Snow in 1980 and, for the present purposes, has the advantage that it is logically possible to speak of learner-control as "both a dimension along which instructional treatments differ, and a dimension characteristic of individual differences among learners". Thus, as Snow points out, "it is perhaps the first instance of an aptitude and treatment variable being potentially definable in common terms" (1980, pp. 157-158).

If learner-control is conceived of as a range or continuum (or more likely a series of continua, for it is possible to exert differing degrees of control over various dimensions), then one end of the range will involve a great degree of learner control over valued instructional functions. Various instructional strategies could be placed at intervals along this continuum, to imply the differing balance of teacher-direction and learner-control.

Although the right-hand end of the continuum is characterized by a high degree of learner-control over many instructional elements, including the setting of objectives, choices about pacing, content and methodology, and assessment of learning outcomes, in the final analysis, it is still a method of conducting instruction, and differs in several important respects from what I will call autodidaxy, or the self-directed learning which takes place outside formal institutional settings.

One Education or Two?

In his autobiography, Edward Gibbon, stated that "every man who rises above the common level has received two educations: the first from his teachers; the second, more personal and important, from himself" (Gibbon, 1907, p. 65). This quote is interesting at two levels. First, it emphasizes the value which Gibbon placed upon self-directed learning or, as it was often called in his time, self education. In this sense, he was expressing a common (though by no means universal) belief in the ennobling power of education generally, and of self-education in particular (Houle, 1961, p. 111). Second, and more important for the present purpose, Gibbon distinguishes "the education obtained from his teachers" from that which he "received from himself". Are these really two educations, or are they just different aspects of one?

In recent years, the notion of lifelong education has provided a unifying conceptual framework for much thinking and writing about educational issues generally.

Despite Yeaxlee's use of the term lifelong education as early as 1929, it has only entered the educational lexicon in the past two decades. From the late 1960s onwards, there has been a series of publications, most of them emanating from Unesco, dealing with the concept itself, and its implications for education worldwide (Cropley, 1977, 1979, 1980; Dave, 1973, 1976; Duke, 1979; Ingram, 1979; Jessup, 1969; Lengrand, 1970; Parkyn, 1973; Skager & Dave, 1977). According to the definition adopted by the Unesco Institute of Education, lifelong education should, amongst other things, "be dependent for its successful implementation on people's increasing ability and motivation to engage in self-directed learning activities" (Cropley, 1979, p. 3).

The relationship between self-directed learning and lifelong education is a reciprocal one. On the one hand, self-directed learning is one of the most common ways in which adults pursue learning throughout their lifespan, as well as being a way in which people supplement (and at times substitute for) learning received in formal settings. On the other hand, lifelong learning takes, as one of its principal aims, equipping people with skills and competencies required to continue their own self-education beyond the end of formal schooling. In this sense, self-directed learning is viewed simultaneously as a means and an end of lifelong education.

Thus, the lifelong project of self-development and self-actualization - as Jankovic et al. put it: " the beautiful and arduous task of becoming a person" (1979, p. 1) - is consistent with, and facilitated by, a system of lifelong education (Skager, 1984, p. 8), and accordingly there can only be one education. In this view, learner-controlled instruction would be contiguous with self-directed learning outside formal institutional settings (autodidaxy), and indeed the indiscriminate application of the term self-direction to both phenomena has done much to blur the distinction between the two.

It is easy to see how the confusion might have arisen. Both phenomena share a number of similarities: stress on the primacy of the learner's purposes; independence of effort on the part of the learner; support or assistance rendered, rather than direct instruction. Moreover one can see why, even at a subliminal level, educationists might want to stress similarities. Autodidaxy is taken to be the paradigmatic case of autonomy in learning; autonomy, in turn, is a central notion within adult education. Autodidacts are known to be single-minded in their commitment to learning tasks, and often achieve high levels of expertise in their chosen areas of inquiry. All in all, if adult educators were able to encourage learners into autodidaxy, or even to define them into autodidaxy, such major instructional issues as motivation, relevance, meaningfulness, independence and so on, would be taken care of, ipso facto. However, let me explore the relationship in more depth.

In the same way that instructional situations may be portrayed as falling along a continuum from almost total teacher-direction at one extreme to virtual learner-control at the other, self-instructional situations are also distinguished from one another by the level of assistance sought. Thus, although the initiative for a learning project rests firmly and indisputably with the learner, it is possible that the autodidact might make extensive use of a guide or helper (or perhaps even more than one) to assist with a range of factors from emotional encouragement, to the location and utilization of specific resources, to management of the learning process itself (Danis & Tremblay, 1985b, p. 286).

This, too, may be portrayed diagrammatically (see Figure 2.2).

Figure 2.2: A Hypothetical Continuum of Autodidaxy and Assisted Autodidaxy

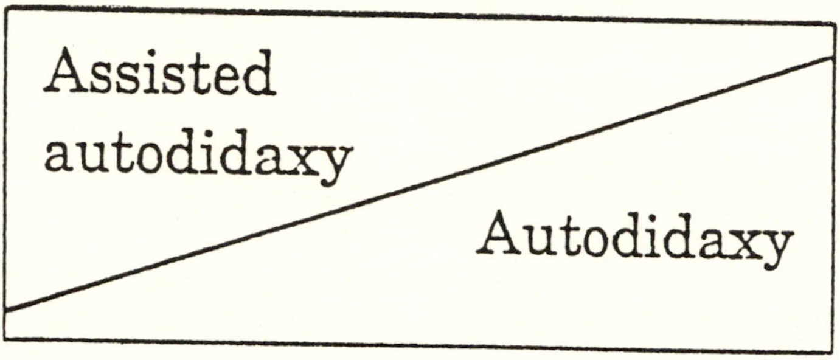

From the point of view of an outside observer, such as a researcher, it might be impossible to distinguish a situation of assisted autodidaxy from one of advanced learner-control. It is as if the two phenomena were interchangeable. This point might best be understood by reference to Figure 2.3.

Figure 2.3: The Relationship Between Autodidaxy and Learner-Control of Instruction.

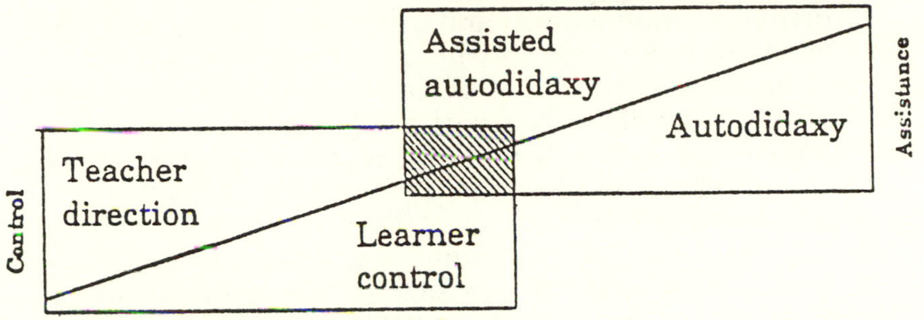

The diagram represents the simple notion that there exists a single continuum from a high degree of teacher-direction to pure autonomous learning or autodidaxy, with an area of overlap in between (the shaded area). This idea is similar to the range of learning situations (from autonomous through traditional institutional settings) discussed by Long (1989, p. 4). The area of overlap represents the intersection of domains where, from the point of view of an outside observer, it is impossible to discern whether the primary orientation is one of instruction or of self-instruction (autodidaxy). However, it is argued here that the notion of a single continuum is misleading. Independent study and assisted autodidaxy, despite their apparent similarity, are not the same. Even if the difference cannot be detected readily by an outside observer, it is still important to the respective participants, because the quality of their interaction is partly dependent on their subjective interpretations of the situation.

What, then, is the difference? It seems to depend on the notion of ownership. In the earlier learner-control diagram (Figure 2.1), it can be seen that there is still a residue, albeit small, of teacher-direction. Even though the instructor might have all but vanished, the ghost of the instructor lingers on, subtly influencing the learner's choices, and even the criteria used to make those choices. Whether symbolically or otherwise, the instructor maintains some degree of control (and hence ownership) over the instructional transaction and, in the final analysis, independent study is still a technique of instruction.

In the autodidactic domain, on the other hand, the learner is frequently unaware of being a learner, much less a student, and hence the image of an instructor is not present to begin with (Thomas, 1967). Both ownership and control are vested in the learner from the outset, and the only question is the amount and type of assistance obtained. One way of envisaging this subtle shift in ownership is to imagine these two continua rotated along their axes through 90°, so that they are viewed edge-on or in elevation, instead of from above (see Figure 2.4).

Figure 2.4: Learner-Control and Autodidaxy as "Laminated" Domains.

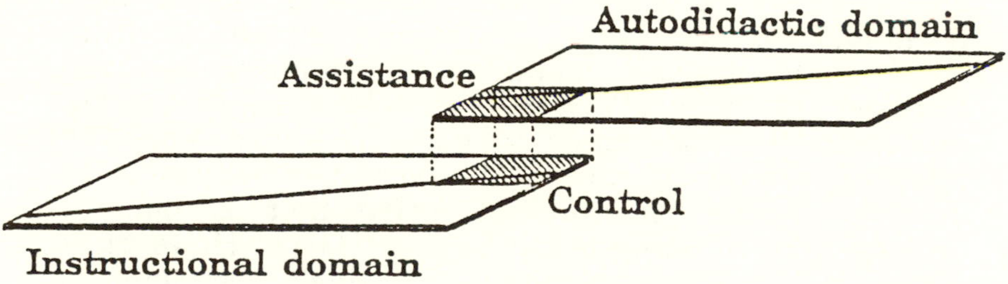

Viewed thus, it can be seen that they are not contiguous at all, but are laminated or layered. One part is concerned with who has control, the other with the assistance obtained by the learner. A researcher or other outside observer may be unable to distinguish one situation from the other. Only the participants can be certain about whether ownership has been transferred to the learner or not, and even they may be unclear, leading to the potential for mismatched expectations.

There are three reasons why it is important to distinguish these two domains from one another: Firstly confusing autodidaxy with methods of instruction may have serious repercussions for theory-building in adult education; secondly, learners and those assisting them may behave differently in the two situations, and this will influence learning outcomes; and thirdly, if there are qualitative differences between the two, then the transition from one plane or level to the other is a matter of great practical and theoretical significance.

The issue of ownership - particularly ownership of the questions which guide a learning endeavor - is actually vital to gaining an understanding both of the operational limits of self-direction in learning, and also of attempts to foster the capability for it (Hynes, 1986, p. 38). Also, as I will show, the issue of ownership has inescapable ramifications for the type of research which can be carried out into self-directed learning, because it implies the need somehow to enter into the mindset of the learner and his or her assistants to be able to distinguish one phenomenon from the other.

<u>Asking Different Questions About Self-Directed Learning</u>
The phenomenon of self-direction in learning has been a recurring theme in education for a very long time (Bouwman, 1982; Houle, 1984; Kulich, 1978; Long and Ashford, 1979; McClintock, 1982; Newsom, 1977; Tough, 1967); indeed, some would argue that self-directed learning is the prototype of all learning (Craik, 1866).

Despite its long and illustrious pedigree, however, as Long (1988, p. 1) points out, the scholarly study of self-direction is comparatively recent, dating probably from the appearance in 1961 of Houle's classic study of twenty-two continuing learners - <u>The Inquiring Mind</u>. Since then, there has been a steady development in the amount of attention to the issue, and a concomitant increase in the number of books, journal articles, conference papers and research reports dealing with aspects of the independent pursuit of learning.

An extensive survey and review of the literature, however (Candy, 1987), reveals that research in the field has been dominated by the positivist/empiricist paradigm (Candy, 1989). Although the pioneering work of Houle (1961) and Tough (1966, 1967) was rich in interpretive detail and description, many later researchers veered toward the safer, but less interesting, approaches afforded by conventional nomothetic research. In the process, they sacrificed understanding of the complexity of individuals' approaches to learning for what has ultimately proved to be unattainable: a generalized, rule-governed theory of independent enquiry (Candy, 1988a). The relatively impoverished state of recent research, combined with one or two promising glimmers of the richness awaiting an alternative approach (see, for example, Boud & Griffin, 1987; Danis & Tremblay, 1985a, 1985b; Spear & Mocker, 1984; Taylor, 1980; Tremblay & Danis, 1984) suggest the desirability of exploring self-direction from an interpretive perspective (Peters, 1988).

The search for law-like generalizations, and for mathematically precise causal relationships is perhaps most pronounced in the domain of learner-control within formal instructional settings, where researchers have frequently assumed that particular teaching strategies or curricular innovations would inevitably lead to changes in the acceptance of responsibility by learners. This tendency is also evident, although to a lesser extent, in research into self-directed learning in everyday situations (autodidaxy) where, as Brookfield (1984, 1985) points out, there has tended to be an overemphasis on the quantitative and quantifiable dimensions of such self-guided learning endeavors, commonly without regard to the quality of learning or of its meaning to individual learners. It seems that the adoption of a predominantly positivistic approach to research has inhibited the emergence of valuable research findings with respect to self direction in learning.

That such preoccupations are manifest in the research literature on self-direction seems particularly ironic, in view of the nature of the phenomenon being studied. If researchers were inquiring into the migration patterns of whole species of birds, for instance, or the behavior of large bodies of water in the open ocean, the search for law-like generalizations may seem appropriate. But self-direction, by its very nature, is distinguished by its concern for individual cases and by its emphasis on the vagaries of human motivation and interest. Researchers have repeatedly shown that self-direction is a highly individual phenomenon, yet individual differences tend to be submerged by research methods which emphasize similarities; an individual person's ability to be self-directing may well vary from one situation to another, yet research methods often ignore such situational differences; the process of self-directed learning (both autodidactic and learner-controlled situations) seems to zig-zag and to follow unpredictable patterns, but researchers have commonly assumed a linearity in the process and have employed research methods based on such means-end logic; finally, learners appear to pay attention to different features of each situation in determining their level and direction of personal autonomy, but researchers have often implicitly assumed that external and publicly observable features are the criteria by which autonomy is to be judged.

In short, some of the very features that appear as paradoxical or problematic in current research could potentially be overcome by the adoption of a research perspective which explicitly allows for such features, rather than ignoring or denying them. In order to acknowledge the unique features of self-directed learning in its various manifestations, what seems called for is a research orientation which emphasizes individuality, which acknowledges situational variability, which takes account of the apparently random and serendipitous nature of human affairs, and which above all gives due prominence to the fact that people are active choosers and participate actively in the creation of the social world of which they are a part.

The interpretive approach, it is suggested, offers such an orientation.

Central to the interpretive approaches are the personal purposes, intentions and frames of references individual actors, in this case the learners themselves, bring to bear in any circumstances. In learning situations, these influence everything from the initial willingness to engage at all, to the help sought and resources used, to the outcomes arising from the learning encounter. Yet it is precisely this perspective that is almost totally absent form most research and writing about self-direction. In the case of assistance sought by learners, little attention is given to the personal significance such help might have for the learner. In the case of an autodidactic project, one rarely encounters descriptions of what the learner feels or what he or she thinks as the project takes shape. In considering the issue of learner-control, few researchers seem sensitive to the fact that the learner's perception of being in control is more vital than some arbitrary set of circumstances engineered by the instructor.

Towards a New Research Agenda in Self Direction

If the preceding argument is accepted, what new directions and revised research questions, might researchers pursue? The purpose of this part of the chapter is to examine major issues in self-directed learning, and to develop a research agenda in the form of a number of recommendations for consideration by interested researchers.

The first corollary of adopting an interpretive perspective is that the researcher becomes aware of precisely whose perspective is being presented. The issue of self-direction at least in formal instructional settings (and to a lesser extent in situations of autodidaxy) can be viewed from the perspective of the learner as well as that of the teacher/trainer/coach/facilitator or helper. Thus, in the discussion which follows, the domain of research interest will be subdivided according to the perspective taken - that of the learner or of the person assisting the learner.

Autonomous Learning from the Learner's Perspective

Despite protestations of learner-centeredness, it is relatively unusual to encounter studies of autonomous learning, whether in formal instructional settings or in the natural societal setting, which represent the situation in the language, and from the point-of-view, of the learner. However, it has been argued that the learner's subjective construing of the situation significantly influences the strategies he or she employs, which in turn is a major factor in the outcomes obtained. This subjective construing includes at least four parts: (1) the learner's view of learning in general; (2) the learner's view of this specific learning endeavor; (3) the learner's view of assistance or direction received; and (4) the learner's view of autonomous learning and the development of personal autonomy. In the remainder of this section, these four aspects will be considered; each of these, in turn, comprises a number of subsidiary elements, related to each other in complex ways.

The learner's view of learning in general. If one were to observe learners approaching a particular learning task, it would be possible to detect a number of different strategies. To take a simple example, confronted with the need to learn a new language, one learner may approach the task with a sort of grim determination, equipped with such paraphernalia as phrasebooks and dictionaries, tape recorders and notepads. Another may choose to live among native speakers, seeking to absorb the language in all the fullness and richness of its cultural context. Such differences in learning strategy could be ascribed to different learning styles, but on what are such differences based? To some extent, learning style preference might be related to personality, but it is also related to the way in which learners view learning itself and this, in turn, depends on two things: their view of knowledge, and their approach to learning tasks.

The learner's view of knowledge. Fundamental to any study of learning - including self-directed learning, must be the learner's view of the nature of knowledge, and how this may affect his or her willingness (or ability) to be self-directed in learning (Candy, 1988b). At one extreme, it is possible to discern the view that knowledge is fixed, enduring and external; that it has to be mastered. Such an understanding implies that learners need study skills in the same way that a mountaineer requires such accoutrements as crampons, ropes and steel spikes (not to mention a head for heights!). People who view knowledge this way assume that some approaches to learning are safer than others, and that one must master the easier parts before launching an attack on the summit. Autodidacts seeing knowledge this way would try to familiarize themselves with the basics of their chosen field, before progressing to advanced levels, in the belief that basic and advanced are somehow properties of the subject matter, rather than of the learner. It will be noted that this view does not in any way imply passivity on the part of the learner, who may well have to undertake massive exertions in order to "appropriate previously constituted knowledge" (Millar et al., 1986, p. 440).

An alternative view of knowledge is that it is labile, evanescent and socially constructed. The learner is involved in actively constructing meanings and hence still requires tools, but different tools. In viewing knowledge thus, the learner becomes responsible for transforming understandings through reflection on experience (Boud, Keogh and Walker, 1985). Learning is not, and cannot be, a matter of rote memorization, nor of simply increasing knowledge, but is instead "an interpretive process aimed at the understanding of reality" (Gibbs et al., 1982, p. 134).

It has already been mentioned that, as learners become more mature they tend to see knowledge differently. Perry's (1970) work suggests that, as students progress through the university, they frequently come to view the subject they are studying in more relativistic terms, and research with autodidacts (e.g., Brookfield, 1981; Nolan, 1981) shows much the same phenomenon.

However, attaining a level of epistemological sophistication in one topic area or domain does not necessarily influence people's view of knowledge more generally. Hence it is possible for someone to have an advanced knowledge of one subject area, yet to regard something unfamiliar as an impenetrable mystery. Not unexpectedly, such a view would dramatically alter the learning strategies employed, the kind of assistance sought, and the learning outcomes obtained.

> Recommendation One. Researchers should examine how learners construe differing subject areas which they are attempting to learn. By virtue of the learners' unfamiliarity with the subject matter, this may entail research techniques which stress analogy and metaphor, and which call on the learners to describe their learning strategies in abstract or metacognitive terms.

The learner's approach to learning tasks. Acting as a sort of bridge between the learner's view of knowledge, on the one hand, and his or her view of a specific learning endeavor on the other, is the understanding of what it means to learn. As part of the research work of the Goteborg Group in Sweden, Saljo (1979) studied people's common-sense conceptions of learning. He did so directly, simply by asking them: "What do you actually mean by learning?". From the answers he has identified five distinct conceptions:

1. Learning as the increase of knowledge;
2. Learning as memorizing;
3. Learning as the acquisition of facts, procedures etc., which can be retained and/or utilized in practice;
4. Learning as the abstraction of meaning; and
5. Learning as an interpretive process aimed at the understanding of reality (Saljo, 1979, pp. 12-14).

One immediately striking feature of these five conceptions is the different views of knowledge which are implied. As Saljo observes, "A prominent feature of especially the second conception described above is the idea that knowledge is external to individuals. In contrast, the essence of conceptions four and five seems to lie very much in the emphasis on the assumption that knowledge is constructed by individuals as a result of an active effort on the part of the learner to abstract meaning from a discourse and also to relate this meaning to an outside reality" (Saljo, 1979, p. 14). Such a difference in the view of knowledge inevitably implies significant differences in the process of learning itself. This distinction is often referred to as the difference between rote and meaningful learning (Novak and Gowin, 1984).

Rote and meaningful learning demand different levels of responsibility to be accepted by the learner. In their experiment with learner-control, Millar et al. (1986) noted that students had two different answers to the question: "What kind of responsibility do I have for learning?" One view, which they labelled the old orthodoxy is typified by the response "I am responsible for appropriating previously constituted knowledge." The alternative new orthodoxy is represented by the view that "I am responsible for transforming my understandings through reflection on experience" (1986, p. 440).

It seems that this difference in perspective is analogous to the distinction between surface and deep-level approaches to learning (Biggs, 1987). The qualitative differences in learning outcomes which derive from learners' taking either a surface or a deep approach have already been discussed. However, very little research has been undertaken into the learning approaches adopted by adults in situations either of autodidaxy or of learner-control.

> Recommendation Two. Researchers should investigate with learners their orientation to new learning tasks (Hayrynen and Hayrynen, 1980), their initial choice of a surface or deep approach and the criteria used in arriving at the choice; their personal definitions of whether learning is essentially a reproductive or a transformational process; and how their views change as they engage further in the learning process.

The learner's view of this specific learning endeavor. When a learner is confronting a new learning task, he or she must make some preliminary judgements about how to approach (or orient himself or herself to) this new domain. The implicit organization of the situation will undoubtedly have an influence, including such tacit dimensions as the degree of structure already present, the nature and amount of assistance available, and other demands such as those of trainers' tests likely to cause situational adjustment. Saljo's work has already been mentioned, in which he discovered that people conventionally distinguish between learning-for-life and learning-for-school. Although this distinction has been shown to influence learners' approaches to learning tasks, it has been little investigated in adult education, even less in the domain of self-direction. Thus, the approach which a learner adopts in any particular learning endeavor will be influenced by the sort of purposes the learner has in mind and by his or her level of previous knowledge of this, or a similar field.

The learner's intentions and purposes. Intentions and purposes, although influential in shaping learners' approaches to learning generally, are rarely addressed in research into self-direction. Imagine the case of two doctors, both interested in learning more about the use of morphine in alleviating chronic pain in cancer patients. The mother of one is dying of cancer; the other is attending a conference and wants simply to be able to speak to colleagues likely to be there. Both are self-directed, both capable learners, but with entirely different levels of concern about, or commitment to, the topic. Surely this will manifest itself in the emotional orientation towards the task and the depth of understanding each might seek?

While one might describe both these situations as instrumental autodidaxy, many learners undertake their projects as ends in themselves. Many hobbyists - the kind studied by Brookfield (1981) for instance - are of this type. They are learning for the sheer joy of the subject - butterflies or steam-traction engines, ecclesiastical architecture or Argentine postage stamps - and their involvement knows no bounds. In the process of such learning, most come to think of knowledge (at least this particular slice of it) in a certain way. They are situationally autonomous in the sense that their motivation for the project comes entirely from within. They become epistemologically autonomous as they enter further and further into their chosen subject, and begin to question established expertise and conventional wisdom.

Experience suggests that what starts off as an instrumental project frequently becomes expressive, and sometimes vice versa! (Havighurst, 1964, p. 18). In their formulation of self-organized learning, Harri-Augstein and Thomas (1976) argue that a learner's strategy is developed in the light of the learner's purposes, but that these latter are not fixed. They write:

> A learning event is peculiar. The learner is purposive and yet it is in the nature of learning that you often cannot know what exactly you are going to learn until you have learned it. This means that the purpose can only be specified completely when it has been achieved ... Effective learning almost always consists of ... cycles in which purposes become progressively more clearly articulated, and the outcomes become more precise and determined and well mapped onto purposes. (p. 15)

In researching learners' purposes, it is important to avoid the assumption that purposes are fixed, and external to the learning act itself. To develop and refine methods of inquiry which reflect the changing nature of self-directed learning is a major challenge for researchers.

> Recommendation Three. Researchers could inquire into the changing nature of the learning tasks as learners engage more fully, and enter more deeply into the material, and into the changing nature of their motivation towards learning endeavors, both in instructional and autodidactic situations. They could also explore, for individual learners, the relation between these emerging purposes and the strategies the learners employ, especially with respect to the selection and use of resources and assistance.

The learner's previous knowledge. It is commonly supposed that when learners confront a domain for the first time, they come to it without any prior knowledge, and hence without preconceptions. Yet this proves to be impossible, especially in adulthood. A person learning a new language must rely on his or her knowledge of other languages for parallels (whether in grammar, syntax or vocabulary); persons learning about childrearing will inevitably refer to similar experiences, their observations of friends and relations and, perhaps most commonly, the experience of their own upbringing; one who seeks to learn physics as an adult will necessarily fall back on past experience, probably an amalgam of everyday experience (Pope, 1983), television and media explanations of phenomena, and half-remembered experiments and formulae from school. Claxton (1982) refers to these domains as gut science, lay science and school science respectively.

In an early experiment in autonomous learning, Mager and Clark (1963) comment, clearly with some surprise:

> In addition to the results just described a rather nagging phenomenon was repeatedly observed. No matter how ignorant the learners appeared to be, no matter how slowly they appeared to learn, no matter how naive they claimed to be, male or female, S's all entered the experiment with some relevant knowledge about electronics. Some Ss knew more than others, of course, and one or two had developed some rather interesting misinformation about the subject. Nonetheless, no S started with zero relevant knowledge. (p. 72)

In recent years, educators have become more aware of the frames of reference that learners bring to bear in undertaking new learning tasks. Recently there has begun a whole stream of research, particularly in science education, into learners' pre-existing understandings of scientific concepts (sometimes referred to as naive theories, misconceptions, or alternate conceptions) and how this affects classroom learning. In discussing the purpose and implications of this line of research, Driver and Erickson (1983) list several underlying assumptions, including the facts that:

1. Many students have constructed, from previous physical and linguistic experience, frameworks which can be used to interpret some of the natural phenomena which they study formally in school science classes; and

2. These student frameworks often result in conceptual confusion, as they lead to different predictions and explanations from those frameworks sanctioned by school science. (p. 39)

> Recommendation Four. Researchers should use devices such as cognitive maps (Buzan, 1978; Fisher et al., 1987; Novak & Gowin, 1984), repertory grids (Kelly, 1955; Candy, 1990; Candy, Harri-Augstein & Thomas, 1985; Thomas & Harri-Augstein, 1985) learning journals and the like, to find out what learners already know about existing domains of knowledge, and how they attempt to reconcile new learning with existing views of knowledge.

The learner's view of assistance or direction received. Learning of any type, including autodidactic learning, is not merely a mechanical function, in which a learner deals with abstract bodies of knowledge and inanimate resources. It is nearly always carried out in the context of interpersonal relationships, with a variety of emotional overtones. The relationship between an autodidact and his or her helpers is often vital to the success of learning project, but relatively little is known about the quality of the relationship from the perspective of the parties involved. In part, it might be expected that a learner's views concerning both help required and obtained, and direction received would relate to his or her self-concept as a learner. However, researchers have been slow to exploit this dimension of the learner's construing. Accordingly, this section deals with the somewhat neglected personal and interpersonal aspects of autonomous learning.

The learner's views concerning help versus direction received. A beginner in any field is likely to turn for help to those from whom help is to be expected. Past experience is the best initial guide in this. If a learner has successfully used libraries before, she or he might well turn to libraries again. If friends have previously provided the needed support and guidance, then it seems likely, at least initially, that the would-be learner would seek such help again. This is just common-sense. But how often is such common sense reflected in educational research? In the search for underlying patterns, generalizable across situations, researchers have often overlooked the simple fact that, from the point-of-view of an individual learner, what he or she is attempting is unique, not generalizable.

Research suggests that those autonomous learners with longer exposure to formal education tend to turn to experts, libraries, or teachers to help them when they want to learn something new. It also appears likely that a disadvantaged single parent, living in an impoverished inner-suburban area, would look to friends and relations for help. What might happen if the situations were reversed; if each learner were forced to rely on the sources of help selected by the other? The disadvantaged learner (who may also have left school at an early age, and mistrust books) would possibly feel confused, anxious and timid when confronted with book knowledge. He or she would probably dismiss it as abstract, irrelevant or too theoretical. The academically competent learner may feel as out-of-place, albeit for a different reason, relying for help and guidance on an assortment of well-intentioned, but ill-informed acquaintances. She or he would be likely to dismiss the advice received as unhelpful, little more than conventional wisdom and unfounded speculation. Thus, what is vital for one learner would be unacceptable to another, and vice versa. The difference resides in the cluster of connotations which each learner has built up on the basis of his or her past experiences, not necessarily on any quality inherent in the form of help itself.

For the sake of the illustration above, it has been decided to use two easily visualized stereotypes, the disadvantaged and impoverished learner versus the middle-class professional with a university education. But people are not stereotypes. Every learner is different.

> <u>Recommendation Five</u>. Instead of striving only for general laws concerning assistance with learning projects, researchers could profitably direct their efforts towards exploring with learners: how they construe various forms of assistance; what criteria they use to decide between competing alternatives

> when the attainment of goals requires some relative loss of autonomy; what criteria they use to distinguish direction from assistance; and what renders one helper acceptable, while another is seen as threatening or inadequate.

Similar comments might be applied to the sort of information sources sought out and utilized by different learners (perhaps books, journals, documentary films and specialized groups by the one; popular magazines, family members or neighborhood groups by the other). Previous research has been directed towards identifying either the inherent qualities of various information sources, or else the pattern of information sources utilized by particular types of learners.

> Recommendation Six. Researchers should attempt to explore with learners how they view various learning resources, and in what way(s) some resources are seen as more helpful or more appropriate than others. They should seek to understand, from the learner's point-of-view, what he or she thinks is required in order to learn.

The learner's view of self-as-learner. Linked to both the assistance sought and resources utilized is the learner's view of himself or herself as a learner. A concept which has gained wide acceptance in recent year is that of learned helplessness which, as popularly understood, means that a person who has suffered prolonged exposure to other-direction may lack the faculties necessary to direct his or her own education: "Academic backgrounds may prove an obstacle to self-directed learning, if the learners have been conditioned to view the teacher as a "Guru", who must be present at all times, assign tasks, set deadlines, test and evaluate progress in order for learning to take place" (Abe, Henner-Stanchina & Smith, 1975, p. 59).

Despite the widespread acceptance of this idea, two alternative explanations may be offered for the phenomenon of learner passivity. One is that of situational adjustment, and the other is the idea of personal learning myths. Situational adjustment refers to the idea that learners are conscious of cues embedded in the learning situation (especially where a teacher or trainer is involved), and that they adjust their behavior accordingly (Becker et al., 1968; Miller & Parlett, 1974; Ramsden, 1988).

Personal learning myths are convictions held by a learner about himself or herself based on past experience. They have four characteristics. Firstly, they are usually debilitating, and inhibit a person's learning potential. Secondly, they are commonly based on the acceptance of someone else's judgement or assessment - for instance parents, teachers or peers - but have been internalized as true by the learner. Thirdly, they tend to be self-fulfilling or self-validating. Fourth and finally, they may either be generalized (e.g., "I'm a failure" or "I couldn't learn if my life depended on it"), or fairly specific (e.g., I can't learn languages" or "I can't do maths").

> Recommendation Seven. Researchers should examine learners' concepts of themselves as learners. This would include trying to ascertain both generalized and subject-specific images of their learning competence; the origins of such notions in their past; how they change or consolidate their self-concept as a learner during the course of a learning endeavor; the particular points in learning experiences (both autodidactic and instructional) where they felt either especially blocked and incapacitated, or else especially competent and capable; and the cues embedded in the learning situation which they believe inhibit or release their potential for exercising control over the learning situation.

The learner's view of autonomous learning and the development of autonomy. One of the most pervasive assumptions in the literature on self-direction is that there exists a connection between the conduct of education and the development and exercise of personal autonomy in some broader sense. For example, this assumption forms the basis of Snedden's (1930) article which includes interviews with two hypothetical adult learners whose respective taste for "self-education" had been shaped by their earlier schooling. In the absence of empirical data, however, this is little more than a "plausible assumption."

Skager (1979) calls for longitudinal studies to establish a connection between educational experiences and the self-directed learning activities of adults in later life. However, with the exception of two Swedish studies (Borgstrom, 1985; Borgstrom & Olofsson, 1983), there is little longitudinal data of any type concerning adults' participation in autodidactic activities, and even less regarding the relationship between educational experiences and personal autonomy in the broader sense. Moreover, in order to test assumptions about situational variability in personal autonomy, it would be necessary to work with adult learners across a range of settings; if possible, matching data about their overt behavior with their subjective evaluation of each situation (Shores, 1985).

> Recommendation Eight. Researchers should undertake long term studies of individual learners with a view to discovering the components of their continuing search for personal autonomy. Researchers should explore with learners: their perceptions of the meaning of autonomy; the opportunities for development of autonomy embodied in various instructional techniques; and the factors in a range of situations which learners perceive as either inhibiting or facilitating the development or exercise of autonomy. Such research should include the same learners' views of different learning situations, as well as different learners' views of the same learning experience.

Autonomous learning from the facilitator's perspective. Having argued so strongly for the adoption of an interpretive paradigm, with its emphasis on the personal perspective of the actors, it might seem strange to advocate research based on the facilitator's point-of-view, especially as one of the major criticisms of present research into learner-control has been its over-emphasis on the teacher's perspective. While this criticism is valid, it is aimed not so much against the inclusion of the teacher's or trainer's perspective, as against the implicit assumption that it is somehow superior, in all respects, to that of the learner.

All instructional situations, and indeed all forms of assisted autodidaxy, rest largely on the quality of the relationship established between the learner and the helper. Such a relationship depends on a genuine responsiveness to the needs of the learner, and it is not, as some have depicted it, a technical one - with the helper acting merely as a resource person - but includes a substantial component of warmth, empathy, authenticity and interpersonal contact. Just as learners construe the situation in which they find themselves, and the sort of help they receive, so do instructors. For instance, in discussing how various learners present themselves to librarians, Smith (1986) distinguishes between confident and timid learners, and she even suggests that the librarian's appraisal will influence how he or she might deal with the learner:

> "I'd probably be more motherly to the sort of person who, you know, looks weak and in need of lots of support. I'd be more jokey and relaxed with a person who is very confident." (p. 251)

The constructions which a learner places on a situation - leading him or her to appear timid or confident - influence the constructions which the helper makes, and these in turn affect he sort of help provided. Thus, research from the point-of-view of the instructor (or, in the case of assisted autodidaxy, the helper) is not just acceptable, it is essential.

> Recommendation Nine. Researchers should study how teachers construe learner autonomy. They should examine the extent to which individual practitioners regard it as a developable capacity, the sort of behaviors they would look for in autonomous learners, and the kinds of practices they believe lead to an enhanced sense of personal control. Ultimately, such research could be used as a way of exploring the teacher's ideological commitments to personal autonomy as an educational goal.

Such inquiries, especially if conducted in an action-research framework, would provide a legitimate focus for in service professional development, as well as a basis for meaningful negotiations between teachers and learners with respect to instructional events and strategies.

It is also worth considering the advantages of investigating autodidaxy, at least in part, through the eyes of those who assist autodidacts with their projects. Only one piece of research has been discovered which adopts such a perspective. Phillips (1980) pursued doctoral students through three years of their studies, interviewing them at monthly intervals. She also separately interviewed their advisers although less frequently, and then juxtaposed the perspective of the learner alongside that of the adviser. The differences in their views of the situation were striking, and serve to emphasize the need for data derived from the perspective of both parties to the teaching/learning transaction.

> Recommendation Ten. Researchers should examine issues such as how the helpers view being approached for assistance, how they construe the learner's need for help, the sort of strategies they employ in trying to meet the learner's needs, and how they sense the learner is nearing independence and hence no longer needs their help.

SUMMARY

Self-direction in learning has become a major theme in educational research, especially in the field of adult education. Despite its popularity, however, there is evidence to suggest that it "remains weakly conceptualized, ill defined, inadequately studied and tentatively comprehended" (Long, 1988, pp. 1-2). In particular, it appears that recent research into self-direction may have become "blocked" or "stalemated", and it is argued that this may be attributed to at least three main causes. The first is the absence of a consistent theoretical perspective underlying the study of self-direction, and the consequent failure to develop a cumulative knowledge base about the phenomenon.

The second cause, which is probably related to the first, is the indiscriminate application of the one term -- self-direction -- to at least four distinct phenomena. These four phenomena are self-direction as a valued philosophical ideal (i.e., personal autonomy), self-direction as the ability and willingness to guide and direct one's own learning, self-direction as the independent pursuit of learning opportunities without institutional support or affiliation (i.e., autodidaxy), and self-direction as the acceptance of responsibility for valued instructional functions in formal education contexts (i.e., learner-control) (Candy, 1987).

The third main cause of this apparent impasse might be attributable to slippage between the research paradigms employed and the nature of the phenomenon being studied. It was asserted that research into self-direction has been dominated by the positivistic paradigm as has research in education generally. However, positivism has been shown to be inappropriate to the study of many educational phenomena, and it seems that the assumptions of positivism are, if anything, particularly antithetical to those underlying self-direction. In studying self-directed learning it would appear that examining the attitudes and intentions of learners is essential to gaining a full understanding of their actions. However, the attitudes and understandings of self-directed learners are intensely personal and idiosyncratic, and are also deeply influenced by the concrete realities of particular situations. They are beyond the reach of conventional positivism, which relies so heavily on observable behavior. As a consequence, it has been proposed that an interpretive approach would probably be more congenial than a positivistic one to the study of self-direction in learning.

In the second part of the chapter, an attempt was made to reframe research into self-direction within the interpretive paradigm. It was observed that research undertaken and reported from the point-of-view of the actors in any situation is relatively rare in adult education, yet such an approach could revitalize research into self-direction. It was stated that, in most learning encounters, the situation may be portrayed either from the perspective of the learner or that of the person assisting the learner. Accordingly, recommendations for research were divided into these two different vantage points.

With respect to research from the learner's perspective, four major themes were suggested: (1) the learner's views of learning in general; (2) his or her intentions or purposes in the situation; (3) his or her attitudes towards direction or assistance; and (4) views of autonomous learning and the development of personal autonomy. What is argued for in this paper is neither the study of the situation per se, nor of the learner, but rather of the learner in the situation. This was the focus of Shores' (1985) dissertation, but little research has been undertaken concerning the learner's in-context construing of autodidaxy, or of the dimensions of learner-control. It was also suggested that research into autonomous learning could be framed from the point-of-view of the person or people providing the learner with assistance. The argument here is not so much against research from this perspective, as against research which implicitly assumes that such a point-of-view is somehow objective and should be shared by the learner.

For the sake of exposition, teachers' and learners' conceptions were subdivided into manageable components: views of knowledge, of resources, of assistance given or received, of self-as-learner, and of the process of learning itself. But the interpretive approach, by its nature, abhors this sort of fragmentation. Instead, it endorses the notion that a person's construction of a situation comprises an integrated whole. One of the criticisms which has been made of the positivist paradigm is the tendency of the latter to alienate research subjects from their contexts, and further to compartmentalize the experiences and perspectives of subjects in artificial ways. Interpretive researchers on the other hand, seek to understand how a person construes a situation in all its complexity; what is regarded as salient, what connections and relationships are perceived by the subject himself or herself. One particularly challenging aspect is the need to develop research approaches which function more like a movie than a snapshot, and which reflect the dynamic and constantly changing nature of learning endeavors.

Overall, what is suggested in this chapter is the acceptance of the person-in-context as the main unit of analysis. What is called for is the attempt to understand how, in any particular situation, self-concept, overall orientation towards learning, shifting patterns of purposes, and frames of reference all interact to create the anticipatory schemes, and influence the strategies used, by either the learner or his or her assistants.

REFERENCES

Abe, D., Henner-Stanchina, C., & Smith, P. (1975). New approaches to autonomy: Two experiments in self-directed learning. Melanges Pedagogiques - 1975. Nancy, France: Centre de Recherches et d'Applications Pedagogiques en Langues, Universite de Nancy.

Ausubel, D.P. (1968). Educational psychology: A cognitive view. New York, NY: Holt, Rinehart & Winston.

Becker, H., Geer, B., & Hughes, F. (1968). Making the grade: The academic side of college life. New York, NY: Wiley.

Biggs, J.B. (1987). Student approaches to learning and studying. Hawthorn, Victoria: Australian Council for Educational Research.

Borgstrom, L. (1985). Self-directed learning and the reproduction of inequalities. Unpublished paper. Stockholm: Department of Educational Research Stockholm Institute of Education.

Borgstrom, L., & Olofsson, L.E. (1983). Participation in study circles and the creation of individual resources. Proceedings of the Twenty-fourth Annual Adult Education Research Conference, April 8-10, 1983, Montreal, Quebec. 13-19.

Boud, D. J. & Griffin, V. (Eds.) (1987). Appreciating adults learning: From the learners' perspective. London: Kogan Page.

Bouwman, P.J. (1982). Self-education in time perspective since the ancient world (from 500 AD). Unpublished D. Ed. dissertation. University of South Africa. (Dissertation Abstracts International, 44 (08A), 2385).

Brookfield, S.D. (1981). Independent adult learning. Studies in Adult Education, 13 (1), 15-27.

Brookfield, S.D. (1984). Self-directed adult learning: A critical paradigm. Adult Education Quarterly, 35(2), 59-71.

Brookfield, S.D. (1985). Analyzing a critical paradigm of self-directed learning: A response. Adult Education Quarterly, 36(1), 6-64.

Buzan, T. (1978). Use your head. London: BBC Publications.

Campbell, V. N., & Chapman, M.A. (1967). Learner-control vs. program control of instruction. Psychology in the Schools, 4(10), 121-130.

Candy, P.C. (1987). Reframing research into "self-direction" in adult education: A constructivist perspective. Unpublished Ed.D. dissertation. The University of British Columbia.

Candy, P.C. (1988a). Key issues for research in self-directed learning. Studies in Continuing Education, 10(2), 104-124.

Candy, P.C. (1988b). On the attainment of subject-matter autonomy. In D. J. Boud (Ed.), Developing student autonomy in learning. (2nd ed). London: Kogan Page.

Candy, P.C. (1989). Constructivisim and the study of self-direction in adult learning. Studies in the Education of Adults, 21(2), 17-38.

Candy, P.C. (1990) Repertory grids: Playing verbal chess. In J.D. Mezirow (Ed.) Fostering critical reflection in adulthood: A guide to transformative and emancipatory learning. San Francisco, CA: Jossey-Bass.

Candy, P.C., Harri-Augstein, E.S., & Thomas, L.F. (1985). Reflections and the self-organized learner: A model of learning conversations. In D.J. Boud, R. Keogh & D. Walker (Eds.), Reflection: Turning experience into learning. London: Kogan Page.

Cheren, M.I. (1983). Helping learners achieve greater self-direction. In R. M. Smith (Ed.), Helping adults learn how to learn. New Directions for Continuing Education, Number 19. San Francisco, CA: Jossey-Bass.

Claxton, G. (1982). School science: Falling on stony ground of choked by thorns? Unpublished paper. London: Centre for Science and Mathematics Education, Chelsea College, University of London.

Craik, G.L. (1866). The pursuit of knowledge under difficulties. (rev edn.). London: Bell & Daldy.

Cropley, A.J. (1977). Lifelong education: A psychological analysis. Oxford/Hamburg: Pergamon Press/Unesco Institute for Education.

Cropley, A.J. (1979). Lifelong education: Issues and questions. In A.J. Cropley (Ed.), Lifelong education: A stocktaking. Oxford/Hamburg: Pergamon Press/Unesco Institute for Education.

Cropley, A.J. (1980). Towards a system of lifelong education: Some practical considerations. Hamburg: Unesco Institute for Education.

Danis, C., & Tremblay, N. (1985a). Critical analysis of adult learning principles from a self-directed learner's perspective. Proceedings of the Twenty-sixth Annual Adult Education Research Conference, March 22-24, 1985, Arizona State University - Tempe, AZ. 138-143.

Danis, C., & Tremblay, N. (1985b). The self-directed learning experience: Major recurrent tasks to deal with. Proceedings of the Fourth Annual Conference of the Canadian Association for the Study of Adult Education, May 28-30, 1985, Montreal Quebec. 283-301.

Dave, R.H. (1973). Lifelong education and the school curriculum. Unesco Institute for Education Monograph No. 1. Hamburg: Unesco Institute for Education.

Dave, R.H. (1973). Foundations for lifelong learning. Oxford/Hamburg: Pergamon Press/Unesco Institute for Education.

Driver, R., & Erickson, G.L. (1983). Theories in action: Some theoretical and empirical issues in the study of students' conceptual frameworks in science. Studies in Science Education, 10, 37-60.

Duke, C. (1976). Australian perspectives on lifelong education. Hawthorn: Australian Council for Education Research.

Fisher, K.M., Faletti, J., Thornton, R., Patterson, H., Lipson, J., & Spring, C. (1987). Computer-based knowledge representation as a tool for students and teachers. Unpublished paper. University of California - Davis.

Gibbon, E. (1907). the autobiography of Edward Gibbon. London: J.M. Dent & Sons.

Gibbons, M., & Phillips, G. (1982). Self-education: The process of lifelong learning. Canadian Journal of Education, 7(4), 67-86.

Gibbs, G., Morgan, A., & Taylor, E. (1982). A review of the research of Ference Marton and the Goteborg Group: A Phenomenological research perspective on learning. Higher Education, 11, 123-145.

Guglielmino, L.M. (1977). Development of the Self-directed Learning Readiness Scale. Unpublished Ph.D. Dissertation. University of Georgia. (Dissertation Abstracts International, 38(11A), 6467).

Hamm, C. (1982). Critique of self-education. Canadian Journal of Education, 7(4), 82-106.

Harri-Augstein, E.S., & Thomas, L.F. (1976). Tools for raising awareness of the learning process. Working paper. Uxbridge, Middlesex: Centre for the study of Human Learning, Brunel University.

Harrison, R. (1978). How to design and conduct self-directed learning experiences. Group and Organizational Studies, 3(2), 149-167.

Havighurst, R.J. (1964). Changing status and roles during the adult life cycle: Significance for adult education. In H.W. Burns (Ed.), Sociological backgrounds of adult education. Papers Presented at a Syracuse University Conference. October 1963, Sagamore, New York. Chicago, IL: Center for the Study of Liberal Education for Adults.

Hayrynen, Y.P., & Hayrynen, S.L. (1980). Aesthetic activity and cognitive learning: Creativity and orientation of thinking in new problem situations. Adult Education in Finland, 17 (3), 5-16.

Himmel, C.E. (1970). A critical review and analysis of self-directed learning methods utilized in the teaching of undergraduate psychology courses. Unpublished Ed.D. dissertation. University of Illinois - Urbana-Champaign. (Dissertation Abstracts International, 31 (05A), 2182).

Houle, C.O. (1961). The inquiring mind: A study of the adult who continues to learn. Madison, WI: University of Wisconsin Press.

Houle, C.O. (1984). Patterns of learning. San Francisco, CA: Jossey-Bass.

Hynes, D. (1986). Theory into practice. In J.R. Baird & I.J. Mitchell (Eds.), Improving the quality of teaching and learning: An Australian case study - The Peel Project. Melbourne, Victoria: The Peel Group, Monash University.

Ingram, J.B. (1979). Curriculum integration and lifelong education. Oxford/Hamburg: Pergamon Press/Unesco Institute for Education.

Jankovic, V., Beauvallet-Caillet, E., Beigbeger, I. et al. (1979). European expert meeting on the forms of autodidactic learning, Paris, October 16-19, 1979. Final report and recommendations. Paris: Division of Structures, Contents, Methods and Techniques, Unesco.

Jessup, F. W. (1969. Lifelong learning: A symposium on continuing education. Oxford: Pergamon Press.

Kasworm, C.E. (1983). Self-directed learning and lifespan development. International Journal of Lifelong Education, 2 (1), 29-46.

Kelly, G.A. (1955). The psychology of personal constructs. (2 Volumes). New York, NY: W.W. Norton.

Kulich, J. (1978). The adult self-learner: An historical perspective. In J.R. Kidd & G. R. Selman (Eds.), Coming of age: Canadian adult education in the 1960s. Toronto: Canadian Association of Adult Education.

Lengrand, P. (1970). An introduction to lifelong education. Paris: Unesco.

Long, H.B. (1988). Self-directed learning reconsidered. In H.B. Long & Associates, Self-directed learning: Application and theory. Athens, GA: Adult Education Department, The University of Georgia.

Long, H.B. (1989). Self-directed learning: Emerging theory and practice. In H.B. Long & Associates, Self-directed learning: Emerging theory and practice. Norman, OK: Oklahoma Research Center for Continuing Professional and Higher Education, University of Oklahoma.

Long H.B., & Ashford, M.L. (1976, Fall). Self-directed inquiry as a method of continuing education in colonial America. The Journal of General Education, 28(3), 245-255.

MacNeil, C. (1967). A comparative study of two instructional methods employed in teaching nutrition: Lecture discussion and self-directed study. Unpublished Ph.D. dissertation. University of Minnesota. (Dissertation Abstracts International, 28 (11A), 4534).

Mager, R.F. & Clark, C. (1963). Explorations in student-controlled instruction. Psychological Reports, 13, 71-76.

Mager, R.F. & McCann, J. (1961). Learner-controlled instruction. Palo Alto, CA: Varian Associates.

McClintock, R. (1982). Reaffirming a great tradition. In R. Gross (Ed.), Invitation to lifelong learning. Chicago, IL: Follett Publishing Company.

Mezirow, J.D. (1981, Fall). A critical theory of adult learning and education. Adult Education (US), 31(1), 3-24.

Millar, C.J., Morphett, A.R., & Saddington, J.A. (1986). Case study: Curriculum negotiation in professional adult education. Journal of Curriculum Studies, 18(4), 429-443.

Miller, C., & Parlett, M. (1974). Up to the mark: A study of the examination game. London: Society for Research into Higher Education.

Newsom, R. (1977, December). Lifelong Learning in London: 1558-1640. Lifelong learning: The Adult Years, 1(4), 19-21.

Nolan, R.E. (1981). Dependency versus autonomy in adult second language learning. Proceedings of the Twenty-second Annual Adult Education Research Conference, April 1-3, 1981, Northern Illinois University, DeKalb, IL. 140-145.

Novak, J.D., & Gowin, D.B. (1984). Learning how to learn. New York, NY: Cambridge University Press.

Parkyn, G.W. (1973). Towards a conceptual model of lifelong education. Paris: Unesco.

Perry, W.G. (1970). Forms of intellectual and ethical development in the college years: A scheme. New York: Holt, Rinehart & Winston.

Peters, J.M. (1988). Toward a new procedure for learning project research. Paper presented at the Joint Meeting of the Adult Education Research Conference and the Standing Committee on University Teaching and Research in the Education of Adults, Leeds, July 23, 1988.

Phillips, E.M. (1980). Education for research: The changing constructs of the postgraduate. International Journal of Man-Machine Studies, 13, 39-48.

Pope, M.L. (1983). Personal experience and the construction of knowledge in science. In R. Boot & M. Reynolds (Eds.), Learning and experience in formal education. Manchester: Department of Adult and Higher Education, The University of Manchester.

Ramsden, P. (Ed.) (1988). Improving learning: New perspectives. London: Kogan Page.

Redditt, R.S. (1973). A quasi-experimental comparison of a group lecture method and a self-directed method in teaching basic electricity at the college level. Unpublished Ed.D. dissertation. University of Tennessee. (Dissertation Abstracts International, 34, (09A), 5599).

Saljo, R. (1979). Learning from the learner's perspective II: Differences in awareness. Reports of the Institute of Education, University of Goteborg, No. 77. Goteborg, Sweden: University of Goteborg.

Shores, W.L. (1985). Study of interactions of adult learners with learning situations. Unpublished Ed.D. dissertation. The University of British Columbia.

Sizemore, B.A. (1979). Forces which affect self-direction and self-responsibility of students. In D.Della-Dora & L.J. Blanchard (Eds.), Moving toward self-directed learning: Highlights of relevant research and promising practices. Alexandria, VA: Association for Supervision and Curriculum Development.

Skager, R.W. (1979). Self-directed learning and schooling: Identifying pertinent theories and illustrative research. International Review of Education, 25, 517-543.

Skager, R.W. (1984). Organizing schools to encourage self-direction in learners. Oxford/Hamburg: Pergamon Press/Unesco Institute for Education.

Skager, R.W. & Dave, R.H. (1977). Curriculum evaluation for lifelong education. Oxford/Hamburg: Pergamon Press/Unesco Institute for Education.

Smith, J.C. (1986). Librarians and self-directed learners. Proceedings of the Twenty-seventh Annual Adult Education Research Conference, May 23-25, 1986, Syracuse University, Syracuse, NY. 249-254.

Snedden, D. (1930). Self-education: A needed emphasis in current proposals for adult education. Journal of Adult Education, 2(1), 32-37.

Snow, R.E. (1980). Aptitude, learner-control and adaptive instruction. Educational Psychologist, 15(3), 151-158.

Spear, G.E. & Mocker, D.W. (1984). The organizing circumstance: Environmental determinants in self-directed learning. Adult Education Quarterly, 35(1), 1-10.

Taylor, M.M. (1980). A conceptual representation of learning from the learner's point of view. Proceedings of the Twenty-first Annual Adult Education Research Conference. May 7-9, 1980, University of British Columbia, Vancouver, BC. 193-198.

Thomas, A.M. (1967). Studentship and membership: A study of roles in learning. The Journal of Educational Thought, 1(1), 65-76.

Thomas, L.F. & Harri-Augstein, E.S. (1985). Self-organized learning: Foundations of a conversational science for psychology. London: Routledge & Kegan Paul.

Tough, A.M. (1966). The teaching tasks performed by adult self-teachers. Unpublished Ph.D. dissertation. University of Chicago. (Dissertation Abstracts International 1861-1972, X1966, 58).

Tough, A.M. (1967). Learning without a teacher: A study of tasks and assistance during adult self-teaching projects Educational Research Series No. 3. Toronto: The Ontario Institute for Studies in Education.

Tremblay, N. & Danis, C. (1984). Manifestations de meta-apprentissage en situation d'autodidaxie. Proceedings of the Third Annual Conference of the Canadian Association for the Study of Adult Education, June 6-10, 1984, Guelph, Ontario. 151-166.

Yeaxlee, B.A. (1929). Lifelong education: A sketch of the range and significance of the adult education movement. London: Cassell & Co.

Chapter Three

SELF-DIRECTED LEARNING AND THE THEORY OF ADULT EDUCATION

Peter Jarvis

Self-directed learning has become quite central to the thinking of many American adult educators, although Adult Education Quarterly has not carried a disproportionate number of papers on the topic. Even so, there have been a number of books on the subject and, naturally, a number of conferences. Brookfield (1988, pp. 13-14) asks why the concept has achieved such popularity among adult educators and he suggests that it reflects the "democratic humanism of our tradition" and whilst he might be correct, it is then important to ask, why has the concept not been so popular among adult educators in the United Kingdom as it has in the United States? There was a self-help tradition in the United Kingdom in the nineteenth century and this is reflected in the historical interest in the subject, (See Graham 1983, Stephens and Roderick 1983). It does appear, therefore, that this is something of a cultural phenomenon as well as onc of interest to learning theorists, but then learning theorists should never neglect the social in their quest to understand the individual.

However, there is a certain degree of nebulousness surrounding the meaning of the concept. This is a point that Brookfield (1988) makes and which is more clearly demonstrated by Caffarella and O'Donnell (1988, pp. 39-61) in their review of the research literature when they concluded that they preferred to retain an open definition - pointing out that "there are many conceptually different definitions to self-directed learning; there appears to be no definitive empirical definition" (1988, p. 57). It is not to be expected that there would be total agreement from researchers in their areas of research but the conceptual question does need to be explored, a point that Mocker and Spear (1982) made in their analysis of lifelong learning and implied by Long (1988, p. 2) when he rightly claims that "conceptualization about what adult self-directed learning is, or is not, varies from weak to non-existent".

At present, the term is used in such a wide manner as to be a "catch-all" concept to cover a variety of different phenomena (see also Brockett and Hiemstra, 1985, pp. 31-33) and whilst this is a perfectly legitimate usage of the term it does not help the growth of theoretical perspectives about the field of study. Hence, it is argued here that it is necessary to explore this concept rigorously, and as a consequence it will be seen that some of the approaches which are called self-directed learning might not actually be self-directed at all whilst others are actually methods of teaching adults, and ones which are used in children's learning in school as well. This will be of no surprise when it is recalled that Tough (1967) first used the term self-teaching to refer to this phenomenon.

There are at least two ways of embarking upon a rigorous analysis of the concept, either to review all of its uses in a manner similar to that undertaken by Caffarella and O'Donnell (1988) or else to go back to the basic elements of learning and self-directedness. This latter approach was implied by Brookfield (1988, p. 15) when he highlighted the semantic difficulties of the term "learning". These difficulties are acknowledged in this analysis but this approach is still considered to be the better one from which to undertake this task. Hence, the first part of this paper seeks to analyze the elements and a model of self-directed learning is constructed and discussed, whilst the second part of the paper examines the implications of the analysis.

ANALYSIS OF THE CONCEPTS OF LEARNING AND SELF-DIRECTEDNESS

Two basic concepts are present within the idea of self-directed learning and both are necessary to this analysis; learning and self-directedness. In order to facilitate this analysis, basic definitions will be adopted. Self-directedness implies that the subject regulates, controls or conducts his or her own learning. Knowles (1980) claimed that this is a feature of adulthood but such a claim may well reflect his own ideological position rather than that of research. Reisman (1950), for instance, showed that some adults are other-directed and Even (1982) has also raised considerable doubts about Knowles' position from the perspective of cognitive styles when she suggested that self-directedness reflects a field-independent style but not a field-dependent one.

Learning is regarded as the process of "transforming experience into knowledge, skills and attitudes" (Jarvis, 1987, p. 8). It must also be recognized that learning is both a number of different processes and also that it occurs in different situations. Perhaps one of the clues to unravelling some of the confusion surrounding the term lies in the fact that learning is such a complex phenomenon, being a number of different processes which occur in different social situations, some of which are not even construed as being education! The significance of this is that there has been conceptual confusion in adult education literature between adult learning and adult education. Education and learning are not synonymous terms although they have sometimes been treated as such, and so the emphasis here must be on learning - not on education.

In some recent research into adult learning, Jarvis (1987) discovered nine different types of learning and, whilst it is unnecessary to examine these in any depth here, it is significant that there was a certain similarity about the stages of the process. However, this research did not relate learning to education in a specific manner and so it is necessary to include other elements in the process and this is following Chene's (1983) analysis of autonomy in self-directed learning. Nine major elements in the learning process are isolated here, namely: disjuncture, decision to learn, setting, aims and objectives, content, method, the actual thinking/reflecting process, assessment and action/outcome. It is recognized that these do not always occur in precisely the same order in each type of learning but this does not raise difficulties for the following analysis.

In their important overview of the material, Mocker and Spear (1982) sought to distinguish between formal, non-formal and informal learning and self-directed learning using the criteria of who controlled the objectives and the means of learning, i.e the self-directed element within this phenomenon. Brockett and Hiemstra (1985) rather unfairly criticize them for suggesting that they had a matrix of four types rather than a continuum, since Mocker and Spear (1982) provided a continuum immediately below their matrix. However, another criticism of their approach is that they only discussed self-directed learning from the perspective of two elements of the learning process, whereas nine have been isolated here. It is, therefore, important that at least each of these nine elements should be examined, and they are discussed in the order presented above.

Disjuncture

In Jarvis's (1987) study of learning, it is suggested that this process begins with a disjuncture between the learner's biography and experience. It is only when this disjuncture occurs that the questioning process can begin which results in learning. However, the concept of disjuncture was not expanded greatly in that initial study, although it is considered to be an important one since it relates to other concepts used with great frequency in the adult education literature, such as needs.

As an initial stage in learning, disjuncture can be self-induced or other-induced, e.g. people can have an experience and realize that they need to learn more before they can cope with a situation in which they find themselves, and so the disjuncture can be self-induced; but other people might, for instance, be informed by their managers in their workplace that they really ought to master some new technique, etc., in order to perform it more effectively, even though they might have thought that they were performing it adequately and, therefore, the disjuncture can be other-induced. Disjuncture between biography and an experience can be construed as a need. Thus the idea of learning need, felt and experienced, can be seen to be a significant element in the concept of disjuncture. Yet this can be taken even further, since individuals can look into the future and wish that they might have a specific knowledge or be able to perform a certain skill which they think might be useful sometime in the future, and so another form of disjuncture is created - between anticipated experience and biography - which might be called a want. But like need, want can also be other-induced!

If the disjuncture, whether it is a need or a want, is other-induced, then can the learning that follows be self-directed? It could be argued that the creation of the disjuncture is not actually part of the learning process and consequently it is superfluous to this discussion, irrespective of whether it is self-induced, or other-induced. Alternatively it might be argued that this is a necessary beginning of the discussion, since it is the start of the learning process, but that it does not impinge greatly upon the type of learning that follows. If this is the case, then even if the disjuncture is created in a teaching-and-learning situation, by the teacher, then it is possible to argue that self-directed learning could actually be teacher initiated, since learners are still able to decide whether they will respond to the disjuncture that has been created. However, this might not be the case in the next stage of the learning.

Decision to Learn

Experiencing a need or a want to learn does not necessarily result in learning. Jarvis (1987) noted that non-learning is a fairly common phenomenon, even when disjuncture has been experienced. Hence, there is a deliberate step between the first stage and the commencement of learning. This stage might involve enrollment in an educational course, or it might involve seeking resources in order to undertake the learning process, and it is at this stage that the autonomy of the person first emerges.

If the need or want has been other-induced in an unequal situation, such as the workplace, then learners might lose their autonomy and be forced to enroll in a course of instruction. But learners might not have anybody else compelling them to learn, at least not overtly, so that it might be claimed that self-directedness emerges here. Knowles (1975) certainly suggests that it is here that self-direction occurs since learners diagnose their own learning needs and take the initiative in implementing their learning strategies, but perhaps Knowles has not analyzed the process as completely as later theorists have. Nor, perhaps, did he look sufficiently at the analyses of social behavior. Reisman (1950) showed that whilst some people are inner-directed, others are other-directed. This raises an initial problem about the concept of self-direction because some people who might appear to act independently, have actually responded because of their reference group and it thus becomes difficult to claim that they are actually self-directed. Whilst there is considerable research on why people participate in adult education, there is less research on relating these psychological types to the learning process *per se*.

However, at the very least it can be shown that there are three possible responses at the point of *decision* to learn, other-directed overtly, other-directed as a result of internal mechanisms and self-directed. Houle's (1988) three types of learners might all fall into the third of these categories - self-directed learners.

<u>Type of Participation</u>

Participation is a term usually restricted to joining an educational class, and this is why it is used here. Two possibilities arise at this point in the learning process, either the learners decide to participate in an educational course or they decide to learn independently. Independent learning was a term that Brookfield first used when he started studying this phenomenon, and like many others it seems to have been lost as the present term has gained popularity. Independent learning might also be a conceptually false term in as much as he (Brookfield, 1985) has shown that all self-directed learning occurs within a social context and Jarvis (1987) has shown that even the internal mechanisms of learning, e.g. the mind and the self, are social. Hence he was right to cease using the term in that sense, but it is used here to indicate a learning process that occurs independently of the educational institution. This highlights a distinction that it is essential to draw, between education and learning: education is the institutionalization of learning but learning is, in one sense, individual. Learning is broader than education and can occur outside of the educational institution, in all other institutions, and even beyond all of them.

Those learners who were earlier classified as self-directed are, in this second stage, now able to decide to learn independently or to enroll in a course in order to satisfy their learning needs or wants, or they can decide to combine the two. It is less likely for those who were classified as other-directed to decide, or even wish, to learn independently or through a combination of the two; although there is a possibility that they may do so, so that any understanding of self-direction at this stage must allow for these eventualities.

<u>Aims and Objectives</u>

This was one of the two elements that Mocker and Spear (1982) utilized in their analysis, and in their discussion they had only two alternatives - control by the learners or by others. Conceptually these two terms are distinct, and they are used with different meanings in curriculum theory, but they are discussed together here since the distinction does not appear to add anything to the discussion. Even so, since their work was published the concept of negotiation has become extensively used in education, so there is a third possibility which now has to be incorporated into the discussion. It will be recognized that where the learners remain outside of the educational institution, it is more likely that they will choose their own aims and objectives, but this is less likely for those who have decided to participate in a course of study. However, learners may have their own aims whilst the teachers have specific objectives for the course and the two may not be in harmony, so that having enrolled the learners may lose some of their autonomy. Additionally, those who have entered the educational institution might be presented with the possibility of negotiating their aims and objectives.

There is a sense in which the relationship between the learners and the teachers is involved here (Chene, 1983) and the following discussion is applicable to this and to each of the next two sections. However, this is not a simple relationship and it has to be carefully examined. Research into teaching styles is still in its infancy but the famous leadership research of Lippitt and White (1958) will suffice in order to make the point. It will be recalled that they isolated three forms of leadership: democratic, authoritarian and laissez-faire. Now the significant thing about this is that it is not necessarily the democratic teacher who encourages either self-direction or negotiation - sometimes there is no opportunity given and the teacher determines that there will be self-direction or negotiation in an authoritarian manner. Sometimes this is called facilitation! Obviously there is non-authoritarian facilitation too, as Hiemstra (1988) shows, but the conceptual problem lies with the more authoritarian approach by the teacher. Is it self-directed, at the level of aims and objectives, content or method, when the teacher has determined in an authoritarian manner that one or more of these aspects will be self-directed or negotiated? It might well be claimed that whilst it appears to be self-directed, in fact it is not truly self-directed learning; and, therefore, there is a question raised in the model that is presented below about the role of the teacher.

It would be possible to extend this argument a little because the teachers might be genuinely democratic in their own minds, but if they are highly respected by the learners then the latter might be influenced by this sense of respect and do what they think the teachers consider best for them. In such instances, the question needs to be raised yet again about the extent to which the learners have genuine autonomy in this situation so that it can be seen how difficult it is for genuine self-directed learning to occur within an educational institution however democratic the teachers might consider themselves to be. However, it might be argued that at each of these three points the self-direction is actually a teaching method, and it should be regarded as such. Additionally, it must be recognized that as children are encouraged to undertake projects and other forms of learning exercise within the school situation, self-direction is a teaching method-but one that is not specifically adult. There is research (eg. Lewin, 1952) that suggests that active participation is more likely to result in behavioral change, and the Lippitt and White (1958) study also shows the advantages of democratic approaches whilst working with children. Hence it must be recognized by adult educators that this is an educational technique and not something specific or unique to adult education.

Content

The next stage in the process is the selection of content and once again there are three possibilities: self-selection, other-selection and negotiation. Self-selection is very possible when the learner has remained outside of the educational institution and is learning for learning's sake, and it will become clear now that this type of person is much closer to Houle's (1988) learning-oriented group.

By contrast, those who are enrolled on a course may be required to complete the set curriculum or even the examination syllabus, and it does not matter how much apparent autonomy the learners have, ultimately they are expected to learn that knowledge, and skill(?), contained within the syllabus. Herein lies a part of the basis of the radical criticism of education-that there is no choice, and ultimately education is a socially and culturally reproductive mechanism. (see Bowles and Gintis, 1976; Freire 1972)

There are some instances where the educational process has high status, such as some forms of university education where the university professor actually determines the shape of the course each academic year, and in these instances the possibility of genuine negotiation emerges - provided that the learners wish to enter into such a situation. If it is forced upon them, then the same types of arguments emerge as have already been discussed.

Method

This was the second element included in Mocker's and Spear's analysis (1982) and much of the foregoing is appropriate in this section also, so that it will not be repeated here. However, it will also be seen from the above discussion that the teachers might have actually decided that it is good for the students to learn independently, or by negotiation, so that contract learning and projects, etc., are encouraged; and, whilst they do have elements of independence within them, they are ultimately teaching methods. The extent to which a teaching method may be equated with self-directed learning is debatable, but it is suggested that if these are decisions by teachers then there is more than an element of other-direction in the process. This might be seen in Gibbs' (1981) excellent book on teaching students how to learn.

Thought/Language

This is deliberately left here as a rather broad element, because there is a tremendous amount of debate possible at this point. For instance, it is possible to discuss this from the perspective of the use of language in thinking, from the perspective of rationality in thought, and from ideas such as intuitive thinking. This discussion is at least another paper, if not a book Although some of this is discussed elsewhere

(Jarvis, 1987, pp. 86-112), some of the outlines will be sketched here in order to indicate the rudiments of the discussion.

In beginning to develop his sociology of knowledge, Karl Mannhein (1936, p. 2) wrote:

> Only in a quite limited sense does the single individual create for himself the mode of speech and of thought we attribute to him. He speaks the language of his group; he thinks in the manner in which his group thinks. These not only determine to a large extent the avenues of approach to the surrounding world, but they also show at the same time from which angle and in which context of activity objects have hitherto been perceptible and accessible to the group or the individual.

No person is an island, and in this sense each person utilizes the language of the group, which must also direct the thought processes to some extent. Hence, it will be noted that in the following diagram there is no totally independent person recorded.

This argument might proceed further to suggest that in most cases people actually follow in the same lines of thought as those who have gone before them, and it is at this point that critical theory becomes significant; and, perhaps one of the reasons why Brookfield (1985) begins to suggest that there needs to be an internal change in consciousness in the learners, since if they have a false consciousness then they will not know what is in their best interests. However, Brookfield is not totally in accord with the critical theorists since he is concerned to relate this change of consciousness to adulthood rather than to emancipation.

However, it will be seen from this discussion that the issues of rationality, consciousness, and critical theory all emerge here, and this is a broader debate than the one being entered into here. Even so, it may be seen that the whole area of self-directed learning has omitted a great deal from its fundamental discussion, and a little of this will be referred to in the second section of this paper. But doubt is cast on the possibility of total autonomy for the person.

Assessment

Often during and almost always at the end of the learning process there is a form of assessment. Of those learners who remain outside of the educational institution it is relatively easy to assess how much they have learned, whether their needs or wants have been satisfied, and whether they have achieved their aims and objectives. However, for those within the educational institution, those following set syllabii, etc., this is a harder process. They may be given the opportunity to engage in a collaborative form of assessment in some situations, but normally the assessment will be other-directed, even if it appears as a form of peer assessment. In these instances its basis is usually if criteria, other than those set by the learner, have been satisfied. However, it might be argued that this and the following element lie beyond the actual learning process and, in this instance, it would be possible for it to be omitted. Indeed, it might be possible to claim that even if the assessment were other-directed and the learners were found not to have achieved the type of expectations that the other had for them - it would be possible for the learners to decide to re-commence learning, and this still might be perceived as a form of self-direction.

Action/Outcome

The outcome of any learning is either innovation or some form of conformity, and this once again need not affect the discussion too closely.

It will be seen from the diagram that there are arrows that flow directly downwards, although the one on the self-directed side is interrupted at the point of language/thought, which indicates that no person is an island and that there must always be certain internal constraints; a point to which further reference will be made in the second part of this paper. However, from henceforth in this paper, the term self-directed learning is restricted to those processes which are predominantly depicted on the left-hand side of the diagram. At the other side of the diagram it will be seen that there is every possibility at every stage for other-directed learning, whilst there are also many opportunities for negotiated forms of learning, or for apparently self-directed elements to occur in the teaching-and-learning process. It is a fact that there are so many possibilities in the middle ground, all of which have been called self-directed learning at one time or another, that this has really added to confusion and to the inexactitude surrounding the terminology. This confusion will only be clarified when the language is more precise.

IMPLICATIONS

Mezirow (1985, p. 27) suggested that:

> There is probably no such thing as a self-directed learner, except in the sense that there is a learner who can participate fully and freely in a dialogue through which we test our interests and perspectives against those of others and accordingly modify them and our learning goals.

Whilst he may be fairly close in his initial claim, it might be more correct to suggest that self-directed learning is the exception in contemporary society rather than the rule-but that may actually be as much a feature of contemporary society as it is of anything else. Houle (1984, p. ix) claims that prior "to the middle of the nineteenth century, learning was accepted without question as a lifelong activity", and he might have added that much less of it was of a formal nature than in modern society. Indeed, many of the historical examples that Houle (1984) himself has chosen indicate that their learning was much closer to the model of the self-directed learner than many examples of the forms of self-directed learning currently discussed within the literature and occurring within stages of the above diagram. This might have been because the formal education system was not as fully developed as it is now; and, the implication of this is that the educational system has helped to hide the self-directed learning that occurs and that the examination systems helps to lessen its status because learners are usually only recognized as having learned when the process has been certificated.

Is it being suggested that contemporary society has removed individuality and freedom from people? A number of inter-related trends occur here that require discussion. In the first instance it is necessary to recognize that:

> the structure of modern society affects man in two ways simultaneously: he becomes more independent, self reliant and critical, and he becomes more isolated, alone and afraid. (Fromm, 1984 ed, p. 90)

These simultaneous processes are important in the sense that most people are free in a variety of ways as a result of the structures of society, although this is only a partial freedom. Yet people feel free. Therefore, even those people who are totally other-directed in their learning are free to opt out of the process if they were to choose to do so - they are free to refuse to participate. This is a negative form of freedom. They may also feel that they are totally self-directed because they feel free to opt out, but then do not act upon that feeling. Hence they continue to feel free; but, in fact, they may have a real fear of freedom, so that Fromm (1984, p. 2) can claim that:

> For the essence of these new systems, which effectively took charge of man's entire social and personal life, was the submission of all but a handful of men to an authority over which they had no control.

Indeed, this conclusion does fit into the fact that people are socialized into a society which is structured in such a manner as to expect conformity to its structures, so that it is only to be expected that individuals reflect their socialization processes and submit to the social pressures of society.

It is, therefore, the exception rather than the rule for people to assume freedom and to act accordingly. This is a positive form of freedom and one less frequently exercised. Hence, this form of self-directed learning is more of an exception in contemporary society rather than the rule and it might be more likely to occur among Houle's (1988) group of people who learn for learning's sake than any other, although even they may well be other-directed somewhere along the learning process.

Hence, it might be asked if people experience a false sense of freedom when they feel that they are free to act? To cite Fromm (1984, pp. 220-221) once again:

> He has become free of the external bonds that would prevent him from doing and thinking as he sees fit. He would be free to act according to his own will, if he knew what he wanted, thought, and felt. But he does not know. He conforms to anonymous authorities and adopts a self which is not his. The more that he does this, the more powerless he feels, the more he is forced to conform. In spite of a veneer of optimism and initiative, modern man is overcome with a profound feeling of powerlessness which makes him gaze towards approaching catastrophes as though he were paralyzed.

> Looked at superficiality, people appear to function well enough in economic and social life; yet it would be dangerous to overlook the deep-seated unhappiness behind that comforting veneer. If life loses its meaning because it is not lived, man becomes desperate.

CONCLUSIONS

It may be seen from the above discussion that underlying the idea of self-directed learning there are profound philosophical issues; and, all that this paper has begun to do is to highlight some of them. It is claimed that much of what appears to be self-directed learning is not really self-directed, but that what Tough was pointing to looked beyond the educational institution and was much closer to self-directed learning than many of the ideas that have more recently been incorporated into the discussion. This incorporation has done little or nothing to add to the theory of adult education nor to the theory of learning - but that there remains a profound concept of self-direction in learning which presupposes an idea of the person-in-society which is both exciting and challenging; people are, according to Fay (1987, p. 48) intelligent, curious, reflective and willful. But are they? This is the assumption of much of the literature on self-directed learning, but one that is questioned here; yet, it is an assumption that really does require more consideration from those who are concerned about self-direction in learning, and this paper has just highlighted one possible philosophical path that that debate might take.

Figure 3.1: A Model of Self-Directed and Other-Directed Learning.

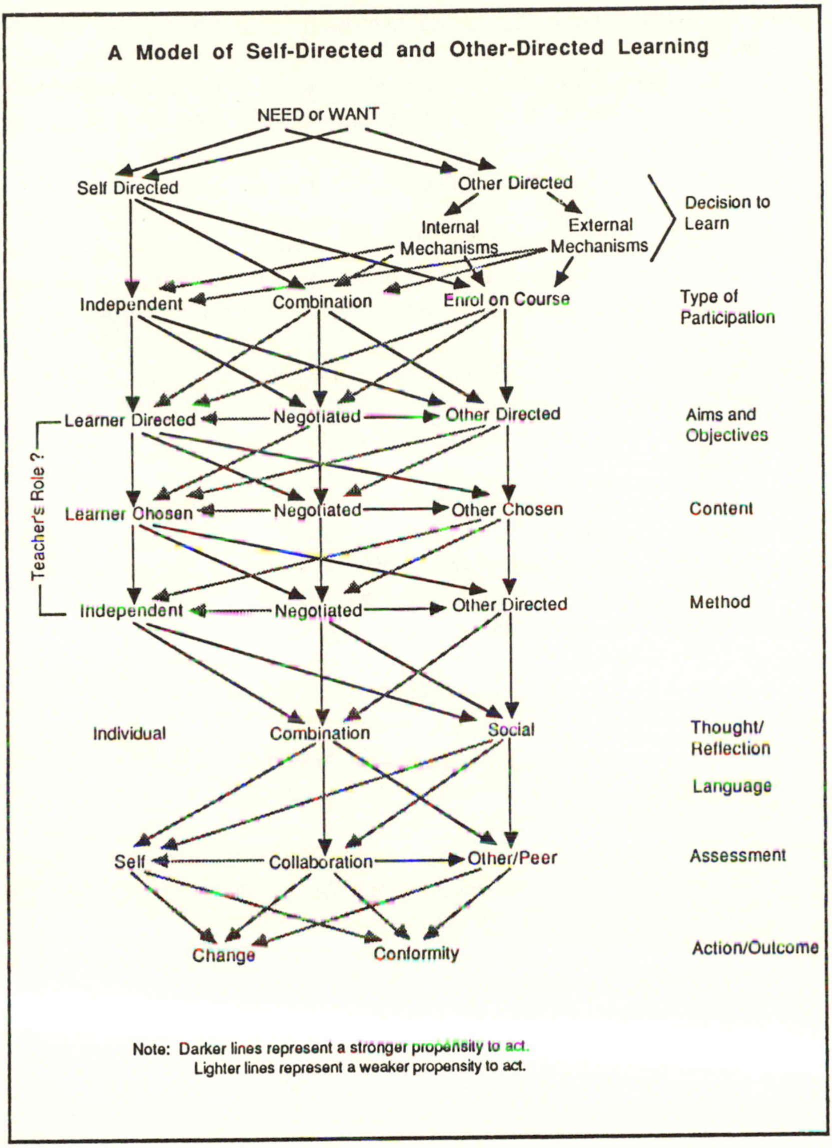

REFERENCES

Bowles, S. & Gintis, H. (1976). Schooling in capitalist America. London: Routledge and Kegan Paul.

Brockett, R. & Hiemstra, R. (1985). Bridging the theory-practice gap in self-directed learning. In S. Brookfield (Ed.). Self-directed learning: From theory to practice. San Francisco: Jossey-Bass, 31-33.

Brookfield, S. D.(editor) (1985). Self-directed learning: from theory to practice. San Francisco: Jossey-Bass.

Brookfield, S. D. (1988). Conceptual, methodological and practical ambiguities in self-directed learning. In H. Long and Associates, Self-directed learning: application and theory. Athens, Georgia: Adult Education Department, University of Georgia, 13-15).

Caffarella, R. & O'Donnell, J. M. (1988). Research in self-directed learning: Past present and future trends. In H. Long and Associates, Self-directed learning: application and theory. Athens, Georgia: Adult Education Department, University of Georgia, 39-61.

Chene, A. (1983). The concept of autonomy: A philosophical discussion. Adult Education Quarterly, Vol 34, No. 1 Fall.

Even, M. J. (1982). Adapting Cognitive Style Theory in Practice. In Lifelong Learning: The Adult Years, Jan., Vol. 5, No. 5, 14-17 and 27.

Fay, B. (1978). Critical social science, (48). Oxford: Polity Press.

Freire, P. (1972). Pedogogy of the oppressed. Harmondsworth: Penguin.

Fromm, E. (1984ed). The fear of freedom, (2, 90, 220-221). London: ARK Paperbacks.

Gibbs, G. (1981). Teaching students to learn. Milton Keynes, Open University Press.

Graham, B. (1983). Nineteenth Century Self Help in Education - Mutual Improvement Societies - The Carlisle Working Men's Reading Rooms (Vol. 2). University of Nottingham, Dept. of Adult Education.

Hiemstra, R. (1988). Self-directed learning: individualizing instruction. In H. Long and Associates, Self-directed learning: Application and theory. Athens, Georgia: Adult Education Department, University of Georgia.

Houle, C.O. (1984). Patterns of learning, (ix). San Francisco: Jossey Bass.

Houle, C.O. (1988). The inquiring mind, (16). Norman: University of Oklahoma. Originally published in 1961.

Jarvis, P. (1987). Adult learning in the social context. London: Croom Helm.

Knowles, M.S. (1975). Self-directed learning. Chicago: Follett Pub. Co.

Knowles, M.S. (1980). The modern practice of adult education. Chicago: Cambridge Book Co.

Lewin, K. (1952). Group Decisions and Social Change in G. Swanson, T. Newcomb, and E. Hartly (Eds.). Readings in social psychology. New York: Holt.

Lippitt, R. & White, R.K. (1958). An experimental study of leadership and group life. In E. Maccoby Readings in social psychology. New York: Holt.

Long, H.B. (1988). Self-directed learning reconsidered. In H. Long and Associates. Self-directed learning: Application and theory. Athens, Georgia: Adult Education Department, University of Georgia.

Long, H.B. & Associates (1988). Self-directed learning: application and theory. Athens, Georgia: Adult Education Department, University of Georgia.

Mannheim, K. (1936). Ideology and Utopia. London: Routledge and Kegan Paul.

Mezirow, J. (1985). A critical theory of self-directed learning. In S. Brookfield (Ed.) Self-directed learning: From theory to practice. San Francisco: Jossey-Bass.

Mocker, D.W. & Spear, G.E. (1982). Lifelong learning: formal, nonformal, informal, and self-directed. ERIC Clearinghouse on Adult, Career and Vocational Education. Columbus: Ohio State University.

Reisman, D. (1950). The lonely crowd: A study of changing American culture. New Haven: Yale University Press.

Stephens, M.D. & Roderick, G.W. (Eds) (1983). Education, University of Nottingham, Dept. of Adult Education.

Tough, A.M. (1967). Learning without a teacher. Toronto: OISE.

Chapter Four

ON THE THEME AND VARIATIONS OF SELF-DIRECTED LEARNING

Lorraine S. Gerstner

Self-directed learning has been lauded as the central concept in adult education (Mezirow, 1985), labeled as a grassroots movement amongst adult educators (Griffin, 1978), proposed as the aim of adult education (Brookfield, 1985), and envisioned as providing a unifying concept for the disparate field of adult education (Knowles, 1980).

In addition to such laudatory comments, there have been hundreds of articles and research studies addressing the merits and substantiating the phenomenon of self-directed learning. (Houle, 1961; Tough, 1971; Coolican, 1974; Denys, 1975; Kathrein, 1981; Zottoli, 1984). Furthermore, there have been several publications focusing almost exclusively on self-directed learning. (Knowles, 1975; Smith, 1982; Skager, 1984; Brookfield, 1985; Long, 1988)

In spite of all this attention and widespread interest there remains a disturbing lack of clarity regarding self-directed learning. At the conclusion of the First North American Symposium on Self-Directed Learning, Long (1988 p. 1) concluded that "adult self-directed learning remains weakly conceptualized, ill defined, inadequately studied and tentatively comprehended". Thus, the question before us is, what is self-directed learning? Is there a shared conceptual understanding of this term or do different people mean different things when they use the term?

The aim of this chapter is to address these questions by exploring the concept of self-directed learning from the philosophical orientations of progressivism, humanism, behaviorism, and the critical perspective. Each philosophical perspective will be briefly reviewed in order to provide a broadened context and background against which to facilitate an understanding of the ideological roots of self-directed learning. Special attention is given to understanding four related concepts which inform the idea of self-directed learning: the self, experience, education and learning. These four concepts will permit us to sharpen our focus by providing a conceptual matrix in which to embed the idea of self-directed learning.

THE INFLUENCE OF FOUR PHILOSOPHICAL PERSPECTIVES

Progressivism

Progressivism writ large represented a humanitarian response to the negative conditions caused by widespread industrialism and immigration during the early years of the twentieth century (Cremin, 1964). The transition from an agrarian to an industrial age generated economic dislocation resulting in migration and immigration as well as dehumanizing political and social conditions in which masses of people attempted to adjust to vastly changing circumstances. The resultant social dislocations necessitated the need for widespread reform. Such reform was not to be reactionary but progressive; a progressive reform movement based on a faith in democracy and education. Progressivism declared that society could and must be improved and that education was the best means for "pursuing social salvation" (Ravitch, 1974, p. 233).

Progressivism and the progressive education movement were at their apex during the first two decades of this century and its intellectual momentum was to immerse and indelibly influence the emerging adult education movement. So profound was this historical juncture that Elias and Merriam have concluded that

"Progressivism has had a greater impact on adult education in the United States than any other school of thought". (Elias and Merriam, 1980, p. 45). Given the impact of progressive thought on the entire field of adult education it is appropriate that we begin our exploration of the concept of self-directed learning from the perspective of progressivism.

The Self as Transactional

Selfhood, for progressive thinkers, is constituted via transactions amongst the organism, its physical, and social environments. According to Dewey (1922), the self represents the unique organization of an individual's habits and interests. These interests are more than subjective, they are patterns of activities which are also objectively influenced and socially stimulated (Boydston, 1970). Thus, interests and habits are actively related to an object of thought which occasions attention. The genesis of the self is found in the dynamic interchange between the individual and the environment and is understood and expressed relative to other selves and society (Lindeman, 1926).

By claiming that interests and habits collectively represent the self, progressives conceived of the self as acquired rather than pre-existent. Selfhood, then, is learned through various situations which promulgate dispositions. The self gradually comes to achieve a mind based on knowledge gained through ongoing transactions. The self has a twofold nature. It is essentially conative, that is comprised of an individual's interests, wants and desires. Through experience and especially educative experiences the self then achieves cognitive capacities involving knowledge and judgement. The ongoing progress of growth and inquiry enables greater self-development and mindfulness and with it increasing individuality (Dewey, 1922).

Progressive Views of Experience, Education and Learning

The very existence of the self is dependent on experience. Experience represents the essence of transaction; for all experience involves a transaction between the individual and the environment. Experience is comprised of two interrelated dimensions. The active dimension of experience involves doing. Experience stimulates us into doing something with it. As we do, we are undergoing the consequences of our doing, which represents the passive dimension of experience. When we consciously consider and reconsider the consequences of our doing, we are able to learn from that experience. Thinking becomes the purposeful endeavor to discover specific connections between what we do and the resultant consequences of that doing (Dewey, 1916). Lindeman (1961, p. 87) advances a similar idea when he offers that "Experience is, first of all, doing something; second,doing something that makes a difference; third, knowing what difference it makes".

Social life had undergone a profound change with the advent of industrialism such that it had become a necessity to reconceive of education for a world which will increasingly be challenged by more change. Hence, it would be impossible to prepare a student for any fixed set of conditions. To ready him for the future life means to give him command of himself. As Dewey commented:

> If our education is to have any meaning for life, it must pass through an equally complete transformation. It remains but to organize all these factors, to appreciate them in their fullness of meaning and to put the ideas involved into complete, uncompromising possession of our school system. To do this means to make each one of our schools an embryonic community life, active with types of occupations that reflect the life of the larger society and permeated throughout with the spirit of art, history and science. When the school introduces and trains each child of society into membership within such a little community, saturating him with

> the spirit of service, and providing him with the instruments of effective SELF-DIRECTION, we shall have the deepest and best guarantee of a larger society which is worthy, lovely and harmonious. (emphasis added - Dewey, 1899, p. 43)

Education, through the reconstruction of experience, is to assist in the birth of the self from random activities. Education is a process of cultivating the self through the formation of fundamental attitudes and dispositions towards nature and humankind. Self direction, then, can be understood as the conscious guidance of experience in order to continue to facilitate further growth and development of the self and mind.

Lindeman recognized the special significance of the progressive ideals of democracy and education for adult education. Adults require educational opportunities which are equal to their charge and circumstances. This is learning which is social in nature and intended to assist adults in making informed choices about political and social issues. The social purpose of adult education is the full operationalization of democracy as a way of life. Adult education, then, is charged with developing social intelligence whereby an adult comes to understand himself and the world in which he lives and is thereby prepared to engage in informed social action.

Through the processes of self-discovery, self-expression, and self-mastery the adult learner will come to gain self-knowledge which permits that person to determine and guide his life course. As Lindeman expressed it:

> The first step toward liberation is taken when an individual begins to understand that which inhibits, frustrates, subjugates him. We learn to be free when we know what we desire freedom for and what stands in the way of our desire. Psycho-therapy has taught us that the first look must be within, not without. Most barriers to freedom have been self-constructed, self-induced... The psycho-therapeutic

> specialist does not "cure" his patient; he merely assists the patient in learning the methods of self-recovery. And the method is self-knowledge. (Lindeman, 1926, p. 70)

Bryson in discussing Adult Education (1936) begins by observing that the modern circumstances of life require self-education. This requirement is occasioned by a maturing self as well as a changing environment. The internal environment or personality can never be considered a finished product. Rather, it is more like a "living plant which is affected by environmental circumstances outside, and by principles of growth within" (Bryson, 1936, p. 9). In order for the personality or self to grow and mature it needs continuous learning.

These reasons coupled with the status accorded to adults make the most characteristic quality of adulthood that of self-directed learning.

> When one begins with the principle that adult education is self-education, that it starts with the student where he is and takes him in the direction in which he wishes to go, any beginning is as good as any other, provided the teacher is good enough. The result should always be the same, namely, a desire for further learning and further self-development. (Bryson, 1936, p. 62)

The ideas of self-discovery and self-education are also found in Mearns' (1940) The Creative Adult: Self-Education in the Art of Living. Mearns amplifies Lindeman's emphasis on individuality, suggesting that it is our unique individuality which contains our creative spirit. Individuality is creative, and thereby artistic, because it uses the material of existence and experience for its own purposes. While individuality cannot be extinguished, it can be restricted. Therefore, adult education should assist persons to discover the artistry which is theirs and to assert such artistry in their daily lives. Mearns is forthright in stating that:

> Adults need a special education to rescue their creative spirit from the annihilating imprisonment of conformity. They hold the responsibility of the world in their charge, they must do a better job of it. (Mearns, 1940, p. 194)

Humanism

Humanism, when broadly conceived, can be thought of as embodying a concern for people in their wholeness (Bugental, 1967). In this regard humanism is an optimistic and affirmative philosophy. For there is more to humanism than just a concern with human beings. Humanism embraces a commitment to human becoming (Matson, 1973). It endorses and encourages a view of human nature as naturally good and as having an innate striving for self-actualization, self-fulfillment, and self-direction (Lamont, 1965; Corey, 1986).

Humanism is affiliated with both phenomenology and existentialism (Elias and Merriam, 1980). From phenomenology it has adopted a concern with the ways in which a person perceives the world and one's own experience in that world. Existential philosophy has contributed the view that knowing and knowledge begins with the person, what Greene (1973, p. 136) calls the "existing self". Further, humanism has also been influenced by pragmatism which offers a theory of experiential knowledge. And finally, there is another influence which is not philosophical but rather social. Humanism throughout its long career has protested against the dehumanizing effects of absolute right and truth and oppressive social and economic factors (Hasting, undated).

The Self-Actional View of the Self

Humanists presume that selfhood is inborn and therefore exists prior to any contact with the external environment. This inner nature or essence, at least initially, is not strong and forthcoming but rather emergent and sentient. It can never be extinguished but it can be distorted or repressed in a hostile environment. However, given a neutral or nurturing environment the self will unfold and reveal its essential benevolence and growth orientation. It is self-actional in that it is motivated or propelled to activity based on its own innate striving for self-actualization. The source of agency and behavior is within the individual (Greene, 1973; Goldstein, 1981).

Selfhood represents the totality of an individual's personality which is comprised of intellectual, emotional, and instinctual elements. (Maslow, 1970) The self is understood to be a process of becoming and self-actualization is the driving motivation encompassing the desire to realize most fully this sense of selfhood. While Maslow and other humanists use the term self, the most fully developed and comprehensive self-theory has been articulated by Rogers. Rogers conceives of the self as a dynamic, creative, organizing core of personality which gives impetus to behavior (Rogers, 1983). Self is to be understood as the ever emergent sense of awareness of being and functioning. Rogers assumes that the self has a natural tendency towards growth and further that this growth tendency is in the positive direction of wholeness, integration, integrity and autonomy. As such, the person is believed to have the need and motivation for self-direction in order to become a fully functioning person.

Self-direction is at the heart of Rogers' conception of the human being. Since the person contains the potential for growth and perception internally, the responsibility "to will to be that self which one truly is, is the deepest responsibility of man" (Rogers, 1961, p. 110). But the opportunity for such growth, development, and unfolding must be provided. It does not occur in a vacuum, nor is it enhanced in harsh, autocratic circumstances. Nor is it discovered only in a therapeutic environment. The process of becoming a fully functioning person is essentially an educational issue because it requires significant learning, lifelong significant learning.

Humanist Views on Experience, Education and Learning
Significant learning is experiential because experiential learning is necessary for the development of fully functioning individuals. Experience represents for Rogers "the highest authority" (1961, p. 23), and as such the "touchstone of validity" for the person.

The aim of education is to assist the person in becoming a fully functioning individual. As Rogers expresses it:

> We can choose to use the behavioral sciences in ways which will free rather than control; which will bring about constructive variability, not conformity; which will develop creativity, not contentment; which will facilitate each person in his SELF-DIRECTED process of becoming which will aid individuals, groups, and even the concept of science to become self-transcending in freshly adaptive ways of meeting life and its problems. (emphasis added, Rogers, 1965, p. 396)

Self-directed learning then refers to the freedom to engage in significant learning. It is essentially an inner, subjective, existential freedom. The freedom to choose one's own attitude and to choose one's own way (Rogers, 1983).

Knowles' view of the self is humanistic while his approach to the adult education process is essentially progressive. Andragogy, as conceptualized and popularized by Knowles posits a set of assumptions which rest on the theological foundation that individuals have the ability to learn for themselves (Knowles, 1980). According to Knowles the adult learner is self-directed by virtue of being psychologically responsible for oneself (Knowles, 1984).

McKenzie in discussing Adult Education and The Burden of The Future (1978) acknowledges that adulthood is generally characterized by independence and self-direction. However, it must be noted that these characteristics are evident when adults are contrasted with children.

McKenzie posits that a different characterization of the adult emerges when we observe him or her in the world and in relation to the larger social, economic, and political forces which are constitutive of that world. Then, we are likely to find significant numbers of adults who are conditioned and even coerced by "ideas of fate, providence, and/or immanent, historical laws" (Merriam, 1984, p. 81).

The issue confronting adult education is not whether adults and children are different, but rather what qualities of adulthood require further development and expression in order to prevent apathy and subordination occasioned by simply yielding to perceived determinate sociohistorical forces. The dangers of determinism, in whatever form, should be countered by adult education which facilitates the development of autonomy.

Behaviorism

Behaviorism, according MacCorquodale (Matson, 1973), is the application of the methods of physical science investigations and explanations to the behavior of organisms. Behaviorists are committed to scientific approaches, techniques, and conclusions that derive from laboratory methods of experimental psychology. Such methodological approaches are considered appropriate to the study and understanding of human beings because since we exist in an ordered and deterministic universe, it follows that humans as part of that universe are subject to a similar order and determination.

Behaviorism as a perspective on the nature of humankind has moved through several developmental periods (Matson, 1973). The first period, referred to as classical behaviorism, encompasses the early experimental work of Pavlov, Thorndike and Watson. The second developmental period is demarcated by the idea of operant conditioning as conceived, developed, and advanced by Skinner. His explanation of operant conditioning sheds light on goal-directed behavior without reference to either mentalistic or neurophysiological influences.

The current and third period of behaviorism is known as cognitive behaviorism or social learning theory. This phase represents a departure from a strictly environmental interpretation of human behavior. Radical behaviorists like Watson and Skinner attempted to explain all human behavior as a function of a stimulus-response phenomenon, a construct that characterizes behavior as directly controlled by external stimuli which elicit a particular response from the individual. Yet, this unidirectional explanation of human behavior is no longer considered comprehensive enough to account adequately for the wide and complex range of human behaviors and actions (Matson, 1973; Bandura, 1977). For social learning theorists, human behavior must be correlated with cognitive, behavioral, and environmental factors. For Bandura:

> ... theorists who exclude the capacity for SELF-DIRECTION from their view of human potentialities restrict their research to external sources of influence. (emphasis added, Bandura, 1977, p. 21)

The Self as Reactive

Generally speaking, the behaviorist conceives of the self or person as a reactive organism, responding primarily to external causes and conditions. The idea of inner, subjective states as explanations for human behavior does not exist in the behavioral paradigm. Mental states and processes, however, are not entirely rejected. What is challenged is the belief that such an entity as the self should be credited as responsible for behavior.

Both classical and radical behaviorism conceive of the self or personality as representing a repertoire of behaviors acquired through a variety of contingencies; "A person is not an originating agent, he is a locus, a point at which genetic and environmental conditions come together in joint effort" (Skinner, 1974, p. 195). For this reason, if we want to know what meaning an experience has for an individual we must examine behavior, not his mind.

<u>Behavioral Views on Experience, Education and Learning</u>
The experience from which knowledge itself is derived is acquired by exploring the full range of contingencies available. (Skinner, 1974) Behavior, which constitutes personality, is determined by past and present events in the external world, not by internal events (Corey, 1986). Within this conceptualization of behavior, the notion of self-determination is simply not possible. Initial thinking and research in the field of behaviorism focused almost exclusively on behavior itself. The emphasis was on how observable behavior was acquired and how it could be changed. Modern behaviorists have introduced a collateral emphasis on cognition and its relationship to behavior. This bidirectional view of behavior is known as cognitive behaviorism or social learning theory. Tolman's work is an early contribution to this emergent view as is that of Schwitzgebel and Kolb (1974). A further elaboration of this idea has been provided by Bandura. Social learning, according to Bandura (1977: VII) "approaches the explanation of human behavior in terms of a continuous reciprocal interaction between cognitive, behavioral, and environmental determinants". Social learning theory acknowledges that individuals are capable of self-directed behavior change. In justifying his conclusion Bandura (1977) observes that if people's behavior were entirely determined by external forces they would behave like weathervanes. That is to say, if stimuli were so singularly potent, people would readily shift their positions and change their behavior with much greater frequency than they do. This, however, is not the case. People adhere to political, social, and religious positions in spite of adverse consequences. This being so, it is necessary to allow that people act on the basis of both observed consequences as well as consequences they create for themselves. Furthermore, the kinds of reinforcements that govern an

individual's behavior change are a result of developmental experiences. Thus, Bandura posits a developmental hierarchy of incentives which include material consequences, symbolic consequences, and social contracting arrangements. At the highest levels of development, individuals regulate their own behavior by self-evaluation and other self-produced consequences. In this model, the development of self-motivation and self-direction requires certain basic functions that are developed through the aid of external incentives. Once people have learned verbal, cognitive and manual skills for dealing effectively with their environment, they are capable of self-management and self-direction.

By acknowledging that individuals have a capacity for self-direction it is possible to develop methods which will assist people to effectively engage in self-control and self-management. Self-direction, though, is not a condition. It is a process, a continual engagement of the individual with changing situations. According to Watson and Tharp:

> SELF-DIRECTION is the ability to actualize one's values. It includes choice of goals, design of strategies, evaluation of outcomes, modification of tactics, and maintenance of valued behavior. (emphasis added, Watson and Tharp, 1977, p. 11)

The Critical Perspective

The fourth influence on self-directed learning is that of the critical perspective. This perspective is different in kind and form from the preceding perspectives. It is necessary to acknowledge that this perspective does not command the same level of abstraction or agreement within its boundaries or amongst its contributors.

Some of the viewpoints included in this umbrella term--critical perspective--are commentaries on the oppressive and dehumanizing nature of certain systems and ideologies. The anarchist tradition, for example, considers public compulsory education as an organized means for limiting individual autonomy by schooling people to accept and internalize the political and social agenda of those already in control. The Marxist position seeks to use personal and informal educational strategies to stimulate awareness of the alienating nature of a capitalistic political economy in order to promote informed social actions toward a more egalitarian, socialist society. While these two approaches critique social values and structures, the Freudian left examines and describes the processes by which authoritarianism and oppression are inculcated within the individual. In addition to examining the structure of educational systems this view also considers family and religious structures and their roles in limiting personal initiative and freedom. The role of education then, is not to condition, but to enlighten individuals as to how they have become subjugated and how they might release and change themselves as a necessary prerequisite to changing society (Elias and Merriam, 1980).

If humanism is representative of an optimistic view of the human condition then the critical perspective represents a negative viewpoint (Held, 1980). In part this is the case because thinkers from within this diverse perspective by and large criticize various intellectual and social systems. Moreover, it is antagonistic in the sense that this perspective negates propositions of universal givens in the realm of human affairs. That is, individuals are not determined to be free agents or objects of environmental control. Nor is the organization or operation of society so determined. This perspective argues that critical social theory is:

> ...designed so as to become part of a self-reflective movement towards a more rational society... It is therefore concerned with identifying the present possibilities for radical change towards a society in which human beings exercise fully their capacity for self-conscious control over social processes, and in which there is an absence of dominative power relationships and ideological consciousness. (Keat, 1981, p. 3)

The Self as Dialectical

The primary elements of the self are the various needs, impulses, and wishes which are continuously in various phases of integration and conflict (Held, 1980). The self is never finished or complete, but rather ever evolving under changing socio-historical conditions. As such, the self can never be conceived nor understood as absolute or in isolation from society. The development of the self is dialectical wherein the self must struggle with its own competing wants and desires as well as confronting dichotomies, opportunities, and limitations which must be realized and surpassed. The individual self is dependent upon the struggle between opposite forces: subject and object, mind and matter, individual and social system. The self only exists in a resistant world because it requires the tension between forces in order to give rise to self-awareness and self-emancipation.

The possibility of creating an autonomous, emancipated, liberated individual can only be sustained if structures which support closed patterns of thought and authoritarian systems are counteracted. Dialectic being and thinking require an ever increasing awareness of the nature of contradictions and opposition and the need to overcome them by way of synthesizing such conflicts into higher stages of knowing. It represents a process whereby the conscious self attempts to come to terms with a chaotic, irrational world through the continuous negation, that is, continuous criticism and reconstruction of knowledge. Selfhood, when so conceived, presumes the ability for transcendence of both the self and the current environment.

The Critical View of Experience, Education and Learning

As mentioned at the beginning of this section, the critical perspective is the most heterogeneous of the perspectives examined. Provided here, then, is an example of the neo-Marxist view in the work of Freire, a Marxist-socialist position in the work of Gelpi, an example of the Freudian left in the contribution of Mezirow, and the thinking of an educational critic in the work of Brookfield.

Freire does not use the phrase self-directed learning. The concept can be inferred from the core assumptions which underpin his philosophy. Freire assumes that human beings are free to create, act, and modify themselves and their world. Further, he believes that individuals change by changing their consciousness. However, people often suffer from false consciousness such that the self's agency, its volition and responsibility, is distorted. A process of conscientization (understanding the context of one's life) is required to gain insight into the nature of one's oppression, and to become self-directing. The process of conscientization is one of problem posing which affirms and facilitates the person in the process of becoming (Freire, 1970). The subject matter of problem posing education is the self and the self's environment. While there are stages of reparation required for conscientization, the ultimate goal is the development of a fully autonomous learner, one who directs himself/herself in reflection and action.

The work of Gelpi (1979) focuses our attention on lifelong education. He conceives of lifelong education as an egalitarian undertaking which has as its purpose social transformation. Transformation, Gelpi believes, can occur through education. But such a transformative process requires a degree of autonomy in relation to social forces. Lifelong education, then, consists of three elements: self-directed learning, acknowledgement of individual motivation, and learning systems which develop into new ways of life. Self-directed learning refers to a person's control over the ends, contents, and methods of education (Gelpi, 1979).

According to Mezirow (1985, p. 17), "No concept is more central to what adult education is all about than self-directed learning". In order to understand the centrality of this concept for Mezirow it is necessary to consider his theory of adult learning and education.

Building on the work of Habermas (1971) and Bateson (1972), Mezirow differentiates three interrelated but distinct kinds and functions of adult learning. Each of these domains of learning are significant because they are inclusive of adult cognitive interests. Furthermore, each domain has its own purpose, content, and methods and each allows for self-directed learning. They are instrumental learning which includes task oriented problem-solving learning required to control the environment, dialogic learning encompassing attempts to understand what others mean when communicating, and self-reflective learning which involves understanding oneself by identifying dependency producing psychological assumptions gained earlier in life.

The purpose of adult education is to enfranchise adults. That is, to enable adults to participate fully as self-directed learners in their quest to explore the meaning of experience. Thus:

> A SELF-DIRECTED learner must be understood as one who is aware of the constraints on his efforts to learn, including the psychocultural assumptions involving reified power relationships embedded in institutionalized ideologies which influence one's habit of perception, thought and behavior as one attempts to learn. A self-directed learner has access to alternative perspectives for understanding his or her situation and for giving meaning and direction to his or her life, has acquired sensitivity and competence in social interaction and has the skills and competencies required to master the productive tasks associated with controlling and manipulating the environment. (emphasis added, Mezirow, 1981, p. 21)

Andragogy, for Mezirow, represents a professional perspective for adult educators. As such, it involves an effort to help adults to learn in a way that enables them to increase their ability to be self-directed learners.

The aim of adult education practice, according to Brookfield (1986, p. 11), is the "nurturing of self-directed, empowered adults". The facilitation of such adult self-directed learning should encourage the critical exploration and analysis of assumptions, knowledge, and behaviors.

Brookfield acknowledges and distinguishes between the two forms of adult self-directed learning. One such form involves the technical elements of self-directed learning such as goal setting, resource identification, strategy selection, and the evaluation of outcomes. Another form of self-directed learning refers to a particular internal change in consciousness. This particular change in consciousness occurs when the learner acknowledges that knowledge, value, and social structures are relative and contextual. Such a change in consciousness makes possible altered perspectives which can transform their personal and social worlds.

Brookfield has long been an advocate of the concept of self-directed learning. Quite recently though he (1988) has come forward to recant much of his previous writing on self-directed learning. Acknowledging a number of conceptual and methodological contradictions, as well as philosophical and semantic ambiguities, he warns that an undue reliance on this concept is dangerous for the field of adult education. He draws special attention to the dual meaning of the word learning. When used as a noun it refers to a change in consciousness. When used as a verb learning refers to a collection of activities and techniques. Thus, confusion abounds when the term self-directed learning appears in the literature. This confusion is no longer acceptable because:

> "it is now past the point where the most often used word in our professional vocabulary and the concept which is most central to our research activities, is still befuddled by confusion and definitional ambiguity." (Brookfield, 1987, p. 7)

Further, he has increasing difficulty in describing any act of learning as fully self-directed. This is because Brookfield has come to conceive of learning as a negotiated transactional process which is neither completely other or self-directed.

SUMMARY AND CONCLUSION

In probing for conceptual clarity this chapter considered four philosophical perspectives which address the idea of self-directed learning. In so doing the metaphor of theme and variations emerged as a useful way to organize our thinking about the range, diversity and complexity of ideas informing the concept of self-directed learning.

Theme and variations, in the world of music, represents a form of musical composition consisting of a singular melodic phrase, played first in its original form and then advanced several times with varied treatments. In the realm of adult education it is important to acknowledge that self-directed learning is the melody over which many of our assumptions about personhood, autonomy, adulthood and freedom are played out. Moreover, the theme of self-directed learning resonates and echoes throughout the field of adult education such that it commands attention and interest. The idea emerges from the literature as a potent concept which bridges numerous philosophical orientations. It is now clear from this examination that it is also an idea which possesses great variation as well.

From the outset, this exploration of self-directed learning sought to probe the inter-related concepts of selfhood, experience, education and learning. Figure 4.1 provides a matrix which illustrates the key findings and allows for easy comparison and contrast of these four concepts.

While there is a similarity in the language used, that is all four perspectives reference to selfhood, experience, education and learning these referents emerge from very different philosophical contexts which alter the meaning of utility of the concept of self-directed learning.

Figure 4.1: SELF-DIRECTED LEARNING MATRIX

	PROGRESSIVISM	HUMANISM	BEHAVIORISM	CRITICAL
SELFHOOD	Organization of habits and interests.	Intellectual emotional, instinctual aspects of personality	Develops in response to external causes and condiitons.	Needs, impulses wishes in various phases of integration.
	Self is acquired thru situations	Self is inborn	Self is reactive	Self is evolving
EXPERIENCE	Transaction between individual and environ-ment	Interaction between individual and environ ment	Exchange between cognitive, behavioral environmental factors	Struggle between opposing forces
EDUCATION	Reconstruc-tion of experience	Fully self-actualized and fully functioning individual	Stimulus-Response consequences	Altered Consciousness
LEARNING	Consideration of and reflec-tion on experience	Experiential	Change in observable behavior	Interpretation of experience

The foregoing inquiry into the meaning of self-directed learning has revealed four variations on the theme of self-directed learning. Figure 4.2 offers a schematic representation of how each perspective conceives and understands the self concept and how selected thinkers have rendered the idea of self-directed learning.

The progressive understand the self as emerging through a variety of transactions amongst the person and his or her physical and social environment. Self-directed learning is essentially understood by Dewey, Lindeman, Bryson, and Mearns as an active pursuit of self-knowledge undertaken in order to understand and direct one's interests, values, and behaviors. Bryson is one of the first theorists to emphasize a dual function for self-directed learning such that it can be understood as a process of instrumental learning as well as a process of self-knowledge.

The humanists conceive of the self as an innate source of agency which is self-actional in its pursuit of self-actualization. Here again we see that self-directed learning is conceived of in several ways. For Rogers and Knowles self-directed learning is an attribute of the the natural personality. Rogers also understands self-directed learning as a process of self-knowledge, while Knowles understands self-directed learning as a process of instrumental learning. McKenzie envisions self-directed learning as exclusively within the instrumental domain.

The behavioral perspective is characterized by three periods of development. The first and second periods, that of classical and radical behaviorism, disallow the idea of self-directed learning and this fact accounts for the absence of any reference to Watson and Skinner in the classification. For the social learning theorists, however, self-directed learning and behavior change reflect the goal setting capacities of an individual who can learn and master

Figure 4.2: Classification of Perspectives on Self-Directed Learning

Perspective / Concept of Self / View of Self-directed Learning	Progressivism	Humanism	Behaviorism	Critical
	transac-tional	self-actional	reactive	dialectic
Personal Attribute		Knowles Rogers		
Self-control/ Management			Bandura Watson & Tharp	
Self-knowledge	Dewey Lindeman Bryson, Mearns	Rogers		Freire Mezirow Brookfield
Instrumental	Bryson	Knowles McKenzie		Mezirow Brookfield Gelpi

the techniques of arranging various reinforcers and environmental conditioners.

For the critical theorists the self is developed in a dialectic relationship wherein struggle and tension are necessary for the self to be realized and released. Here too, theorists of this persuasion understand self-directed learning in several ways. Both Mezirow and Brookfield acknowledge that self-directed learning can be applicable in the domains of both instrumental learning and self-knowledge. For Gelpi it is understood as a process of instrumental learning, while Freire emphasizes the process of self-knowledge.

Thus, at one end of the scale self-directed learning is understood as a personal attribute based on the premise that the capacity for self-directedness is an intrinsic characteristic present in human beings. Self-directed learning, as it relates to self-control/self-management, refers to the techniques of goal selection by predetermining outcomes and arranging contingencies. Self-directed learning, as it relates to self-knowledge, refers to the discovery and understanding of oneself as well as the capacity to create and reconceptualize. On the other end of the scale is self-directed learning, as it relates to instrumental learning which refers to the process of acquiring information and skills necessary for the effective management of the environment

In conclusion, we do not have a univocal concept of self-directed learning. Instead we have four variations on the theme of self-directed learning which function not only to describe and explain this phenomenon, but also to enjoin action.

REFERENCES

Bandura, A. (1977). Social learning theory. Englewood Cliffs, N.J.: Prentice Hall.

Batson, G. (1972). Steps to an ecology of mind. New York: Basic Books.

Boydston, J. (Ed.) (1970). Guide to the work of John Dewey. Carbondale: Southern Illinois University Press.

Brookfield, S.D. (1988). Conceptual, methodological and practical ambiguities in self-directed learning. In H. Long and Associates: Adult self-directed learning: Application and theory. Athens: University of Georgia Press.

Brookfield, S.D. (1986). Understanding and facilitating adult learning: A comprehensive analysis of principles and effective practices. San Francisco: Jossey Bass.

Brookfield, S.D. (Ed.) (1985). Self-directed learning: From theory to practice. San Francisco: Jossey Bass.

Bryson, L. (1936). Adult education. New York: American Co.

Bugental, J.F. (Ed.) (1967). Challenges of humanistic psychology. New York: McGraw Hill.

Coolican, P.M. (1974). The Learning Style of Mothers of Young Children. Dissertation abstracts international, 35, 783A-784A.

Corey, G. (1986). Theory and practice of counseling and psychotherapy. (3rd ed.). Monterey: Brooks/Cole.

Cremin, L.A. (1964). The transformation of the school: Progressivism in American education, 1876-1957. New York: Vintage.

Darkenwald, G.S. and Merriam, S.B. (1982). Adult education: Foundations of practice. New York: Harper and Row.

Denys, L.O.J. (1975). The Major Learning Efforts of Two Groups of Accra Adults. Dissertation abstracts international, 35, 579A.

Dewey, J. (1969). Outlines of a critical theory of ethics. New York: Greenwood Press.

Dewey, J. (1938). Experience and education. New York: Macmillan.

Dewey, J. (1922). Human nature and conduct. New York: Henry Holt and Co.

Dewey, J. (1916). Democracy and education: An introduction to the philosophy of education. New York: Macmillan.

Dewey, J. (1899). The school and society. Chicago: University of Chicago Press.

Elias, J.L. and Merriam, S. (1980). Philosophical foundations of adult education. Florida: Krieger.

Freire, P. (1985). The politics of education. South Hadley, MA: Gergin and Garvey.

Freire, P. (1970). Pedagogy of the oppressed. New York: Herder and Herder.

Gelpi, E. (1979). A future for lifelong education. Volumes 1 and 2 (Manchester Monographs No. 13) Manchester, England: University of Manchester.

Goldstein, H. (1981). Social learning and change: A cognitive approach to human services. New York: Tavestock Pub.

Greene, M. (1973). Teacher as stranger: Educational philosophy for the modern age. Belmont: Wodsworth.

Griffin, V. (1978). Self-Directed Adult Learners and Learning. In G. Selman (Ed.), Learning, 2. Toronto: Canada.

Habermas, J. (1971). Knowledge and human interests. Boston: Beacon Press.

Hastings, J. (Ed.) (undated). Encyclopedia of religion and ethics. New York: Scribner and Sons.

Held, D. (1980). Introduction to critical theory: Horkheimer to Habermas. Berkeley: University of California Press.

Houle, C.O. (1961). The inquiring mind: A study of the adult who continues to learn. Madison, WI: University of Wisconsin Press.

Kathrein, M.A. (1981). A study of the self-directed continued professional learning activities of members of Illinois Nurses Association. Unpublished dissertation, University of Maryland.

Keat, R. (1981). The politics of social theory. Chicago: University of Chicago Press.

Knowles, M.S. (1984). Andragogy in action. San Francisco: Jossey Bass.

Knowles, M.S. (1980). The modern practice of adult education. From pedagogy to andragogy. Chicago: Follett.

Knowles, M.S. (1975). Self-directed learning: A guide for learners and teachers. Chicago: Follett.

Knowles, M.S. (1973). The adult learner: A neglected species. (2nd ed.). Houston Gulf.

Lamont, C. (1965). The philosophy of humanism. New York: Basic Books.

Lindeman, E.C. (1926). The meaning of adult education. New York: New Republic. (Reissued in 1961 by Harvest House Publ., Montreal).

Long, H.B. and Associates (1988). Self-directed learning: Application and theory. Georgia: University of Georgia.

Maslow, A.H. (1970). Motivation and personality. New York: Harper and Row.

Matson, F.W. (Ed.) (1973). Without/within: Behaviorism and humanism. Brooks/Cole.

McKenzie, L. (1978).. Adult education and the burden of the future. Washington, D.C.: University Press of America.

Mearns, H. (1940). The creative adult: Self-education in the art of living. New York: Doubleday and Co.

Merriam, S.B. (Ed) (1984). Selected writings on philosophy and adult education. Florida: Krieger.

Mezirow, J. (1985). A critical theory of self-directed learning. In Brookfield, S.D. (Ed.) Self-directed learning: From theory to practice. San Francisco: Jossey Bass.

Mezirow, J. (1981). A critical theory of adult learning and education. Adult Education, 32, 3-27.

Mezirow, J. (1971). Toward a theory of practice. Adult Education Journal, 21, 135-147.

Ravitch, D. (1974). The great school wars: New York City, 1805-1973. New York: Basic Books.

Rogers, C.R. (1983). Freedom to learn for the 80s. Ohio: Merrill.

Rogers, C.R. (1965). The place of the person in the new world of the behavioral sciences. In F.T. Severin (Ed.) Humanistic Viewpoints in Psychology. New York: McGraw Hill.

Rogers, C.R. (1961). On becoming a person: A therapist's view of psychotherapy. Boston: Houghton, Mifflin Co.

Schwitzgebel, R.K. and Kolb, D.A. (1974). Changing human behavior: Principles of planned intervention. New York: McGraw Hill.

Skager, R. (1984). Organizing schools to encourage self direction in learners. Oxford: Pergamon Press.

Skinner, B.F. (1953). Science and human behavior. New York: Free Press.

Skinner, B.F. (1976). About behaviorism. New York: Vintage.

Smith, R.M. (1982). Learning how to learn: Applied theory for adults. Illinois: Follett.

Thomas, J.E. (1982). Radical adult education: Theory and practice. Nottingham: University of Nottingham.

Tough, A. (1971). The adult's learning projects. Toronto: Ontario Institute for Studies in Education.

Watson, D.L. and Tharp, R.G. (1977). Self-directed behavior: Self-modification for personal adjustment. California: Brooks/Cole.

Watson, J.B. (1913). Psychology as the Behaviorist Views It. Psychological review, 20, 158-177.

Zottoli, J.V. (1984). Self-Directed Learning in Public Management Masters Program. Dissertation abstracts international, 45, 264A.

Chapter Five

SELF-DIRECTED LEARNING - A GROWTH PROCESS?

Gordon Eisenman

In the last two decades the concept of self-directed learning has been the focus of much attention and study by adult educators. Certainly, more recognition has been given to self-directed learning research in the last 20 years than any other comparable span in history. The proliferation of self-directed learning studies revealed in literature reviews (Tough, 1978; Mocker and Spear, 1982; and Caffarella and O,Donnell, 1987) indicates the importance adult educators place on self-directed learning. These reviews present evidence that there is self-directed learning taking place in the vast majority of adults. Adult learners plan and conduct personal learning projects using a variety of techniques and resources while differing in background, learning style, incentive, self-perception, and personality. While much has been written, no consensus of opinion among adult educators has been reached as to the origin of self-directed learning in individuals. Indeed, there is not even agreement as to a definition of the term "self-directed learning". There is no last word on self-directed learning, only continuing words. More research will follow. The fact remains, however, that self-directed learning in a conceptual development stage is an important segment of the discipline's knowledge base and will continue to be a major concept in the field of adult education (Caffarella and O'Donnell, 1987; Brookfield, 1984).

With regard to the origins of self-directed learning, two divergent opinions seem to have emerged among the adult educators. One view is that self-directed learning is a function of a person's experience (Bonham, 1987). In particular, researchers have found correlations between self-directed learning and adults' formal educational experiences (Bejot, 1981; Hassen, 1982; Long and Agyekum, 1983, 1984; Sabbaghian, 1980). This correlation between formal education and self-directed learning suggests the presence of extrinsic variables in the early life of the person that contribute to the development of a tendency toward independence in learning. The other prevailing opinion regarding the origin of self-direction in the individual is that self-directed learning is a function of a natural maturation process that develops as persons age. An underlying theme of Malcolm Knowles' assumption of adult learning is that adults possess both a deep need to be self-directing and to be seen by others as being self-directing (1970 and 1980). While not stating a theory as to the origin of that self-direction, Knowles does assert that the adult's past experience plays an important role in the current learning endeavors. This theoretical construct of a person's readiness for self-directed learning seems to infer that individuals possess an innate tendency for growth in self-direction as they advance toward adulthood. It does not appear, however, that each person arrives at adulthood with the same amount of self-directedness in their educational endeavors (Tough, 1979).

Experience is an active ingredient in both of the above opinions regarding the origins of self-directed learning. It should be noted, however, that one group emphasizes experience that influences individuals by means of external variables, and the other recognizes experience as the catalyst that unlocks the internal tendency to be self-directing.

Little research (Skager, 1984; Torrance and Mourand, 1978) has been conducted into childhood self-directed learning. In a cognate area, however, there have been hundreds of studies relating to significant variables leading to academic achievement in children. Jenks (1979) and Coleman (1966) have shown that the total socio-economic factors in the child's background bear a strong relation to academic achievement. There are also several characteristics of family life that influence the academic achievement of children. The most common are the beliefs or attitudes of parents and the behaviors of parents relative to the learning of their children at home and school. While strong evidence exists that the parents' positive regard for the school has considerable association with their children's success in school (Christopher, 1967; Garbarion, 1982; and Moss and Kagan, 1961), direct parent-child interactions appear to be better measures of educationally relevant home factors.

Research of school effectiveness places an emphasis upon strong institutional leadership and teacher expectations for students. Research data on teacher expectation has revealed that many teachers treat high- and low-achieving students differently, and that teachers' expectations appear to be associated with student achievement. Literature reviews have shown this to be a consistent view of researchers (Brophy and Good, 1974; Cooper, 1979; Braun, 1976; and Smith, 1980). Teacher classroom practices as well as behaviors are significant in developing and maintaining high academic achievement for students (Rutter and others, 1979; Squires, 1980; Brookover and others, 1982; and Wynne, 1980).

If then, as research indicates, children are influenced by external forces such as parents and teachers to achieve academically in a structured school setting, is it possible that the self-directed learning factor in these same students could also be influenced by parents and teachers?

Because of its close ties with the educational experiences, cognitive ability was also considered in this study as a possible enhancement for self-directed learning.

Cognitive ability or intelligence from the standpoint of this literature review centers around individual differences in intellectual skill and common cognitive developmental patterns. First, that people differ in their intellectual skill (Bee, 1985) is an incontestable fact and it was this supposition that gave rise to the development of intelligence (IQ) tests. Binet (1916) structured the first IQ tests as predictors of academic success in school and such tests are still used principally for that reason. While high intelligence test scores do not guarantee academic achievement, research has shown a correlations factor between scores and grades of about .60 (Sattler, 1974). Such a correlation suggests that children with high IQ scores will tend to be at the top of their classes and that those with low scores tend to be at the bottom academically.

Intelligence test scores are good predictors of both present and future school success (Eichorn and others, 1981). These researchers have shown that preschool children who test high will likely be good students in elementary school. The same pattern holds true for those children in upper elementary grades. Those with superior IQ scores will tend to be at the upper half of their class in high school. Researchers have not reached the point where they can make the statement that IQ is the causal factor in performance, but they can say that intelligence can be used to forecast academic success.

A second incontestable fact regarding cognitive ability is that children develop in predictable patterns. Many researchers who have studied cognitive ability believe "intelligence develops. Behavior becomes increasingly complex and abstractly organized with age" (Butterfield, Silado, and Belmont, 1980). Piaget's theory of cognitive development has become the dominant theory explaining how children learn. In Piaget's (1970) view, heredity, environment, and maturation (the process of growing up) all interact in the development of intelligence. Children attempt continually to adapt to their environment.

It is the general belief among adult educators that self-directed learning is a function of a person's experiences in general (Bonham, 1987), and the educational experience in particular (Bejot, 1981; Hassan, 1982). Since cognitive ability is highly correlated with education (Eichorn and others, 1981) the possibility exists that cognitive ability and self-directed learning are also correlated. Little research (Chickering, 1969; Gunzburger, 1980) however, has been conducted in the area of intelligence as it relates to self-directed learning. Chickering (1969) in studying independent study students at Goddard College noted "the measures of intelligence, information, and academic skills in reading, writing, and critical thinking do not differentiate the independent student from the norm" (p. 40). Stated another way, there was no correlation between cognitive ability and self-directed learning. Gunzburger (1980) came to a similar conclusion in comparing the 1956 Chicago Pritzker School of Medicine student entrance test scores to the same students' independence in continuing education some fourteen years later. He found that entrance test scores did not identify the extent to which individuals later become independent continuing learners. In their comprehensive literature review of self-directed learning, Caffarella and O'Donnell (1987) assert that more research is needed in the area of intelligence as it relates to self-directed learning. It should be noted also that to date no study has dealt with children's cognitive ability and self-directedness in learning.

In summary, intelligence tests have shown people to differ in cognitive abilities even though they develop intellectually in similar pattern. Both heredity and environment seem to play roles in cognitive development, though researchers and theorists do not agree as to the amount of variance for each. It has been shown that both self-directed learning and cognitive ability are correlated with the educational experiences. It seems reasonable then to assume that self-directed learning and cognitive ability might also be related. Two researchers (Chickering, 1969; Gunzburger, 1980) seem to contradict this notion but more research is needed before dofinitive statements can be made.

Cognitive development becomes increasingly more complex and abstractedly organized with age. Piaget, whose cognitive development theory remains dominant in explaining how children learn, views heredity, environment and motivation as interacting in the cognitive development process.

The purpose of this study was to determine the extent to which the self-directed learning readiness present in parents and teachers is related to the level of self-directedness in their children. This study also sought to determine whether student scores on the Self-Directed Learning Readiness Scale (SDLRS) correlated with student scores on the Cognitive Abilities Test. An additional purpose of this study was to obtain base line data and set the format for a longitudinal study to test the adult education assumption that as persons mature they become increasingly more and more self-directed in their approach to learning. It is possible that follow up studies will re-test the subjects in this study in subsequent years to determine if indeed they are increasing in their self-directed learning readiness.

In an effort to verify the presence of experiential factors in early life as they relate to SDL and to explore cognitive ability association with SDL, 289 students out of a total population of 758 fifth grade students in the Clarke County, George School District were administered the Self-Directed Learning Readiness Scale (SDLRS). Of the completed forms, 209 were usable. Scores from the students' Cognitive Abilities Test were obtained from student files and used to compare with SDLRS scores. Also included in the sample were SDLRS scores from 18 fifth grade teachers and 41 parents (27 mothers and 14 fathers) representing 33 households. Correlations were analyzed between teacher and student SDLRS scores, between parent and student SDLRS scores, and between student SDLRS and Cognitive Abilities Test scores. Correlations were considered to be significant at the .05 level. Correlations for each of the three hypothesis, however, were found to be non-significant at the .05 level. The following section is a discussion of the findings relating to the three hypothesis.

PRESENTATION OF FINDINGS

Instruments

The Self-Directed Learning Readiness Scale. The Self-Directed Learning Readiness Scale (SDLRS), a 58-item Likert type scale, was designed to show the degree to which persons perceive themselves to have skills and attitudes commonly associated with self-direction in learning. Guglielmino (1977) developed the SDLRS using a three-round Delphi survey involving fourteen recognized experts in the field of self-directed learning. The finished instrument was administered to 307 individuals. After several revisions the scale was estimated by Guglielmino to have a reliability coefficient of .87. For additional information on the scale, see Guglielmino (1977).

The SDLRS has been the instrument in many studies since 1977 (Long and Agyekum, 1983, 1984; Torrance and Mourad, 1978; Sabbaghian, 1979; Savoie, 1979; Caffarella and Caffarella, 1983; Kasworm, 1982). According to Brockett (1985), two major directions of self-direction have been explored using the scale. The first is the relationship between self-directed learning and other psychological variables such as creativity (Tourance and Mourad, 1978) and self-concept (Sabbaghian, 1979). The second thrust has been the use of the SDLRS as a diagnostic instrument. Brockett cites, for example, Savoie (1979) who used the SDLRS to predict success for nurses in whose jobs learners were expected to possess high levels of self-direction. These cited studies are representative of the many investigations which have used the SDLRS. From such studies there appears to be general agreement and support for the validity and reliability of the instrument.

Guglielmino later designed an elementary (E) version of the SDLRS using similar questions to the adult version but with simpler wording. The elementary version of the SDLRS has been used with children as young as fifth grade (Torrance and Mourad, 1978). In order to determine the possibility of using the E version with younger children, this researcher asked the opinion of four elementary school teachers as to the lowest grade they believed the test could be administered successfully. All four indicated fifth grade. Based on previous research (Torrance and Mourad, 1978) and the opinion of professional teachers, it was determined that fifth grade would be the student population for this study.

The Cognitive Abilities Test. The Cognitive Abilities Test is a revision and extension of the Lorge-Thorndike Intelligence Test. In addition to the verbal and nonverbal sections that were part of the Lorge-Thorndike, a quantitative section has been added. Tests are available for kindergarten through grade 12. This study used the Multi-Level Edition which encompasses grades 3-12. The Cognitive Abilities Test is administered annually to students in grades 2-5 of the Clarke County, Georgia School District.

Data Gathering

To provide the data base form which the analyses could be made, letters were sent to the parents of every fifth grade student in the Clarke County, Georgia School District. The purpose of the letter was to request parental approval for their child's participation in the self-directed learning readiness testing. Two hundred eighty-nine positive parental forms were returned.

The 289 students were administered the elementary version of the SDLRS and their teachers completed the adult version. After screening the finished scales for completeness, proper signatures and other relevant factors, 209 acceptable student scales and 18 teacher scales were identified. A second letter along with two adult versions of the SDLRS was sent to the homes of the 209 students. Parents in these homes were asked to complete the scale. The 33 responding households yielded 27 mother and 14 father completed forms. Student scores from the Cognitive Abilities Tests (quantitative, verbal and nonverbal sections) were obtained from student records.

Data Analysis

As reported above, data consisted of parent, teacher and student scores on the SDLRS, and student scores from the Cognitive Abilities Test. SDLRS data were grouped by school classes for the purpose of comparing teacher and student scores. Parent scores were coupled with their child's scores.

Data were analyzed using the interactive microcomputer statistical analysis package, STATISTIX, from NH Software. Scores from each group were visually inspected by means of scatter diagrams and histograms and statistically treated with the Person Product Moment. Because some of the data were not normally distributed, all data were treated also with the Spearman Rank Correlations test. Null hypotheses not meeting the .05 level of significance were retained. Listed below are the hypotheses tested in this study along with an accompanying data analysis.

Hypothesis 1: There is no significant relationship between teacher SDLRS scores and student SDLRS scores.

The SDLRS score was calculated by adding the values of 1, 2, 3, 4, or 5 marked for each of the 58 items on the scale. Using the above procedure, a total score was computed for each participant. The lowest possible total score was 58 and the highest possible 290.

Once the scales were scored, the data were visually examined so as to determine if there was a trend in the data and/or if differences existed between teacher and student scores. A histogram of students indicated that the spread of student SDLRS scores closely aligned with a normal curve but having a slight skewing to the right. To assist in the visual analysis, a scatter diagram was made of the total score for students and teachers. This diagram was developed by first ranking the student and teacher scores from lowest to highest and then plotting the student scores that were associated with the teacher scores. The diagram visualization indicated that the correlation between teacher and student scores was small. This visualization was supported by both the Person Product Moment and the Spearman Rank Correlations tests with correlation coefficients of 0.0331 and 0.0301 respectively. Since the correlation did not meet the .05 level of significance, the hypothesis was retained.

Hypothesis 2: There is no significant relationship between parent SDLRS scores and student SDLRS scores.

Only 33 of 209 households responded by completing the adult version of the Self-Directed Learning Readiness Scale. These 33 households yielded scores for 27 mothers and 14 fathers. Though neither was of sufficient sample size to allow for conclusions to be made, it is interesting to note a correlation trend in the mother's scores and student scores. The Spearman Rank Correlation Test yielded a correlation coefficient of .03621. As a result of the extremely small sample size of the father's scores, no attempt was made to analyze the data.

Hypothesis 3: There is no significant relationship between student SDLRS scores and student Cognitive Abilities Test scores.

Histograms for verbal, quantitative, and nonverbal sections of this test reveal a more evenly distributed range of scores from lowest to highest. Such variation from the normal curve raises questions regarding the validity of the Pearson Test for this particular set of data since that test assumes that variables are normally distributed. Therefore, to further test the data the Spearman Rank Test was performed on all data.

Scatter diagrams comparing student scores on the SDLRS and student scores on the Cognitive Abilities Test (verbal, quantitative, and nonverbal sections) were designed by ranking the various scores and plotting the SDLRS scores against the Cognitive Abilities test scores. Visual inspection yielded noticeably low correlation between SDLRS scores and verbal, quantitative, and nonverbal scores. A Spearman Rank Correlations test substantiated the visual observations by revealing low correlations of 0.0863 (verbal), 0.1181 (quantitative), and 0.0867 (nonverbal).

Scatter diagrams corroborated the low correlations between the SDLRS scores and the Cognitive Abilities Test scores by showing a relatively strong trend of correlations between quantitative, and nonverbal vs verbal. Since the correlations between the SDLRS scores and the Cognitive Abilities Test scores did not meet the .05 level of significance, the hypothesis was retained.

SUMMARY OF FINDINGS

Null hypotheses numbers 1 and 3 were statistically tested and found to not meet the .05 level of correlation significance. They were, therefore, retained. Because of insufficient parental response, no conclusion was reached regarding hypothesis 2.

Discussion of the Findings

Hypothesis number one that there is no significant relationship between teacher SDLRS scores and student SDLRS scores was retained. Even though earlier related research (Jencks, 1979; Brookover and others, 1979; Levine and Stark, 1981; Smith, 1980; and Bruner, 1960) had shown parents and teachers to be highly influential variables in their children's development of academic ability, moral judgement, and social adjustment, that same relationship regarding self-direction in matters of learning approaches was not evident in this study. Correlation coefficients for teacher scores vs student scores as calculated by the Spearman Rank Correlation and the Person Product Moment tests were 0.0301 and 0.0331 respectively. Because these correlations were non-significant, null hypothesis number one was retained.

These findings might be attributable to the school grade of the children (fifth). Thomas Good (1980) found that teacher influence on student achievement and behavior is greater in primary grades when students still accept teacher authority roles and have not yet taken cognizance of their own power to be independent. Children are also influenced by external variables (authority figures in this case) when they are of early preschool age, when parents seem to allow them more freedom to explore. Greater restrictions are placed upon the child's personal choices as the child approaches school age. As children move through elementary, middle, and high school years, they are less likely to be influenced by the adults in their lives. If this is true in these related areas of child development, then perhaps it could be speculated that parents and teachers of preschoolers and early grade children have a greater opportunity to prompt the course of self-direction in their children. It seems reasonable, too, that perhaps the adult who spends more time with the child has the greater chance for making an impact upon the child's behavior. In this regard, it is interesting to note that (even though the correlation was not within the significance level) the correlation of mother and child was higher (0.3621) than the teacher and student (0.0331).

Even though no conclusion from this study's data can be drawn as to adult influence upon the child's self-directedness, other researchers (Deci and Ryan, 1981; Skager, 1984) believe that there is the possibility that adult influence upon the child has the potential to be an inhibition as well as an enhancement for the child's self-direction. In contrast to the adult education assumption that humans tend to increase in their ability to be self-directing in learning approaches as they increase in age, Deci and Ryan state that "for young children, self-directed learning is a fact of life. They are curious, they go to things that interest them, they marvel at each new discovery" (p. 1). A transformation seems to take place as the child ages. Much of their learning seems to come from regulated instructions by parents and teachers. The intrinsic motivation is replaced by extrinsic pressure from significant adults. Thus, the child becomes dependent upon the adult to dictate what should be learned and how to learn. The adult (teacher/parent) even evaluates the child's learning progress. Some adult educators (Dressel and Thompson, 1973; Guglielmino, 1977; and Knowles, 1975) concur, arguing that many adults fail to develop self-direction in learning because of early experiences of strict teach classroom control that retards autonomy.

Following the above line of reasoning, one could speculate that children are born with the innate ability to be self-directed and do indeed exhibit self-directed learning during the preschool years as they explore their world. At the onset of formal schooling, children are quickly regimented into a dependent mode by teachers (and by parents at home). Much of the child's autonomous spirit is suppressed. The self-directed learning tendencies remain submerged throughout the formal training years but begin a push toward the surface in the middle and high school. The teen years, then may not be so much a period of rebellion as they are an effort to once again find the autonomy that was theirs from the beginning. Early in adulthood when persons finish formal training and move from their parents' house, the significant other influence is largely removed. It is then that the natural tendency to be self-directed resurfaces in various areas of life including approaches to learning.

To emphasize the above "suppressed" self-directed learning suggestion, a parallel observation can be drawn between the learning approaches used by preschoolers and by adults. Child developmentalists (Piaget, 1952; Bee, 1985) have shown that preschool children discover new knowledge by solving problems that face them. While much of their solutions are by trial and error, preschoolers nevertheless use problem solving as their primary vehicle to learning. Adults, according to Knowles (1980), also seek knowledge as a means to solve situational problems. "To adults, education is a process of improving their ability to deal with life problems they face now. They tend, therefore, to enter an educational activity in a **problem-centered** frame of mind?" (p. 48, emphasis added).

School children, on the other hand, according to Knowles (1980), see education as a gathering and storing of curriculum information to be used later in life. "Children tend, therefore, to enter any educational activity in a **subject-centered** frame of mind" (p. 48). As discussed earlier, however, it is likely that it is actually adult (parent/teacher) dominance and suppression that creates the appearance that children pass through a non-self-directed stage. Perhaps it is that adults create a synthetic learning atmosphere for children.

Skager (1984) and Knowles (1980) believe that the major attention of formal school curriculum should be placed on the process of developing skills that would enable students to know how to learn. While these educators do not suggest neglecting content, they believe students will ultimately learn more if they learn how to learn. Skager (1984) suggests that there are elements in most schools' learning structures that inhibit the process of learning skills growth. These elements include (1) using memorization as principal method of learning; (2) focusing on answers rather than the procedure through which the answers were reached; (3) teacher imposition rather than student voluntarism; and (4) developing teacher control strategies. Skager believes that developing a more democratic school atmosphere will result in greater student self-directedness.

In summary, because young children seem to be more susceptible to adult authority, it could be speculated that teachers and parents can be either an inhibition or an enhancement to the self-directedness of their children regardless of their own level of self-directedness. As other studies have suggested (Dressel and Thompson, 1973; Guglielmino, 1977; and Knowles, 1975), it seems plausible that the innate human tendency to be self-directing may be suppressed in children by teachers and parents during the formal education years. Once the individual has graduated and moves away from the parental home, self-directedness resurfaces.

Hypothesis number two that states there is no difference between parent Self-Directed Learning Readiness Scale scores and the scores of their children remained without conclusion for lack of sufficient responses from parents. Only 16 percent (33) of the households returned a completed scale. These 33 households yielded 27 mother and 14 father scores. There are a number of possible reasons for the limited cooperation from parents in this study. One might be a lack of time. More families today are finding two incomes necessary to provide the basics for the home. If this is true, then it could be speculated that parents do care about the welfare of their children and are willing to sacrifice time with the family in order to provide material stability in the household. This same line of reasoning may be applied to the single parent home where the parent has no choice but to work in order for the family to survive. In such cases, then it is not a matter of parental apathy toward education but rather a greater parental concern for food, clothing, and shelter.

The other side of this issue is that perhaps a significant number of parents are not concerned enough about the education of their children to have that positive regard toward learning which leads to academic nurturing of the children and displays supportive attitudes for the school (Christopher, 1967; Garbarino, 1982; Moss and Kagan, 1961; and Morrow and Wilson, 1961). In informal interviews during the course of this study, teachers cited the lack of parental support as a leading contributor to the poor academic performance of many students in their classrooms. Could it be that lack of parental concern is also a factor in the low correlation between parent and child scores in self-directedness?

The lack of correlation of SDLRS scores between teachers and students and parents and children (hypotheses 1 and 2) might also suggest that the matter of self-directed learning development might not be so much one person (adult) influencing another person (child), but rather might be the result of a maturation process that takes place in varying degrees in all humans. This notion would be in keeping with theories postulated by developmentalists Maslow (1954) and Rogers (1969) who both believed that human development is a natural process that takes place with age. While this maturation does not proceed at the same pace nor does each person reach the same levels, "such an orientation to the adult learner...focuses upon the **process** of development" (Darkenwald and Merriam, 1982, p. 87). Knowles (1980) also makes a case for self-directed learning as a maturation process. While he does not give reasons for nor state how this maturation takes place, Knowles (1980) says that "as a person matures, his concept moves from one of being a dependent personality toward one of being self-directed human being" (p. 39).

Hypothesis number three that there is no significant relationship between student Self-Directed Learning Readiness Scale scores and student Cognitive Abilities Test scores was retained. The Spearman Rank Correlation statistical tests revealed correlations of only 0.0863 for student vs verbal, 0.1181 for student vs quantitative, and 0.0867 for student vs nonverbal. These findings are in keeping with earlier research results (Chickering, 1969; Gunzburger, 1980) which suggest that the capacity to be a self-directed learner is not associated with intelligence. It may be that self-directed learning is a trait to be found generalized in the population. This is not to imply that each person has the same amount of innate capacity for self-direction, but rather to intimate that the population as a whole might possibly be born with varying tendencies toward self-directed learning.

Such reasoning would also tend to support Oddi's (1987) call for viewing self-directed learning from a personality perspective rather than from a process of self-instruction or natural maturation. Oddi believes that personality is a relatively constant factor that would furnish a consolidated and comprehensive basis for research in self-directed learning.

As she points out, theory and research on self-directed learning have concentrated on self-instructional procedures that include such steps as needs assessment, goal setting, learning plans, learning activities, and evaluation. Oddi (1986) cites theorists Bruner (1961), and Dewey (1951) in saying that most learning, however does not take place through the instructional process. Learning occurs most often through individual personalities "characterized by initiative and persistence in learning over time through a variety of modes, such as the modes of inquiry, instruction, and performance proposed by Houle (1980)" (Oddi, 1986).

In designing the Oddi Continuing Learning Inventory scale, Oddi identified three dimensions which she labeled (1) Proactive Drive vs Reactive Drive which focused on the individual's skill to begin and continue learning intrinsically; (2) Cognitive Openness vs Defensiveness which centers upon the learner's receptivity to change; and (3) Commitment to Learning vs Aversion to Learning which encompasses the notions of learning for learning sake (Houle, 1986), attitude of continuous learning, learning through various modes (oddi, 1986). According to Oddi (1986):

> These three dimensions of the self-directed continuing learner's personality were assumed to be interrelated and mutually reinforcing: They combine to enable this individual to extract information and learn from life, be it via self-planned learning projects, participation in formal or informal group learning activities, or reflection on personal performance and life experiences. The pleasure and satisfaction derived from learning enhance the individual's self-confidence and promote further receptivity to learning; thus, the self-directed continuing learner tends to initiate and persist in learning, exhibiting a trend of behavior directed toward increasing growth and self-fulfillment through learning. (p. 99)

Such a notion would tend to judge self-direction from the perspective of a life thrust or continuing engagement rather than as single planned occurrences.

It is also somewhat surprising to note that even though some adult educators (Brockett, 1985) have criticized the SDLRS for being tied too closely with academic achievement in the context of formal school experience, self-directed learning in this study did not significantly correlate with cognitive ability. Even though cognitive ability tests are not necessarily a predictor that a person <u>will</u> achieve academically, it is an indicator that the individual <u>has</u> the capacity for academic success. Perhaps it is not the ability factor or the amount of formal schooling that causes some adults problems in completing the SDLRS but rather the memories of negative formal school experiences (Guglielmino, 1977).

<u>Implications</u>

The findings of this study have implications for both theory and practice. Based on the results of this study there is an indication that parents and teachers need not be necessarily highly self-directed in their own lives in order for their children to be self-directed. The correlation coefficients for teacher and student scores on SDLRS was only 0.0301 (Spearman Rank Correlation) and mother and student was 0.3621. If future studies sustain these findings, theories regarding modeling as it relates to self-direction may have to be rethought. A number of educators (Garbarino, 1982; Christopher, 1967; Moss and Kagan, 1961) believe that parents who demonstrate or model lofty ideals for education raise children who succeed academically in school. While this notion may hold true for academic success, such may not be the case for influencing the level of self-direction of the child. The lack of significant SDL correlation levels in adults and children in this study might suggest modeling notions need to be rethought as they relate to self-directed learning. That is, modeling self-directed learning by adults does not necessarily mean that children will emulate SDL in their learning approaches. This study, examining the relationship between the levels of self-directed learning readiness present in parents, teachers and their children, may then be a step toward achieving a clearer understanding of role modeling as it relates to self-directedness in children.

This study also suggests that the adult education assumption of a developing self-directed learning readiness may rather be an emergence of suppressed self-directed learning readiness. It is possible that children are born with varying levels of self-directedness that are suppressed by parents and teachers during the formal school years. As the young adults leave the restraints of home and school, their early childhood self-directedness surfaces. If this "suppressed-emergence" notion is found to be valid, then there are implications here for a possible realignment of adult education thought on the origins of self-directed learning.

From a practical standpoint, it may be possible for parents and teachers to encourage and nurture the natural self-directional tendencies in their children. It could be that parents who find ways to foster autonomy in the home such as being aware of the child's need for exploration and within reason allowing the child room for discovery, may encourage self-direction. Stated another way, parents and teachers who refrain from suppressing the child's natural tendency for self-direction may in the long run produce an adult that demonstrates strong self-direction in most areas of life including learning approaches. Studies have shown that giving children choices helps enhance their self-directedness (Zuckerman and others, 1978; Swann and Pittman, 1977). Parents and teachers need not create an atmosphere of total freedom in order for the child to experience a perception of autonomy. Instead of discouraging the natural curiosity of the child with a "no, don't do that" environment, it might be advantageous to create several alternatives from which the child may select. Arranging for the child to choose from a number of adult initiated choices might very well be an avenue toward sharpening self-directed learning skills in the young.

Another possible method for fostering intrinsic motivation in children might be positive competence feedback. When children are successful in accomplishing a task and are complemented for their attainment, they seem to become more engaged in the activity and will pursue the activity longer than those who receive no feedback (Anderson, Manoogian, and Reznick, 1976; Blanck, Jackson, Reis, 1979; Harackiewicz, 1979).

Skager (1978) offered eight guidelines for fostering self-directed learning in the classroom. They are (1) flexibility in the learning situation; (2) encouragement of choice; (3) teaching a facilitating activity; (4) learners as their own evaluation agents; (5) democratic relationships in the learning situation; (6) capitalizing on intrinsic motivation; (7) multi-pathed problem solving; and (8) incorporating learning outside of the school. These guidelines parallel the thinking of other researchers such as Berlyne (1965), Eisner (1968), and Knowles (1970, 1980). In summary, perhaps parents and teachers would do well to look for positive rather than negative approaches to educating children in their efforts to enhance self-directed learning levels.

Recommendations for Future Study

This study has generated information relevant to factors surrounding possible origins and development of self-directed learning in individuals. Concurrently, it has stimulated further questions regarding the genesis and ontogeny of self-directed learning. Therefore, additional research in several areas is recommended.

Future studies seeking to identify correlations between adult (parents or teachers) self-directedness and that of their children might observe different age levels in children. Certainly, it would enhance the knowledge base if preschoolers were compared with their parents. In the same manner, self-direction levels in older children perhaps in middle and high school might be compared with teacher and parental levels of self-directedness.

Research is needed to verify the notion that parents and teachers might tend to suppress the self-directedness of children from about school age until the end of formal education and leaving of home. One possible approach to testing the notion would be to observe the same children from birth through the early elementary grades noting changes, if any, in the children's level of self-directedness as the transition is made from the informal to formal school setting.

Self-directed learning theory could also possibly be enhanced by an expanded examination of the belief that personality is a key factor in determining the origins of SDL. Research topics might center around the three dimensions described by Oddi (1986) which are (1) proactive drive vs reactive drive, (2) cognitive openness vs defensiveness, and (3) commitment to learning vs apathy or aversion to learning.

Another potentially profitable study is the continuation of the longitudinal study begun here. A retesting of the children in this study every two to three years might prove valuable in testing the adult education assumption that as people mature they have a tendency to become more and more self-directing in their learning approaches.

In summary, it is hoped that research in the area of the origins and development of self-directed learning will continue to be pursued so that adult educators will have a better understanding of the phenomenon of self-directed learning and thus be in a position to assist adult learners become all they can be.

REFERENCES

Anderson, R., Manoogian, S.T., & Reznick, J.S. (1976). The undermining and enhancing of intrinsic motivation in pre-school children. Journal of Personality and Social Psychology, 34, 915-922.

Armor, D. & others (1976). Analysis of the school preferred reading program in selected Los Angeles minority schools. Baltimore: Maryland State Department of Education.

Bayha, R. A. (1983). Self-directed learning readiness of Northwest Missouri farmers as related to learning resource choice and valuing (Doctoral dissertation, Kansas State University, 1983). Dissertation Abstracts International, 45, 50A.

Beder, H., Darkenwald, G., & Valentine, T. (1983). Self-planned professional learning among public school adult education directors: A social network analysis. Proceedings of the Twenty-Fourth Annual Adult Education Research Conference.

Bee, H. (1985). The developing child. New York: Harper and Row.

Bejot, D. D. (1981). The degree of self-directedness and the choices of learning methods as related to a cooperative extension program. Unpublished doctoral dissertation, Iowa State University.

Berlyne, D. E. (1965). Curiosity and education. In J. D. Krumboltz (Ed.), Learning and the educational process. Chicago: Rand McNally.

Binet, A., & Simon, T. (1916). The development of intelligence in children. Baltimore: Williams & Wilkins.

Blanck, P., Jackson, L., & Reis, H. T. (1979, September). Effects of verbal praise on intrinsic motivation for sex-typed tasks. Paper presented at the American Psychological Association Convention, New York.

Bonham, A. E. (1987). Theoretical and practical differences and similarities among selected cognitive and learning styles of adults: An analysis of the literature (Doctoral dissertation, The University of Georgia, 1987). Dissertation Abstracts International, 48, 2788A.

Braun, C. (1976). Teacher expectation: Socio-psychological dynamics. Review of education Research, 46, 185-213.

Brockett, R. G. (1983). The relationship between life satisfaction and self-directedness among older adults. Lifelong Learning Research Conference Proceedings, No. 5. College Park: Department of Agriculture and Extension Education, University of Maryland.

Brockett, R. G. (1985). The relationship between self-directed learning readiness and life satisfaction among older adults. Adult education Quarterly, 35(4), 210-219.

Brody, E. B., & Brody, N. (1976). Intelligence: Nature, determinants and consequences. New York: Academic Press.

Brookfield, S. (1981). Independent adult learning. Studies in Adult Education, 35(1).

Brookfield, S. (1984). Self-directed learning: A critical paradigm. Adult Education Quarterly, 35(1).

Brookfield, S. (1986). Understanding and facilitating adult learning. San Francisco: Jossey-Bass.

Brookover, W. B. & Lezotte, L. W. (1979). Changes in school characteristics coincident with changes in student achievement. East Lansing, MI: Institute for Research on Teaching, College of Education, Michigan State University.

Brookover, W. B. & others (1979). School social systems and student achievement: Schools can make a difference. New York: Praeger.

Brookover, W. B. & others (1982). Creating effective schools: An inservice program for enhancing school learning climate and achievement. Holmes Beach, FL: Learning Publications.

Brookover, W. B. & Schneider, J. M. (1975). Academic environments and elementary school achievement. Journal of Research and Development in Education, 9, 82-91.

Brophy, J. E. & Good, T. L. (1974). Teacher-student relationships: Causes and consequences. New York: Holt, Rinehart & Winston.

Brophy, J. E. (1976). Teacher behavior and its effects. Journal of Teacher Education, 71, 773-750.

Bruner, J. (1961). The Process of education. Cambridge, MA: Harvard University Press.

Butterfield, E. C., Siladi, D., & Belmont, J. M. (1980). Validating theorities of intelligence. In H. W. Reese & L. P. Lipsitt (Eds.), Advances in child development and behavior (Vol. 15). New York: Academic Press.

Caffarella, R. S. & Caffarella, E. P. (in press). Self-directedness and learning contracts in adult education. Adult Education Quarterly.

Caffarella, R. S. (in press). Self-directed learning: A critical paradigm revisited.

Caffarella, R., & O'Donnell, J. (1987). Research in Self-Directed Learning: Past, Present and Future Trends. In H. Long and Associates (Eds.), Self-directed learning: Application and theory. Athens, GA: Adult Education Department, The University of Georgia.

California State Department of Education (1980). Report on the special studies of selected ECE schools with increasing and decreasing reading scores. Sacramento: Office of Program Evaluation and Research.

Carpenter, M. G. (1981). Self-actualizing and other selected characteristics of adults enrolled in correspondence study: A comparative study (Doctoral dissertation, University of Georgia, 1981). Dissertation Abstracts International, 42, 2435A.

Chickering, A. W. (1964). Dimensions of independence. Journal of Higher Education, 35, 38-41.

Christopher, S. A. (1967). Parental relationship and value orientation as factors in academic achievement. Personnel and Guidance Journal, 45, 921-925.

Cobb, J. E. (1978). Self-directed learning of prospective parents. Unpublished doctoral dissertation, Kansas State University.

Coleman, J. S. & others (1966). Equality of educational opportunity. Washington, D.C.: Government Printing Office.

Collican, P. M. (1974). Self-planned learning: Implications for the future of adult education (Tech. Rep. No. 74-507). Syracuse: Syracuse University.

Cooper, H. (1979). Pygmalion grows up: A model for teacher expectation communication and performance influence. Review of Educational Research, 49, 389-410.

Cross, K. P. (1981). Adults as learners: Increasing participation and facilitating learning. San Francisco: Jossey-Bass.

Darkenwald, G. G., & Merriam, S. B. (1982). Adult education: Foundations of practice. New York: Harper & Row.

Dave, R. H. (1963). The identification and measurement of environmental process variables that are related to educational achievement. Unpublished doctoral dissertation, University of Chicago.

Deci, E. L., & Ryan, R. M. (1981). Curiosity and self-directed learning: The role of motivation in education. Urbana, IL: ERIC Clearinghouse on Elementary and Early Childhood Education. (ERIC Document Reproduction Service No. ED 206 377)

Deroos, K. K. B. (1982). Persistence of adults in independent study (Doctoral dissertation, University of Minnesota, 1982). Doctoral Abstracts International, 43, 47A.

Dewey, J. (1951). Democracy and education (original work published in 1916). New York: The Macmillan Co.

Doss, D. & Holley, F. A. (1982). A cause for national pause: Title 1 schoolwide projects (ORE Publication No. 81.55). Austin, TX: Office of Research and Evaluation, Austin Independent School District.

Dressel, P. L. & Thompson, M. M. (1973). Independent study. San Francisco: Jossey-Bass.

Edmond, R. (1981). A discussion of the literature and issues related to effective schooling (Vol. 6). St. Louis: CEMREL, Inc.

Eichorn, D. H., Hunt, J. V., & Honzik, M. P. (1981). Experience, personality and IQ: Adolescence to middle age. IN D. H. Eichorn, J. A. Clausen, N. Haan, M. P. Honzik, & P. H. Mussen (Eds.), Present and past in middle life. New York: Academic Press.

Eisenman, J. G. (1986, March). Unpublished interview with Malcolm Knowles at the Georgia Adult Education Annual Meeting.

Eisner, E. W. (1968). Instructional and expressive educational objectives: Their formulation and use in curriculum. In W. J. Popham and others (Eds.), Instructional Objectives. Chicago: Rand McNally.

Garbarino, J. (1982). Children and families in the social environment. New York: Aldine Publishing Co.

Geisler, K. K. (1984). Learning efforts of adults undertaken for matriculating into a community college. Unpublished doctoral dissertation, Texas A & M University.

Glenn, B. C. (1981). What works? An examination of effective schools for poor black children. Cambridge, MA: Center of Law and Education, Harvard University.

Good, T. (1980). Classroom expectations: Teacher-pupil interactions. In J. McMillian (Ed.), The Social Psychology of School Learning. New York: Academic Press.

Goodson, B. D. & Hess, R. D. (1975). Parents as teachers of young children: An evaluative review of some contemporary concepts and programs. Palo Alto, CA: Stanford University Press.

Gordon, I. J. (1970). Parental involvement in compensatory education. Chicago: University of Illinois PRess.

Guglielmino, L. M. (1977). Development of the self-directed learning readiness scale (Doctoral dissertation, University of Georgia, 1977). Dissertation Abstracts International, 38, 6467A. (University Microfilms No. 78-06004)

Gunzburger, L. (1980). Characteristics identified upon entrance to medical school associated with future participation in professional education (Doctoral dissertation, University of Chicago, 1980). Dissertation Abstracts International, 41, 2572A.

Harackiewicz, J. (1979). The effects of reward contingency and performance feedback on extrinsic motivation. Journal of Personality and Social Psychology, 37, 1352-1363.

Hassan, A. M. (1982). An investigation of the learning projects among adults of high and low readiness for self-direction in learning (Doctoral dissertation, Iowa State University, 1981). Dissertation Abstracts International, 42, 3838A.

Havighurst, R. J. (1952). Developmental tasks and education. New York: David McKay.

Hess, R. D. (1969). Parental behavior and children's school achievement; implications for Head Start. In E. Grotberg (Ed.), Critical issues in research related to disadvantaged children. Princeton, NJ: Educational Testing Service.

Hiemstra, R. (1976). The older adult's learning projects. Educational Gerontology: An International Quarterly, 1, 227-236.

Hiemstra, R. (1980). Policy recommendations related to self-directed learning. Occasional Paper No. 1. Syracuse: Syracuse University.

Houle, C. O. (1961). The inquiring mind. University of Wisconsin Press.

Houle, C. O. (1984). Patterns of learning. San Francisco: Jossey-Bass.

Hunter, M. G. (1979). Final report of the Michigan cost-effectiveness study. East Lansing: Michigan Department of Education.

Iverson, B. K., & Walberb, H. J. (1982). Home environment and school learning: A quantitative synthesis. The Journal of Experimental Education, 50.

Jencks, C., & others (1979). Who gets ahead. New York: Basic Books, Inc.

Kamin, L. J. (1974). The science and politics of IQ. Hillsdale, NJ: Erlbaum.

Kasworm, C. E. (1982). An examination of self-directed contract learning as an instructional strategy. Innovative Higher Education, 8(1), 45-54.

Kathrein, M. A. (1981). A study of self-directed continuing professional learning of members of the iLlinois Nurses' Association: Content and process (Doctoral dissertation, Northern Illinois University, 1981). Dissertation Abstracts International, 42, 1902A.

King, L. (1979). An attributional analysis of student achievement, related behavior and expectancy effect. Unpublished doctoral dissertation, University of Alberta, Alberta.

Knowles, M. K. (1970). The modern practice of adult education: Andragogy versus pedagogy. New York: Association Press.

Knowles, M. K. (1973). The adult learner: A neglected species. Houston: Gulf Publishing Co.

Knowles, M. K. (1975). Self-directed learning. New York: Association Press.

Knowles, M. K. (1980). The modern practice of adult education (rev. ed.). New York: Cambridge Press.

Kratz, R. J. (1978). The effect of programs which foster self-directed learning on the dropout rate, the length of stay, and the preference for self-directed learning of adult basic education students (Doctoral dissertation, State University of New York at Albany, 1978). Dissertation Abstracts International, 39, 1236A.

Leean, C., & Sisco, B. (1981). Learning projects and self-planned learning efforts among undereducated adults in rural Vermont--final report. Washington, D. C.: National Institute of Education.

Levine, D. U., & Stark, J. (1981). Extended summary and conclusions: Institutional and organizational arrangements and processes for improving academic achievement at inner city elementary schools. Kansas City, MO: University of Missouri-Kansas City, school of education, Center for the Study of Metropolitan Problems in Education.

Little, D. (1979). Adult learning and education: A concept and analysis. In P. Cunningham (Ed.), Yearbook of adult and continuing education, 1979-80. Chicago: Marquis Academic Media.

Long, H. B. (1986). Test-retest reliability of Guglielmino's self-directed readiness scale: A summary report. Unpublished report.

Long, H. B., & Agyekum, S. K. (1983). Guglielmino's self-directed learning readiness scale: A validation study. Higher Education, 12(1), 77-87.

Long, H. B., & Agyekum, S. K. (1984). Multitrait-multi-method validation of Guglielmino's self-directed learning readiness scale. Proceedings of the Twenty-fifth Annual Adult Education Research Conference, 194-198.

Long, H. B., & Associates (1988). Self-directed learning: Application and theory. Athens, GA: Adult Education Department, University of Georgia.

Marjoribanks, K. (1979). Family environments. In H. J. Walberb (Ed.), Educational environments and effects. Berkeley, CA: McCutchan Publishing Corp.

Maslow, A. H. (1954). Motivation and personality. New York: Harper & Row.

Maslow, A. H. (1972). The farther reaches of human nature. New York, Penguin Books.

Mezirow, J. (1985). A critical theory of self-directed learning. In S. Brookfield (Ed.), Self-directed learning: Theory and practice (pp. 17-30). San Francisco: Jossey-Bass.

The Minnesota adoption studies: Genetic differences and maleability (1983). Child development, 54, 260-267.

Mocker, D., & Spear, G. (1982). Lifelong learning: Formal, informal, and self-directed learning. Kansas City: Center for Resource Development Education, University of Missouri-Kansas City. (ERIC Document Reproduction Service No. ED 220 723).

Moore, M. G. (1973). Toward a theory of independent learning and teaching. Journal of Higher Education, 44.

Morris, J. F. (1977). The planning behavior and conceptual complexity of selected clergymen in self-directed learning projects related to their continued professional education. Unpublished doctoral dissertation, University of Toronto, Toronto.

Morrow, W. R., & Wilson, R. C. (1961). Family relations of bright high-achieving and under-achieving high school boys. Child Development, 32, 501-510.

Moss, H. a., & Kagan, J. (1961). Stability of achievement and recognition-seeking behavior from early childhood through adulthood. Journal of Abnormal and Social Psychology, 62, 504-513.

Murphy, J. F., & others (1982). Instructional leadership: A conceptual framework. Learning effectiveness project working paper.

Mussen, P. H. (Ed.) (1970. Carmichael's manual of child psychology, Vol. 1, (3rd ed.). New York: Wiley.

New York State Department of education (1974). Reading achievement related to educational and environmental conditions in 12 New York City elementary schools. Albany, NY: Division of education evaluation.

New York State Department of Education (1974). School factors influencing reading achievement: A case study of two inner city schools. Albany, NY: Office of Education Performance Review.

New York State Department of education (1974). Three strategies for studying the effects of school processes. Albany, NY: Bureau of School Programs Evaluation.

Oddi, L. F. (1984). Development of an instrument to measure self-directed continuing learning (Doctoral dissertation, Northern Illinois University, 1984). Dissertation Abstracts International, 46, 49A.

Oddi, L. F. (1986). Development and validation of an instrument to identify self-directed continuing learners. Adult education Quarterly, 36, 97-107.

Oddi, L. F. (1987). Perspectives on self-directed learning. Adult Education Quarterly, 38(1), 21-31.

Oscanyon, F. S. (1977). How can I teach my students to learn on their own? Educational Theory, 27, 98-104.

Penland, P. R. (1979). Why do some urban schools succeed? Bloomington, IN: Author.

Plomin, R. & deFries, J. (1980). Genetics and intelligence: Recent data. Intelligence, 4, 15-24.

Purkey, S., & Smith, M. (1982). Too soon to cheer? Synthesis of research on effective schools. Educational Leadership, December 1982.

Research Information Service (1981). Teacher expectation and student perceptions: A decade of research (Good). 38(5).

Rich, D. (1979). Families as educators of their own children. In R. S. Brandt (Ed.), Partners: Parents and schools. Alexandria, VA: Association for Supervision and Curriculum Development.

Rogers, C. (1951). Client-centered therapy. New York: Houghton-Mifflin.

Rogers, C. (1969). Freedom to learn. Columbus, OH: Merrill.

Rosenthal, R., & Jacobson, L. (1968). Pygamalion in the classroom: Teacher expectation and pupil's intellectual development. New York: Holt, Rinehart and Winston.

Rutter, M., & others (1979). Fifteen thousand hours: Secondary schools and their effects on children. Cambridge, MA: Harvard University Press.

Rymell, R. C. (1981). Learning projects pursued by adult degreed engineers (Doctoral dissertation, North Texas State University, 1981). Dissertation Abstracts International, 42, 936A.

Sabbaghian, Z. S. (1980). Adult self-directedness and self-concept: An exploration of relationships (Doctoral dissertation, Iowa State University, 1980). Dissertation Abstracts International, 40, 3701A.

Sattler, J. M. (1974). Assessment of children's intelligence. Philadelphia: Saunders.

Savin-Williams, R. C. (1979). Dominance hierarchies in groups of early adolescents. Child development, 50, 1106-1110.

Savoie, M. L. (1980). Continuing education for nurses: Predictors of success in courses requiring a degree of learner self-direction (Doctoral dissertation, University of Toronto, 1980). Dissertation Abstracts International, 40, 6114A.

Scarr, S. (Ed.) (1981). Race, social class, and individual differences in I.Q. Hillsdale, NJ: Erlbaum.

Sexton-Hesse, C. A. (1984). Assuming responsibility for self-directed learning in professional practice: The contributions of psychosocial factors. Proceedings for the Twenty-Fifth Annual Adult Education Research Conference.

Schackelford, R. A. (1983). Self-directed learning projects among black adults in Havana, Florida (Doctoral dissertation, The Florida Sate University, 1983). Dissertation Abstracts International, 44, 647A.

Shirk, J. C. (1983). Relevance attributed to urban public libraries by adult learners: A case study and content analysis of 81 interviews (Doctoral dissertation, Texas A & M University, 1983). Dissertation Abstracts International, 45, 53A.

Skager, R. (1984). Organizing schools to encourage self-direction in learners. Hamburg: Unesco Institute for Education.

Skaggs, B. J. (1981). The relationship between involvement of professional nurses in self-directed learning activities, loci of control, and readiness for self-directed learning measures (Doctoral dissertation, University of Texas at Austin, 1981). Dissertation Abstracts International, 42, 1906A.

Smith, M. (1980). Meta-analysis of research on teacher expectation. Evaluation in Education, 4, 64-68.

Smith, R. M. (1982). Learning how to learn: Applied learning theory for adults. New York: Cambridge Books.

Spartz, J. L., & others (1977). Delaware educational accountability system case studies: Elementary schools grades 1-4. Dover: Delaware Department of Public Education.

Spear, G. E., & Mocker, D. W. (1984). The organizing circumstance: Environmental determinants in self-directed learning. Adult Education Quarterly, 35(1), 1-10.

Squires, D. A. (1980). Characteristics of effective schools: The importance of school processes. Philadelphia: Research for Better Schools.

Stearns, M. S., and others (1973). Parent involvement in compensatory education programs: Definitions and findings. Menlo Park, CA: Stanford Research Institute.

Strong, M. (1977). The autonomous adult learner. Unpublished master's thesis, Department of Adult Education, University of Nottingham.

Swann, W. B., & Pittman, T. S. (1977). Initiating play activity of children: The moderating influence of verbal cues on intrinsic motivation. Child Development, 48, 1128-1132.

Torrance, E. P., & Mourad, S. (1978). Some creativity and style of learning and thinking correlates of Guglielmino's self-directed learning readiness scale. Psychological Reports, 43, 1167-1171.

Tough, A. M. (1967). Learning without a teacher: A study of tasks and assistance during adult self-teaching projects Educational Research Series, No. 3). Toronto: Ontario Institute of Studies in Education.

Tough, A. M. (1971). The adult's learning projects. Toronto: The Ontario Institute for Studies in Education.

Tough, A. M. (1979). The adult's learning projects (2nd ed.). Toronto: The Ontario Institute for Studies in Education.

Trisman, D. A., & others (1976). A descriptive and analytic study of compensatory reading programs: Final report (Vol. 2, PR-75-26). Princeton, NJ: Educational Testing service.

Venezky, R. L., & Winfield, L. F. (1979). Schools that succeed beyond expectations in reading (Studies on Education Technical Report No. 1). Newark: University of Delaware.

Verner, C. (1964). Definition of terms. In G. Jensen and others (Ed.), Adult education: Outlines of an emerging field of university study. Washington, D.C.: Adult education association of the U.S.A.

Weber, G. (1971). Innercity children can be taught to read: Four successful schools. Washington, D.C.: Council for Basic Education.

Weinstein, R., & others (1980, April). Student perceptions of differential teacher treatment. Paper presented at the annual meeting of the American Educational Research Association, Boston, MA.

West, C., & Anderson, T. (1976). The question of preponderant causation in teacher expectancy research. Review of Education Research, 46, 185-213.

Wynne, E. A. (1980). Looking at schools: Good, bad, and indifferent. Lexington, MA: D.C. Heath.

Zuckerman, M., Porac, J., Lathin, D., Smith, R., & Deci, E. (1978). On the importance of self-determination for intrinsically motivated behavior. Personality and Social Psychology Bulletin, 4, 443-446.

Chapter Six

ANALYSIS OF PRACTICAL THINKING IN SELF-DIRECTED LEARNING

John M. Peters

In a previous chapter on "Self-direction and Problem Solving: Theory and Method" (Peters, 1989), I argued that self-directed learning can be understood as a problem-solving process. I also suggested a methodology for studying self-directed learning as problem solving. The method is known as the Action-Reason-Thematic Technique (ARTT), and it is being used to collect and analyze verbal accounts by adults of their problem-related learning experiences. This chapter extends the earlier discussion of the concepts of problem solving and practical thinking, and also presents a case example of data generated by ARTT.

PRACTICAL THINKING AND PROBLEM SOLVING

Models of technical rationality such as formal models of instruction or formal models of problem solving fail to accommodate the nature of self-directed experiences. Most formal systems of problem solving and learning have been based on a notion of deduction that does not account for the type of reasoning and acting in ordinary problem-solving situations and learning that takes place in those situations (Winograd, 1980; Neisser, 1976). We must look elsewhere for descriptive and explanatory frameworks.

One such framework is grounded in the concepts of practical thinking and practical problem solving, and in the broader constructs of activity theory (Vygotsky, 1978; Leont'ev, 1979). Practical thinking is, according to Castaneda (1975), "finding out or deciding what to do" about some problem or need (p.5). Scribner (1986) refers to it as "thinking that is embedded in the larger purposive activities of daily life and that functions to achieve the goals of those activities" (p.15). It is similar to the kind of thinking involved in what Dreyfus and Dreyfus (1986) refer to as "knowing that" (vs "knowing how"), which is "the sort of ability we all use...when we go about our everyday tasks" (p.29). Finally, Johnson, Johnson and Little (1985) refer to "operative knowledge" as being different from textbook knowledge, and describe operative knowledge as the kind of knowledge organized to do tasks. It is operative knowledge that allows a person to plan, to decide, and to take goal-directed action. Practical thinking is embedded in operative knowledge and is crucial to the acquisition and use of operative knowledge.

Practical thinking is instrumental to the achievement of mental activities, such as deciding on the best materials to use in building a piece of furniture, and manual activities, such as making the furniture. Scribner points out that practical thinking is not the type of thinking involved in the performance of isolated mental tasks undertaken as ends in themselves, such as solving a textbook arithmetic problem. Thus, practical thinking research is not concerned with underlying cognitive abilities or structures of intelligence, but rather is concerned with the functions of thinking. Its locus is in a system of activity. Thus the researcher interested in practical thinking would "select as her object of analysis not an isolated mental process or task in itself but an integral action directed toward some specifiable end and accomplished under specifiable circumstances" (Scribner, 1986, p.16). The unit of analysis is the person's actions, or intended actions, and the purpose of such research is to understand how thinking is tied to action as it is regulated by factors in the actor's life-world.

On the view that self-directed learning is a purposive, self-monitored activity by the learner which involves thinking and reasoning about experiences and objects in his/her environment, a close association can be said to exist between the concepts of self-directed learning and practical thinking. Moreover, the aims of research in the area of practical thinking and the aims of research in the area of self-directed learning are similar. Theorists and researchers in both areas are concerned with learning activities that take place mainly outside formal institutional contexts. They are also concerned with understanding the antecedents and consequences of individual learning episodes in natural settings, though investigators of practical thinking more often than not couch their inquiries in the construct of practical or nonformal problem solving. They share one other characteristic as researchers - both operate in a relatively new area of inquiry, and their works are scattered throughout the literature. However, I find the literature sources in the area of practical thinking to be much more informative than our literature in adult education, about the dynamics of the relationship between learning and related acts of thinking, reasoning and problem solving.

Some of the more interesting research in the area of practical thinking and problem solving is being done by Scribner (1986), Sternberg and Wagner (1985, 1986), Murtaugh (1985), and Goodnow (1986, 1976). Their works consistently differentiate practical thinking from theoretical or academic thinking, leading to the claim that something other than academic intelligence accounts for skilled accomplishment of everyday, real-world tasks. While the collective heading for their works is usually called "practical intelligence", the kind of thinking involved is almost always referred to as practical thinking. They have studied practical thinking in job-related settings, everyday settings outside of occupational pursuits, life-span development of practical thinking skills, and in terms of cultural differences in practical thinking (Sternberg and Wagner, 1986).

Scribner's studies, and those of her students, were of actions taken by workers in a milk-processing plant, in bars and restaurants, in engineering offices and in auto repair shops. Combining ethnographic and experimental techniques, their focus was on work tasks in routine situations. Although tasks in these environments were usually well-defined and work goals were often highly-structured and socially determined, Scribner and her colleagues reported that their studies produced results similar to studies of adults in nonoccupational settings (Murtagh, 1985; Carraher, Carraher and Schliemann, 1984). It was from results of these studies and others that Scribner proposed a model of skilled practical thinking, in which she describes it as having five characteristics (Scribner, 1986, pp.21-24):

(1) "Skilled practical thinking involves problem formulation as well as problem solution" (p.21). This feature may best be understood in contrast to formal problem solving models which assume a given problem and a correct solution to that problem. In Scribner's studies, "expertise in practical problem solving frequently hinges on an apt formulation or redefinition of the initial problem. Murtagh (1985) found that, in everyday tasks such as supermarket shopping, actions are not necessarily controlled by problems. Given the problem of how to find the best buy among available products, shoppers interested in best buys computed price differences only in those situations in which they could do simple arithmetic, ignoring more complicated price-unit comparisons altogether. These shoppers "shifted the problem space", to accommodate their own ability to solve the problem as they redefined it.

(2) "Skilled practical thinking is marked by flexibility solving the "same problem" now one way, now another, each way finely tuned to the occasion" (p.22). Scribner maintains that formal models do not account for the variability in ways people go about accomplishing tasks and solving problems which appear to be the same across work and everyday situations. Suchman (1985), Kusterer (1978) and Schon (1983) all documented workers' propensities for devising short-cuts and novel ways of solving problems on the job, even in the most routine of work environments. This is seen by Suchman and others as a form of practical problem solving, in which intelligent use is made by people of their circumstances and other people, in order to reach their goals.

(3) "Skilled practical thinking incorporates features of the task environment (people, things, information) into the problem-solving system" (23). Scribner's notion of the role of the task environment goes beyond the contextualist view that the problem solver's cognition is a function of context. She emphasizes "the inextricability of task from environment, and the continual interplay between internal representations and operations and external reality throughout the course of the problem-solving process" (p.23). She also points to a similar idea about the mutual constitution of subject and object expressed in activity theory (Leont'ev). According to Scribner's analysis, environmental factors assume a functional role in the person's problem-solving process "only through the initiative and constructive activities of the problem solver" (p.23).

(4) "Skilled practical thinking often seeks those modes of solution that are the most economical or that require the least effort" (p.25). This involves fitting the mode of solution to circumstances surrounding its use, and sometimes redefining the problem to fit the simplest solutions available.

(5) "Practical thinking involves the acquisition and use of specific knowledge that is functionally important to the larger activities in which problem solving is embedded" (p.26) The role of setting and task-specific knowledge is well documented in practical problem-solving. The consistent finding of studies of practical thinking and problem solving has been that "experts differ from novices primarily in the amount and organization of their knowledge about the task, rather than in underlying cognitive abilities" (Wagner and Sternberg, 1986, p.54).

These characteristics of practical thinking, when mapped onto descriptions of self-directed learning episodes, strongly suggest questions about these episodes which could become the focus of research into self-directed learning. The following are several questions that roughly parallel characteristics in Scribner's model:

(1) How does the learner attempt to recast or transform a problem he/she is called upon to solve in order to relate it to their own experiences?

(2) What are the strategies which a learner employs in the conduct of making decisions and taking actions?

(3) What is the documentary or situational information utilized by a learner in making decisions -- the aspects of a situation which the learner attends to or ignores?

(4) What are the kinds of additional information which the learner seeks, or which the learner provides out of his own knowledge, given a problem?

(5) What are the goals or purposes served by different learner actions and decisions, and the rationales related to these goals?

(6) What are the premises or lines of reasoning on which the learner bases his/her decisions?

(7) What are the short-cuts, or rules of thumb which guide the learner's decisions?

Most of these questions (especially the first five) are similar in form to questions asked by adult education researchers who study self-directed learning. However, they differ in terms of their underlying assumptions and intended interpretation of answers to the questions.

It is assumed that the environment within which self-directed learning activities occur will play a strong functional role in shaping those activities, especially as they are responsive to intentional actions taken by the learner. Another assumption is that the learner's beliefs, rules, wants and other aspects of domain knowledge that are part of the learner's reasoning structure also play a functional role in decisions and actions. The focus of these questions, therefore, is on the interplay between situational elements and internal representations of reality, or what Leont'ev (1981) refers to as the mutual constitution of subject and object. Such a focus calls for a particular method for collecting information about the dynamics of self-directed learning, and ARTT, introduced earlier, fills that role.

ARTT is an interview-analyze-interview cycle of interactions between the researcher and his/her subject. The researcher-interviewer solicits verbal descriptions of actions taken by the subject to learn something, including an account of reasons cited by the subject for taking the actions. These actions and reasons are analyzed for their structure and content, and at least one additional interview is conducted to verify the results from the first interview, and to fill in gaps in the first account. This cycle may be repeated until the researcher is satisfied that the subject has fully described his or her actions and supporting reasons. These reasons and actions are reduced to their essential meaning by the researcher as the interview progresses, always in tandem with the subject, so that at the end of the process the essential *themes* of the subject's learning experience can be identified and described, along with the detailed features of the learner's *actions* and *reasons*.

Several graduate students and I have begun to accumulate cases of learning and problem solving experiences of adults, many of which have been subjected to analysis by using the ARTT (Farris, 1982; Ihlenfeld, 1982; Sanders, 1983; Banks, 1983; Lazzara, 1985; Drew, 1989). Dozens of cases have been collected and more are being added to the collection as we gain experience in using the technique. One case, resulting from an interview I did with a colleague as a part of a National Institute of Education funded research project, is especially suited to the topic of this chapter. A version of this case was reported by Banks, 1983.

<u>Case of the Bow-Maker</u>

The interviewee was an adult who faced the problem of protecting his home from burglars. His solution, while unconventional, nonetheless provided an interesting and richly detailed example of a self-directed learning experience. The interview was designed to elicit two broad kinds of descriptions: (1) <u>What</u> the subject did to solve his problem, including how he went about learning what he needed to know; and (2) <u>why</u> he chose these actions. The interview process was subject-centered, and I asked one question at a time, probed for explanations, mirrored the subject's responses, avoided leading questions, and generally allowed the subject to tell me what happened and why, all the while accepting his description, not mine, as the best representation of his experience.

The subject set out to build a cross-bow, to use as a weapon in case his house was entered by someone (his neighborhood had experienced a high rate of crime). Here is the synopsis of his story:

> My wife and I are concerned about the rise in crime and protection of our property. I decided we needed some type of weapon to use as a deterrent to crime. We didn't have the money to spend on a gun so I started thinking about building a weapon. I like the idea of self-sufficiency, trying to survive on native materials through pioneer efforts. I believe the art of creating something on my own is in itself a valuable practice.
>
> So I decided to build a cross-bow. I had been reading about bows recently and the idea of creating something unique yet useful appealed to me. I thought about the design of a bow and what construction would entail. When I work on projects, I generally make the construction process a learning process as well. I want to be able to understand the mechanics of whatever I construct and I like building objects on my own. In order to do this, I play a game with myself. The game is to make as much of the object as I can without looking at a manufactured version of the product. I depend heavily on mental images of the product and when I have a pretty good idea of how it should look and work, I make a drawing. This drawing serves as a template for the actual construction process.
>
> Because I believe in self-sufficiency, I tried to make the first model of the bow out of materials I have on hand. I like to see if the model looks, feels, or works the way I had envisioned. It is only at this point that I seek out information from outside sources such as the library to research the kind of material appropriate for use. When I do it this way, I have a much greater appreciation of how the product is made. When I'm satisfied that I have sufficient knowledge and skills, then I make a complete working version.

This story was actually constructed out of the interview protocol, itself a verbatim transcript of an audio recording of the interview. The raw material for this story was a list of intended ideas expressed by the subject during his account, which looks like the following excerpt from a longer interview:

I: What did you do next?

S: Well, I decided that sometime during that weekend that if I'm going to do it, I've got to draw it.

I: Draw it?

S: The triggering mechanism

I: Why did you decide to draw it?

S: I do everything visually.

I: Tell me more about that...

S: I can recreate on paper almost the exact dimensions that would be required to actually have done it. I can recreate levers, angles, pull...

I: And you first visualize....?

S: Yes. In this case, I had a mental picture of merry ole England and William Tell raising a cross bow to his shoulder, and I stepped, visually, into his shoes and raised the cross-bow to my shoulder to get the feel of what it is to fire the bow. I wanted to get the feel, the texture of the experience. I didn't create one where I was standing on a golf course aiming at a tree or something like that. I had to use the context of something I already had visited before.

I: Please tell me what you mean by having already visited before...

S: Well, by that I mean I had read, somewhere, the story of William Tell, and the boy with an apple on his head, etc.

I: You said that you put yourself in that picture...

S: Correct.

I: Why was that?

S: If I'm visualizing the early stages of a product or the visualization that represents the product, I always put myself in it.

I: Regarding the triggering device, what led you to that visualization?

S: I had seen several bows, or pictures of bows, and their stocks and strings were clear in my mind, but their triggers, or their trigger mechanisms, were hidden, being inside the stock. So I had to imagine what one looked like. I remember something about a brown bow on display at the Smithsonian, but less clearly what its trigger looked like.

I: What did you do at this point?

S: I visualized what such a mechanism might be like, by thinking about how it must be constructed in order to do what it is supposed to do...resist several hundred pounds of pressure and yet release at the slightest touch of a finger...

I: Tell me more...

S: As I drew the possible triggering mechanisms, I thought of parallels to the mechanism.

I: Parallels?

S: What I mean by that is, I thought of pins, springs, connectors on things I was already familiar with, such as the spring on my tiller carburetor, and on my go cart engine.

(Interview protocol continued, but omitted here)

The interview protocol was segmented into single expressions of ideas, and these were listed as they occured in the transcript. Conjunctive sentences were separated into two or more statements, false starts were eliminated, and some statements were paraphrased but intentions were preserved. These intended ideas served as the units of analysis.

Next, intended ideas that describe actions taken toward the subject's goal were separated from the total list and recorded on a sheet of paper (or computer document). In the bow-maker case, the list of actions is long, and follows below:

1. I decided that I needed some type of weapon.
2. I decided to produce for myself some sort of weapon.
3. I thought about a bow and arrows as a weapon.
4. I decided to make a bow.
5. I put the idea aside for a while.
6. After several weeks had passed, I started thinking about the bow.
7. I decided to build something unique.
8. I conjured an image of William Tell with a bow.
9. I decided to build a cross-bow.
10. I asked myself questions about the design.
11. I decided to draw the triggering mechanism.
12. I mentally rehearsed the kind of triggering mechanism that I could invent or copy.
13. I visualized different types of triggering mechanisms by using concepts of various related items.
14. I decided at that point to resist looking at models of bows and their triggering mechanisms.
15. I decided to design a few select triggering mechanisms.
16. I looked about my house for wood.

17. I made several prototype stocks.
18. After again putting the project aside, I went to the library.
19. I decided on the type of wood and type of bow to make.
20. I went to the lumber yard and purchased a piece of maple wood.
21. I began work on the piece of maple.
22. I examined a manufactured cross-bow at a sports store.
23. I made a new stock for my cross bow.
24. I decided to invent a connecting device to fit the bow to the stock.
25. I went to K-Mart and walked the hardware aisles, looking for ideas.
26. I connected the bow to the stock and test-built the bow.

The next phase of the analysis involved a search among the remaining items on the total list of intended ideas for reasons that were given in support of each action. Sometimes a reason is given immediately following a statement of an action step, and sometimes one or more reasons are found at some distance on the list. So, the analyst, faced with the need to reconstruct the subject's intended account as accurately as possible, uses the context provided by each and every statement to decide on the appropriate placement of reasons with actions.

The goal at this stage of the analysis is to reconstruct "arguments" used by the person in accounting for or justifying his actions, using an argument analysis procedure developed by Nolt (1984). A practical argument is a set of reasons cited in support of a conclusion, leading to an action.

The following is an excerpt from a full analysis, with several action steps omitted for purposes of discussion and to conserve space. The arguments are numbered the same as the actions listed above. For each argument the action is stated first and italicized, and supporting reasons are listed under each action. Reasons that fit together are located side-by-side and should be read in the following manner: "I took action x, for the reasons y and z." For example, Action step 10 would read. "I asked myself questions...." (because) "When a project is new to me..." and "I had not done this project..."

Action step 10: *I asked myself questions about the design of the cross bow*

When a project is new to me, I learn about it by asking myself questions.	I had not done this project before now.
I use questions as a way to gather information.	I wanted as much information as possible.
	I wanted to know what I needed in the way of information and tools.

Actions step 11. *I decided to draw the triggering mechanism*

If I am to build it, I've got to draw it.	I wanted to recreate the exact dimensions of the triggering mechanism.
I always draw things before I make them.	I wanted to build something I had not built.

Action step 12. *I mentally rehearsed the kind of triggering mechanism that I could invent or copy*

I use imagery to get the texture of an experience.	I wanted to see how the mechanism would fit in the weapon, and the weapon in my hands.
If I can visually create a product can make it.	I wanted a model of the mechanism

Action step 13.	*I visualized eight or nine different types of triggering mechanisms by using concepts of various related items.*
I use experience I've had with other items or tasks and transfer it to new ones.	I wanted to adapt something that I knew would work to the triggering. work to the triggering mechanism.
	Mechanisms of this type have features in common.

Action step 14.	*I decided at that point to resist looking at models of bows and their triggering mechanisms*
I like to see for myself how accurately I can build a device without prior direct knowledge.	I wanted to build something I had not done before.
I learn by thinking about and doing something myself.	I wanted to do this alone.
I get satisfaction out of creating something new for me, although it might have been created by others.	Others had created bows and made made them available.
My philosophy of survival assumes a need to learn to do for ones self.	I wanted to practice survival techniques.

(Skip actions 15-16)

Action step 17:	*I made several prototype stocks*
If I am to test my ideas I need to, measure against a working model.	I wanted to test my image of w bow.
I use whatever is on hand.	I had some wood lying about.

Action step 18:	*I went to the library*
I go to the library when I need information I can't find elsewhere.	I wanted information on archery and kinds archery and kinds of wood needed I was unable to find information at home or from friends.

(Skip actions 19-21)

Action step 22:	*I examined a manufactured cross bow at a sports store*
When I reach a certain stage of design, I look at a manufactured version of whatever I'm making.	I had reached a stage of needing needing more than I could visualize.
When I find a manufactured item I need as a model, I memorize it.	
If I memorize a product, I can duplicate it.	I wanted to file the image for use at a later time.

(Skip actions 23-24)

Action step 25:	*I went to K-Mart and walked the (hardware) aisles, looking for ideas*
If I browse in stores, something usually catches my eye and connects with my idea.	I wanted an item that would convert into a connecting device for the bow and stock.

Action step 26:	*I connected the bow to the stock and test-built the cross bow*
A project needs to come to a close and be tried out.	I wanted to finish the job.
	A shelf brace did the trick.

Discussion of Argument Analysis
The seven questions posed earlier in this chapter will serve to focus this discussion of the protocol analysis. The essence of each question is repeated for ease of interpretation.

Question One: *Recasting or Transforming the Problem*. The problem was as the bow-maker defined it, and the problem changed from time to time over the course of his project. At one level, the problem was how to protect his home. At another level, the problem was how to select a particular weapon that could be used in defense of his home, should the worst happen. At still another level, the problem was how to understand a triggering mechanism that he had never fully seen first hand... and so on. Sometimes the problem was how to make something, and at other times the problem was how to understand something. No single problem directed the whole process, instead several problems at different times drove different decisions and actions. Sometimes an action would present another problem, such as when the bow-maker tried using a very light wood for his stock, only to find that he had to learn how to compensate for recoil and resistance evoked by pulling the bow string on his weapon.

The bow-maker was constantly using his environment and his experience for problem formulation and re-formulation. The decision to make a prototype out of materials found in his garage, the attempt to recall how William Tell would have used the bow, and his decision to walk the aisles of a hardware store for ideas, all contributed to regular re-thinking of his problem. This is another way of saying that things in his environment and patterns of information formed out of his own experience helped shape his solutions and his problem.

Question Two: *Strategies employed by the learner.* "Strategies" is a general term that here refers to the bow-maker's approach to solving his problem(s). His specific action steps, listed above, are representative of his strategies, but are not entirely constitutive of them. His reasons must also be taken into account, as well as the overall context within which he formulated his problem and solutions. His overall approach can thusly be characterized in terms of these features of his experience.

The bow-maker's approach was nonlinear, in terms of his action steps, and he actually appeared to follow no overall strategy. However, this apparent lack of strategy may be due to a lack of a conventional standard against which to compare his approach, rather than a problem with the approach itself. His strategy may have been to begin the project and let the events instruct him on steps to take next. He seemed to be goal-directed, even though not all of his goals were formulated at the beginning of his project. His decision to avoid looking at models in favor of figuring out the bow structure for himself is a kind of strategy. We could call this an instance of creative problem solving (the bow-maker was certainly creative), but that label is usually reserved for instances in which people are afforded considerable latitude to arrive at an appropriate solution to a set problem. In the bow-maker's case, the problem itself was created and re-created, and sometimes there was little choice among solutions available. There seems to be no ready label for his strategy, but that in itself is no tragedy.

A person's approach to solving a problem is largely a function of the amount and organization of his knowledge about the task at hand, and a very important area of knowledge in any problem situation is self-knowledge (Wagner and Sternberg, 1986). Knowledge of self is defined by Wagner and Sternberg as "knowledge that an individual has about his or her individual motives and goals that might be useful in maximizing productive accomplishment" (p.55). Knowing the kind of learner one is can be of great importance in selecting actions appropriate to one's particular environment and that best fit one's own needs and interests. The bow-maker clearly knew himself as a learner, and appeared to tacitly understand how best to adjust his actions and circumstances to meet his particular way of approaching tasks such as making the cross-bow. For example, he knew when to set the problem aside, and when to return to it. Indeed, such pauses seemed the natural thing to do for the bow-maker. He knew that drawing an object before attempting to make it was an essential decision aid, and he knew that he functioned best when he was able to visualize the outcome of a task. This is a conceptual orientation, or a metaknowledge, that helps to distinguish this learner from others less skillful.

Question Three: *Information used by the learner.* His situation, or immediate environment, was the primary source of information for the bow-maker's project. There was a sense in which he was "informed" by objects in his environment, and he attached meaning to each according to its functional role in producing the bow. He first chose what was on hand (e.g, available wood for making a prototype stock), or he invented what he needed. Only when his own ideas and available resources were exhausted did he seek out conventional sources of information, such as the library and sporting goods stores. Even then, commercially-available cross-bows served as models for additional inventions. The bow-maker's modes of solution came into being around his means of solution.

Question Four: *Additional information sought by the learner.* The bow-maker sought information that he did not initially possess, but only as he needed it and when he needed it. He also sought only problem-specific information, while general information about weapons, home-protection systems, hunting and other related topics went unstudied. His own experience with woodworking served him well, as he was able to transfer some of his knowledge of wood composition, strength and flexibility to decisions about choice of proper wood for his stock and bow. Similarly, knowledge about spring and lever mechanisms proved useful in his attempt to design a triggering mechanism for his cross-bow. Again, the functional requirements of his project largely dictated which aspects of his own past experience would play a role in shaping his immediate experience with the bow.

Question Five: *Goals served by actions*. Just as available means in his situation helped shape the modes of his problem solution, the bow-maker's goals were in large part a function of his particular environment, and his actions were both stimulated and constrained by conditions in that environment. He initially took action to achieve the goal of protecting his home, but his options were limited by available funds and his personal values concerning possession of firearms. He also pursued his longer-standing goal of learning to develop stronger survival skills, and the way he chose to protect his home gave him yet another opportunity to develop those skills (In this instance, the bow-making decision rekindled an old goal). He then added a goal of winning a "game" as he challenged himself to make something without first examining an actual model of it. His actions, therefore, were multi-goal directed, and these goals were formulated as he went along. Some provided direction for actions, and some were sparked by other actions.

Questions Six and Seven: *Premises and rules-of-thumb*. I combined these two questions because they address the strongest feature of ARTT - its ability to uncover beliefs, rules, wants, and intentions expressed by the interviewee that guiding their choice of actions in such projects as the bow-maker's. These aspects of an interviewee's verbal account of learning and problem solving also make up the content and structure of his/her reasoning, or premises for taking actions. Rules are another name for short-cuts, or rules-of-thumb used in decision making. Beliefs and wants reveal how the learner perceives himself in relation to his life-world. Some examples of the bow-maker's expressions of these aspects of his thinking follow.

Action step 11 was driven by the belief that "If I am to build it, I've got to draw it", and the motive to "recreate the exact dimensions of the triggering mechanism". Moreover, the bow-maker cited a rule there also, asserting "I always draw things before I make them," and another motive, "I wanted to build something I had not built (before)." These are clearly premises and lines of reasoning, but they are also themes of the bow-maker's life-world, insofar as they represent recurring ways of thinking, acting and ways of interacting with things in his world. He attached meaning to the things in his environment in the context of the problem as he understood it, at each stage of the problem solving process as he alone structured it. Objects, and his vision of himself in physical relation to the objects, became the structure within which he developed meanings. Thus, when he told me about what he did, and why he did it, he was describing these meaning structures.

GENERAL OBSERVATIONS AND CONCLUSION

The case illustrates how poorly textbook models of learning processes represent self-directed learning experiences. The cross bow builder followed few principles of pedagogy as he worked his way through the problem and learned what he needed to know in order to solve it. Instead of laying out his learning needs, identifying his objectives and carefully mapping his strategy for achieving his objectives, he "made the road as he traveled it". Indeed, he didn't even look for a model or prototype of his bow until very late in his project, instead opting for trying his own hand at making a prototype before looking at a specimen of what he had in mind in the first place. Had this project been directed by a teacher, I believe the teacher would have at least begun with a demonstration of the Real McCoy, then shown how this student could make one for himself. But there were other factors involved in this learner's choices, such as his need to learn survival skills, to be self-sufficient, to challenge himself and perhaps to entertain himself, by doing it himself. Regarding the situational information attended to by this learner (question one), it is safe to say that he selected aspects of his project and his environment which furthered his interests in self-sufficiency, creativity, and the satisfaction of directing his own experiences.

Although this analysis is based on a single case, and no attempt is made to generalize to other cases of self-directed learning, it illustrates the potential of the concept of practical thinking for our interest in understanding the dynamics of self-directed learning. In particular, it sheds light on the role the environment plays in problem and solution formulation, goal setting, and information selection and interpretation. It also points to the potential explanatory power provided by knowledge of the content and structure of learners' reasoning associated with their actions. One can find in reasoning structures evidence of how learners attach meaning to features of the in learning environment, the problem, modes of solution, and so forth. Phenomenalists are interested in describing and understanding the life-world of people, in terms of meaning structures that constitute themes in their lives. Themes are recurring ideas, actions and ways of thinking that depict individuals' interactions with other people and things in their world. The concept of practical thinking would seem especially useful in understanding how meaning structures mediate learning in problem-solving situations.

Finally, the Action-Reason-Thematic Technique seems especially suited to the collection of verbal accounts of self-directed learning experiences. As we collect and analyze additional data, we can look for regularities in learning situations, regularities in the meanings of interpretations applied to situations, and regularities in the problem solving and learning actions produced by adults. Even as we do that, however, we should keep abreast of the work our colleagues are doing in the area of practical problem solving and thinking.

REFERENCES

Banks, B. (1983). Problem solving in nonformal settings by literate and nonliterate adults. Unpublished Ed.D dissertation, North Carolina State University, Raleigh.

Carracher, T.N., Carraher, D.W., & Schliemann, A.D. (1985). Mathematics in the streets and in the schools. British Journal of Developmental Psychology, 3, 21-30.

Castaneda, H. (1975). Thinking and doing: The philosophical foundations of institutions. Dordrecht, Holland: D. Reidel.

Drew, (1989). A method for understanding critical thinking. Unpublished doctoral dissertation, University of Tennessee, Knoxville.

Dreyfus, H., & Dreyfus, S. (1986). Mind over machine. New York: Free Press.

Farris, J. (1982). Problem solving activities of administrators in higher education. Unpublished E.D. dissertation, University of Tennessee, Knoxville.

Goodnow, J.J. (1976). The nature of intelligent behavior: Questions raised by cross-cultural studies. In L.B. Resnick (Ed.), The nature of intelligence. New York: Erlbaum.

Goodnow, J.J. (1986). Some lifelong everyday forms of intelligent behavior: organizing and reorganizing. In R. Sternberg and R. Wagner (Eds.), Practical intelligence: Nature and origins of competence in the everyday world. New York: Cambridge University Press.

Ihlenfeld, J. (1982). Problem solving strategies of selected managers. Unpublished M.S. thesis. University of Tennessee, Knoxville.

Johnson, P., Johnson, M., and Little, R. (1985). Expertise in trial advocacy: Some considerations for inquiry into its nature and development. Campbell Law Review, 7, 119-143.

Kusterer, K.C. (1978). Know-how on the job: The important working knowledge of "unskilled" workers. Boulder, CO: Westview.

Lazzara, P.J. (1985). Foundations for a method for knowledge analysis. Unpublished Ph.D. dissertation, University of Tennessee.

Leont'ev, A.N. (1979). The problem of activity in psychology. In J.V. Wertch (Ed.), The concept of activity in Soviet psychology. White Plains, NY: Sharpe.

Murtagh, M. (1985). The practice of arithmetic by American grocery shoppers. Anthropology and Education Quarterly, 16, 186-192.

Neisser, U. (1976). General, academic, and artificial intelligence. In L. Resnick (Ed.), The nature of intelligence. Hillsdale, NJ: Erlbaum.

Nolt, J.E. (1984). In formal logic: Possible worlds and imagination. New York: McGraw-Hill.

Peters, J. (1989). Self direction and problem solving: Theory and method. In H. Long and Associates (ed.), Self-directed learning: Emerging theory and practice. Norman, OK: University of Oklahoma.

Sanders, F. (1983). Problem solving and reasoning by industrial managers. Unpublished M.S. thesis, University of Tennessee.

Schon, D.A. (1983). The reflective practitioner: How professionals think in action. New York: Basic Books.

Scribner, S. (1986). Thinking in action: Some characteristics of practical thought. In R. Sternberg and R. Wayner (Eds.), Practical intelligence: Nature and origins of competence in the everyday world. New York: Cambridge University Press.

Sternberg, R., and Wagner, R. (1986). Practical intelligence: Nature and origins of competence in the everyday world. New York: Cambridge University Press.

Suchman, L.A. (1985). Plans and situated actions: The problem of human-machine communication. Palo Alto, CA: Zerox Corporation.

Vygotsky, L.S. (1978). Mind in society. Cambridge, MA: Harvard University Press.

Wagner, R., and Sternberg, R. (1986). Tacit knowledge and intelligence in the everyday world. In R. sternberg and R. Wagner (Eds.), Practical intelligence: Nature and origins of competence in the everyday world. New York: Cambridge University Press.

Winograd, T. (1980). What does it mean to understand language? Cognitive Science, 4, 209-241.

Chapter Seven

ADULT SELF-DIRECTION IN LEARNING: A META-ANALYTIC STUDY OF RESEARCH USING THE SELF DIRECTED LEARNING READINESS SCALE

Sandra McCune, Lucy M. Guglielmino &
Gonzalo Garcia, Jr.

During the past 12 years, a number of researchers have conducted empirical studies using Guglielmino's (1977/1978) Self-Directed Learinging Readiness Scale (SDLRS) to examine and explore the phenomenon of self-direction in learning. By analyzing and synthesizing these research efforts, this meta-analysis provides a broad picture of the results of previous research.

The Self-Directed Learning Readiness Scale (SDLRS) is a self-report questionnaire with 58 Likert-type items and is described to subjects as "a questionnaire designed to gather data on learning preferences and attitudes toward learning" (Guglielmino, 1977/1988, p.115.) Guglielmino (1977/1978) surveyed the literature and then conducted a Delphi survey involving 14 authorities to identify characteristics associated with self-direction in learning. The survey results were used as a basis for the construction of items for the SDLRS. After the items were reviewed and revised the instrument was administered to 307 subjects in Georgia, Canada, and Virginia. Item analysis and factor analysis data were used to select items for revision and to estimate the parameters of the test. Revised and added items brought the item total to 58.

Numerous studies have provided evidence of the reliability and validity of the SDLRS. Guglielmino (1977/1978) reported a Cronbach-alpha reliability coefficient of .87 for the 41-item scale. The latest reliability estimate, based on a varied sample of 3,151 adults responding to the SDLRS, was .94 (Pearson split half). (Guglielmino, 1988). Wiley (1981) calculated a Cronbach-alpha coefficient of .910 and a test-retest reliability coefficient of .793 for the SDLRS. Finestone (1984) reported Cronbach-alpha coefficients of .91 and .95 in his validation study of the SDLRS.

In addition, the content validity of the SDLRS was supported by the literature search and the use of the opinions of experts by Guglielmino (1977/1978). Internal and predictive validity of the SDLRS have been demonstrated (Brockett, 1982). A number of studies (Curry, 1983; Finestone, 1984; Hassan, 1981/1982; Long & Agyekum, 1983, 1984, 1988; Sabbaghian, 1979/1980; Savoie, 1979/1980; Torrance & Mourad, 1978) have supported the construct validity of the SDLRS.

The SDLRS is produced by Guglielmino and Associates in five forms: elementary level Form E; adult level Forms A and B and self-scoring; and the ABE form. The SDLRS-ABE was developed in response to critics (e.g., Brockett, 1982; Brookfield, 1984) who questioned the validity of the SDLRS for populations with low levels of educational attainment. In its various forms, the SDLRS is at the present the most widely used instrument for assessing self-direction in learning (McCune, 1988). In addition, "It is the best instrument now available" that "can provide reliable and valid predictions" of adult self-direction in learning (Long & Agyekum, 1988, p. 264).

PURPOSE

Glass (1976) introduced the quantitative method of meta-analysis, whereby the findings of a large number of research studies can be statistically analyzed and organized into a meaningful whole from which general conclusions can be drawn. Meta-analysis allows the researcher to examine the influence of relevant study characteristics on the outcome of the statistical analysis. Using the procedure of meta-analysis, the purpose of this paper was to statistically integrate the summary findings of empirical SDLRS research studies in order to accurately describe the state of knowledge regarding adult self-direction in learning as measured by the SDLRS.

METHOD

The application of meta-analysis to the present study involved four steps:

1. A comprehensive search of the literature was conducted to identify empirical studies which used the SDLRS to examine adult self-direction in learning. Individuals who had placed orders for the SDLRS were contacted and asked to provide information on any publications resulting from their research. Computer retrieval searches were also conducted, using the following data bases: Educational Resources Information Center (ERIC), Dissertation Abstracts, Nursing and Allied Health Literature (NAHL), MEDLARS, PsycLIT, and Social Science Citation Index. In addition, the DIALOG information Retrieval Service was used to search the Adult Education Quarterly and the Journal of Continuing Education in Nursing. The automatic retrieval search was augmented by manual searches of indices and journals as well as proceedings of the annual Adult Education Research Conference. All bibliographic references of retrieved studies were examined to identify further studies that might be included.

2. Every effort was made to acquire all published and unpublished studies that would be appropriate for use in the meta-analysis. Dissertations or not-readily-accessible journal articles were ordered through interlibrary loan. Copies of dissertations unavailable through interlibrary loan were purchased from University Microfilms International or the National Library of Canada. All studies obtained were examined; some were dismissed from inclusion in the meta-analysis. Causes of elimination included: use of children as subjects (since this

study focused on adult self-direction in learning), failure to report statistics that were sufficient for calculating or meaningfully approximating an effect size, and use of an abbreviated version of the scale.

3. Once the appropriate research studies were identified and located, a coding instrument was developed so that data from the individual studies could be collected (see appendix A). The coding instrument was pilot-tested on several studies that had been dismissed from the analysis. For each study, each product-moment correlation coefficient (or a statistic that was converted into a product-moment correlation coefficient) was coded as the effect size, which served as the dependent variable. If the study finding was reported as a Spearman's rho, point-biserial correlation coefficient, or a Cramer's phi, this statistic was recorded as the effect size. Glass et al. (1981) compiled a set of guidelines for converting a number of different summary statistics (such as t and F) into product-moment correlation coefficients (see Appendix B). Where it was meaningful to do so, these formulae were employed in converting study findings into correlation coefficients when the findings were reported as other statistics. For some studies it was not meaningful to convert the findings into correlation coefficients so the findings of these studies could not be included in the meta-analysis. The effect size functioned as a scale-free measure of the study findings so that studies could be combined and examined simultaneously. Independent variables coded for this meta-analysis were:

(1) year of publication;
(2) form of publication;
(3) sample size;
(4) mean age of the sample;
(5) mean educational achievement level;
(6) mean SDLRS score;
(7) median socioeconomic status (low, medium, or high);
(8) subject gender;

(9) ethnic mix (less than 25% white, 25%-75% white, or over 75% white);
(10) student status of subjects (yes or no);
(11) gender of principal investigator;
(12) study quality (on a scale from 1 to 3) based on seven criteria adapted from Hembree, 1984: problem identification, population description, sampling procedure, quality of instruments, data analysis,conclusions, and report readability;
(13) the variable associated with adult self-direction in learning for the recorded correlation coefficient.

4. Each correlation (effect size) along with the 13 coded independent variables was entered into various procedures of the statistical software package SPSS* (SPSS, Inc. 1986). Data analysis was broken into two phases: (a) extraction of descriptive statistics, and (b) application of statistical techniques (mainly, calculation of summary statistics and correlational analysis) to the effect size data. Because the studies analyzed were not intended to be a sample but rather the population itself (with some margin of retrieval error), inferences about the population are not entirely appropriate. However, in the interest of readability and completeness, inferential statements were made as if the set of studies were a sample. No weighting scheme by sample size was used in this meta-analysis because the researchers felt this approach would give undue emphasis to larger studies. Where a correlation was observed between sample size and effect size, a t-test was used to determine whether the unweighted (by sample size) mean effect size was statistically different from the unweighted mean effect size. To avoid the risk of using nonindependent data, if a study had two or more correlation coefficients for which the independent study variables were exactly the same, an average of these correlation coefficients was recorded as the effect size.

RESULTS

As a result of the literature search, 35 studies* which used the SDLRS to examine adult self-direction in learning were identified. Of these, 6 were eliminated from the data analysis: 2 studies used children as subjects, 3 studies failed to report statistics that were sufficient for calculating or meaningfully approximating an effect size, and one study used a 10-item version of the SDLRS which was inappropriate for this study.

The remaining 29 studies, consisting of 21 dissertations and 8 journal articles, comprised the data for this investigation.

Descriptive Statistics

A total of 4596 subjects were represented in this meta-analysis. The gender of the subjects was 66.2% female and 33.8% male. The mean number of subjects included in each of the 29 studies was 158, ranging from 31 to 753 subjects. The mean age of the subjects was 37.5 years, ranging from 17 to 75 years. The mean educational achievement level was 14.4 years of formal schooling, ranging from 10.4 to 20 years. The mean SDLRS score for all samples was 227.7, ranging from 185.3 to 246.8.

The socioeconomic status of the subjects was difficult to assess. Information about socioeconomic status was provided in only 14 studies, of which 13 used middle-class subjects. Racial composition, like socioeconomic status, could not be readily determined. Only two of the nine studies which reported this information were studies with less than 25% white. Four of the studies were over 75% white, with the remaining three studies consisting of a mixed racial composition.

Sixty-two percent of the studies used students as subjects. The principal investigator was female in 18 studies and male in 11 studies. On a scale of 1 to 3 (where

* A list of the studies is available from the authors at the Department of Mathematics and Statistics, Stephen F. Austin State University, Nacogdoches, TX 75962.

1 indicates low and 3 indicates high), the mean study quality was 2.3, ranging from 1.7 to 2.9. None of the studies was classified as low quality (more than two standard deviations below the mean).

Analysis of Effect Size Data

A total of 109 effect sizes were obtained from the 29 studies, in which adult self-direction in learning (as measured by the SDLRS) was investigated in association with a variety of demographic and psychosocial/behavioral variables. These variables were examined for commonalities and then placed into broad categories descriptive of the nature of the relationship under study. Altogether the researchers identified nine different major variable categories that had been sufficiently investigated (at least five studies) in relation to adult self-direction in learning as measured by the SDLRS. Those variables for which fewer than five studies investigated the variable in relationship to adult self-direction in learning were designated other and omitted from subsequent analyses. The demographic variables were:

(1) Age
(2) Gender
(3) Race
(4) Educational attainment level

The psychosocial/behavioral variables were:

(5) Autonomy, consisting of the following component variables: internal locus of control, self-reliance, self-motivation, peer ranking as an independent learner, and faculty rating as an independent learner.
(6) Dependence, consisting of the following component variables: external motivation, preference for structure, external locus of control, and lack of independent response.

(7) Growth orientation, consisting of the following component variables: creativity, originality, fluency, openness, initiative, future orientation, positive view of learning, cognitive and ethical development, self-development, problem-solving ability, and desire to escape from a dull and boring environment.

(8) Degree of involvement in self-directed learning (SDL) activity, consisting of the following component variables: number of learning projects, number of hours spent in SDL, and degree of participation in extension education.

(9) Perceived contentment, consisting of the following component variables: life-satisfaction, positive mood tone, perceived health, successful job performance, and social contacts.

Table 7.1 summarizes the findings of the meta-analysis for each of the major variable categories.

The overall effect size (ES), which may be interpreted as the average correlation of the variable with adult self-direction in learning, and the number (N) of studies from which it was calculated are recorded. If the correlational analysis indicated that one or more selected independent study variables--specifically, sample size, mean age of the subjects, mean educational achievement level, mean SDLRS score, subject gender, or study quality--significantly ($\alpha = .05$) influenced the magnitude of the ES being examined, the study variable, the correlation coefficient (r) the p value, and number (n) of values that were used to calculate r are listed; otherwise, none is recorded in the table.

For ease of presentation the variable categories will be separated into two groups, based on whether the possibility of interaction between the effect size and any of the independent study variables exists. Group 1 includes

Table 7.1: Summary of Meta-Analysis Findings for the Major Variable Categories in the 29 Adult Self-Direction in Learning Research Studies using the SDLRS.

Variable Category	ES	N	Influential Study Variable	r	p	n
Age	.048	14	mean age	-.594	.013	14
Gender	.083	13	percent female	.636	.010	13
Race	- .030	5	none	-	-	-
Educational Attainment Level	.269	10	none	-	-	-
Autonomy	.217	5	none	-	-	-
Dependence	- .124	6	mean SDLRS score	-.986	.009	6
Growth Orientation	.215	9	none	-	-	-
SDL Activity	.270	5	none	-	-	-
Perceived Contentment	.259	6	none	-	-	-

the variables for which examination of Table 7.1 reveals no statistically significant (= .05) correlation between any of the independent study variables and magnitude of the average correlation. Variables in this group are race, educational attainment level, autonomy, growth orientation, perceived contentment, and involvement in SDL activity.

Those for which Table 7.1 shows a statistically significant (= .05) correlation between selected independent study variables and the magnitude of the average correlation comprise Group 2. Included in this group are age, gender, and dependence.

Group 1:

To aid in assessing the practical meaning of the average correlation of the variable categories in Group 1, the following modified guidelines adapted from Cohen (1977) were adopted:

below .100	negligible relationship
.100-.242	slight relationship
.243-.370	moderate relationship
above .370	marked relationship

Thus, the conclusions are that involvement in SDL activity (ES=.270), educational attainment level (ES=.269), and perceived contentment (ES=.259) are moderately related to adult self-direction in learning; both autonomy (ES=.217) and growth orientation (ES=.215) are slightly related to adult self-direction in learning; and the relationship between race and adult self-direction in learning is negligible (ES=-.030).

Group 2:

Assessment of the average correlations of the variable categories in Group 2 is confounded by the influence of independent study variables. The average correlation between age and adult self-direction in learning is .048, but correlational analysis indicated the relationship is more pronounced for younger subjects (r = - .549). The average correlation between gender and adult self-direction is .083, but correlational analysis indicated the relationship becomes more pronounced as the percent of female (r = .636) in the population increases. The average correlation between dependence and adult self-direction in learning is -.124 , but correlational analysis indicated the negative relationship is more pronounced for those with higher SDLRS scores (r = -.886).

REFERENCES

Brockett, R. (1982). Self-directed learning readiness and life satisfaction among older adults (Doctoral dissertation, Syracuse University, 1982). Dissertation Abstracts International, 44, 42A.

Brookfield, S. (1984). Self-directed adult learning: A critical paradigm. Adult Education Quarterly, 35, 59-71.

Cohen, J. (1977). Statistical power analysis for the behavioral sciences. New York: Academic Press.

Curry, M. (1983). The analysis of self-directed learning characteristics in older adults engaged in formal learning activities in two settings (Doctoral dissertation, Kansas State University, 1983). Dissertation Abstracts International, 44, 1293A.

Finestone, P. (1984). A construct validation of the self-directed learning readiness scale with labour education participants (Doctoral dissertation, University of Toronto, 1984). Dissertation Abstracts International, 46, 05A.

Glass, G. (1976). Primary, secondary, and meta-analysis of research. Educational Researcher, 5, 3-8.

Guglielmino, L. (1978). Development of the self-directed learning readiness scale (Doctoral dissertation, University of Georgia, 1977). Dissertation Abstracts International, 38, 6467A.

Guglielmino, L. (1988). (Item - test correlations and reliabilty estimate for 3151 respondents to the SDLRS). Unpublished data analysis.

Guglielmino, L., & Guglielmino, P. (1988). Self-directed learning in business and industry: An information age imperative. In H.B. Long (Ed.), Self-directed learning: Application and theory (125-148). Athens, GA: Adult Education Department of the University of Georgia.

Hassan, A. (1982). An investigation of the learning projects among adults of high and low readiness for self direction in learning (Doctoral dissertation, Iowa State University, 1981). Dissertation Abstracts International, 42, 3838A.

Hembree, R. (1984). Model for meta-analysis of research in education with a demonstration in mathematics education: Effects of hand-held calculators (Doctoral dissertation. University of Tennessee, 1984). Dissertation Abstracts International, 45, 10A.

Long, H.B., & Agyekum, S. (1983). Guglielmino's self-directed learning readiness scale. Higher Education, 12, 77-87.

Long, H.B., & Agyekum, S. (1984). Teacher ratings in the validation of Guglielmino's self-directed learning readiness scale. Higher Education, 13, 709-715.

Long, H.B., & Agyekum, S. (1988). Self-directed learning readiness: Assessment and validation. In H. B. Long (Ed.), Self-directed learning: Application and theory (pp. 253-266). Athens, GA: Adult Education Department of the University of Georgia.

McCune, S. (1988). A meta-analytic study of adult self-direction in learning: A review of the research from 1977 to 1987 (Doctoral dissertation, Texas A&M University, 1988). Dissertation Abstracts International, 49, 11A.

Sabbaghian, Z. (1980). Adult self-directedness and self-concept: An exploration of relationships (Doctoral dissertation. Iowa State University, 1979). Dissertation Abstracts International, 40, 3701A.

Savoie, M. (1980). Continuing education for nurses: Predictors of success in courses requiring a degree of self-direction (Doctoral dissertation, University of Toronto, 1979). Dissertation Abstracts International, 40, 12A.

SPSS, Inc. (1986). SPSS* User's Guide. New York: McGraw Hill.

Torrance, E.P., & Mourad, S. (1978). Some creativity and style of learning and thinking correlates of Guglielmino's self-directed learning readiness scale. Psychological Reports, 43, 1167-1171.

Wiley, K. (1981). Effects of a self-directed learning project and preference for structure on the self-directed learning readiness of baccalaureate nursing students (Doctoral dissertation, Northern Illinois University, 1981). Dissertation Abstracts International, 43, 01A.

Chapter Eight

STRUCTURAL ANALYSIS OF THE SELF-DIRECTED LEARNING READINESS SCALE: A CONFIRMATORY FACTOR ANALYSIS USING LISREL MODELING

Russell F. West and Ernest L. Bentley, Jr.

Interest in self-directed learning during adulthood has grown steadily over the past twenty years as researchers focused on the natural process of learning that occurs outside of institutional settings. Much of the early research on self-directed adult learning was stimulated by Alan Tough (1971) who studied learning projects of adults and later the process of intentional change (1982), including the role of self-directed learning in the change process. This learning projects research tradition has been extensive. Many different studies have been completed, such as Fair's study of elementary teachers, Field's study of low literate adults in Jamaica, John's study of practicing pharmacists (cited in Tough, 1978) and a study of urban and rural adults in Tennessee (Peters & Gordon, 1974). This learning projects research tradition has been criticized in recent years for having a narrow focus (Oddi, 1987) and for promoting a commitment to the research method, rather than an interest in answering important research questions (Brookfield, 1984). The early learning projects research highlighted the importance of self-directed adult learning which, subsequently, has dominated much of the adult education literature (e.g., Knowles, 1975; Smith, 1983) over the past fifteen years. This research tradition also led others to take different approaches in defining and studying self-directed learning.

The Self-Directed Learning Readiness Scale (SDLRS) was developed by Guglielmino (1978) as a result of this heightened interest in self-directed learning brought about, in part, by the learning projects research tradition. This 58 item self-report instrument was developed for use in assessing an individual's readiness to engage in the self-directed learning process. According to Guglielmino (1978):

> The instrument was developed for use by educational institutions or individual learning facilitators in their efforts to select suitable learners for programs requiring self-direction in learning and to screen learners to determine their strengths and weaknesses in self-direction in learning in an attempt to guide them into situations in which they can best utilize and develop their potential in this area (p. 29).

The original 41 item SDLRS was developed through a three round delphi process in which 14 experts in self-directed learning were asked to identify important personality characteristics of self-directed adult learners. The instrument was administered to a sample of 307 high school junior and seniors, college undergraduates and noncredit students that were enrolled in university enrichment courses. A principal components factor analysis with orthogonal rotation was used to identify eight factors which best represented the structure of the intercorrelation matrix for the items on the scale. The factors were labeled as follows: openness to new learning opportunities, self-concept as an effective learner, initiative and independence in learning, informed acceptance of responsibility for one's own learning, love of learning, creativity, positive orientation to the future and ability to use basic study skills and problem-solving skills. While revisions have been made in the test items and the scale has been lengthened from 41 to 58, the instrument is still reported to measure these eight factors.

Since its development, the instrument has been used extensively to assess readiness for self-directed learning. A number of doctoral students have used the SDLRS in completing dissertations (e.g., Savoie, 1979; Sabbaghian, 1979; Hassan, 1981). Researchers have also studied the psychometric properties of the scale. In the original research, Guglielmino (1978) found an internal consistency of .87 for the total 41 item scale, as did Brockett (1985) with the 58 item version. Construct validity research has shown that total SDLRS score is positively related to measures of originality, creative experiences and achievements, and right hemispheric style of learning (Torrance & Mourad, 1978a). In another study these authors found significant relationships between the creativity subscale of the SDLRS and gifted students' abilities to think creatively (Torrance & Mourad, 1978b). In assessing the predictive validity of the SDLRS, Crook (1985) found a significant relationship between total SDLRS score and yearend nursing grades, although the relationship was not strong. Crook also found a significant correlation between SDLRS scores and peer nominations of self-directed learners after the first year of school. Hassan (1981) reported that in a study of 77 randomly selected adults, those with higher SDLRS scores had engaged in a greater number of learning projects, thus supporting the validity of the construct. Long and Agyekum (1984), however, failed to find a significant relationship between SDLRS total score and faculty ratings of self-directedness.

While the SDLRS has been used extensively in studying the self-directed learning process, the measurement instrument has also been criticized. For example, Brockett (1985) suggested that the instrument is not appropriate for those adults with low levels of educational attainment because the SDLRS "is very much oriented toward learning through books and schooling (p. 21)." While noting the importance of the SDLRS in the development of self-directed learning theory and practice, Brockett (1983) suggested that the SDLRS would not be appropriate in assessing self-directed learning readiness outside of educational institutions. Brookfield (1984) has also been critical of this approach to studying the self-directed learning process. More recently, Oddi (1987) has been critical of the SDLRS because she claims that it was developed from a process perspective rather than from a psychological characteristics perspective.

While previous researchers have looked at the measurement integrity of the SDLRS through the assessment of measurement reliability and validity, the implied measurement model underlying the instrument has not been assessed using the more recent confirmatory factor analysis (CFA) procedures using maximum likelihood estimation (Joreskog & Sorbom, 1984; Joreskog & Sorbom, 1988). Confirmatory factor analysis represents an approach to analysis in which a measurement model is specified in advance, with this information being built in to estimation procedures (Bollen, 1989). Confirmatory factor analysis is more appropriate for testing theoretically derived models, since it is much more flexible than the traditional exploratory factor analysis model. The EFA model requires that the following assumptions are made; 1) all latent variables are correlated with each other or none of the latent variables are correlated 2) all latent variables affect all observed variables 3) errors of measurement associated with observed variables are uncorrelated 4) each observed variable is affected by only one measurement error 5) measurement errors are uncorrelated with latent variables (Carmines, 1986). Most of these assumptions are not required in the CFA model. This allows the researcher to analyze more substantive models and impose "substantively motivated" constraints (Long, 1983, p. 12), which then can be tested or confirmed. Using CFA the researcher is able to constrain some correlations to equal zero while others are left free to vary. Factor intercorrelations can also be constrained to be equal. Using CFA, individual item loadings on latent variables can be estimated or constrained to zero, (whereas in EFA each item must load on each latent variable). Using CFA, the researcher is also able to specify the existence of correlated measurement errors (Bollen, 1989). According to Gorsuch (1983):

> Exploratory factor analysis should be reserved only for those areas that are truly exploratory, that is, where no prior analyses have been conducted. If prior analyses have been conducted then either those results or a strong theory challenging those results should be used as a hypothesized structure in the new study...confirmatory factor analysis is much more theoretically important [than EFA] and should be the much more widely used of the two major factor analytic approaches (p. 134).

In discussing the utility of confirmatory analysis using the LISREL (LInear Structural RELations) model (Joreskog & Sorbom, 1988a), Hayduk (1987) suggests that:

> The joy of LISREL is that it provides opportunities for an active interplay between theory, modeling and estimation. This rapprochement forces users to become experts at their theory, rather than mere number crunchers (p. xv).

The purpose of the present study was to assess the fit of the eight factor measurement model underlying the SDLRS with CFA procedures using the LISREL model and maximum likelihood estimation. In addition, several alternative measurement models were assessed that represented the readiness for self-directed learning construct.

METHOD

Subjects

In this study SDLRS instruments were sent to 16 different elementary, middle and high schools across the state of Tennessee, as part of a larger assessment package associated with a large professional development program for schools entitled TN LEAD. All teachers and administrators in the schools were asked to complete the SDLRS. The median response rate from the schools was 93%. The lowest response rate was 75%. A total of 439 individuals actually completed the SDLRS. Seventy-seven percent of the respondents were female. Forty-six percent of the respondents were working at the elementary school level. High school and middle school personnel made up 30% and 17% of the sample, respectively. Ninety-four percent of the respondents were classroom teachers. Ninety percent of the respondents were white. The average age of the respondents was 41. The typical respondent had between 13 and 14 years of teaching experience.

Procedures

The 58 item SDLRS was administered to every teacher and administrator in the 16 participating schools. The data were recorded on optical scan sheets to facilitate scoring. In order to assess the adequacy of the 8 factor model, the number of items was reduced from 58 to 33. The factor loadings found in a previous study provided by Guglielmino (personal communication, January 8, 1989) were used to trim the full model in the following way: 1) only those items that had previously loaded .40 or higher on a factor were retained and 2) only those items whose secondary loadings were less than .30 were retained. The application of these criteria resulted in the deletion of 25 items that loaded in an "ambiguous" fashion in the previous study. In utilizing these restrictions, the intent was to work with a smaller set of items with good psychometric properties. Each of the 33 items that remained was thought to have a substantial loading on only one factor in the specified model.

Model Specification

The LISREL model of Joreskog and Sorbom (1988a) was used to specify the initial eight factor measurement model. This model is symbolized as follows:

$$x = \Lambda_x \xi + \delta$$

where each x value is a person's score on a particular item which is dependent on a latent variable or factor (ξ) and a unique error term (δ). Using the LISREL model, the pattern of loadings of individual items on latent variables can be specified, as can variances/covariances between factors and the pattern of variances/covariances between unique components of the model.

In this analysis, no correlations were assumed to exist between error terms. Appropriate loadings of items on factors were specified, while the remainder were set equal to zero. In the orthogonal solution, the correlations between latent variables or factors were set equal to zero. In the oblique solution, they were estimated. Each specified item/factor relationship represented a theoretically expected loading on a factor while each zero specified no relationship between an item and a factor. To estimate the model, the variances of the factors were assigned a value of 1.0 to fix the measurement scale.

Data Analysis

The raw data were processed using PRELIS (Joreskog & Sorbom, 1988b) for microcomputers prior to running the LISREL analysis. Normalized scores on each item were created in PRELIS and the interitem correlations were obtained. The resulting correlation matrix was then input into LISREL for analysis. The microcomputer version of LISREL VII (Joreskog & Sorbom, 1988a) was used to estimate the several different models of interest. LISREL VII was used to estimate the desired components in each model (i.e., the factor loadings, correlations between latent variables and unique components). LISREL VII provided an estimate of how well the theoretically derived model and its implied variance/covariance matrix ($\hat{\Sigma}$) could reproduce the sample variance/covariance matrix (S). The chi-square goodness-of-fit test was used to test the congruence between $\hat{\Sigma}$ and S. Large chi-square values indicated large differences in the $\hat{\Sigma}$ and S matrices. The chi square measure indicated the extent to which the matrix derived from theory was congruent with the observed data. The chi-square goodness-of-fit test has been shown to be artificially inflated when sample size is large (Joreskog & Sorbom, 1988a), and is most appropriately used in conjunction with other measures of fit. Bollen (1989) suggests that the chi-square goodness-of-fit test be interpreted with caution. In addition, the ratio of chi-square to degrees of freedom was also calculated. It has been suggested that a chi-square/degrees of freedom ratio of no more than 2 or 3 can be used to identify a good fit (Carmines & McIver, 1981). The Adjusted Goodness-of-Fit Index (AGFI) was also used to examine the adequacy of the model. The AGFI can range in magnitude from 0 to +1 and is interpreted as the amount of the total variances and covariances in S that are predicted by $\hat{\Sigma}$ (Bollen, 1989). The AGFI represents the relative amount of variance/covariance explained by the particular model.

The chi-square goodness-of-fit test for nested models (Long, 1983; Hayduk, 1987) was used to examine the adequacy of the correlated factors models, over and above the more restrictive orthogonal models. This test was conducted by taking the differences between chi-quare values for each pair of oblique/orthogonal solutions, along with the associated differences in degrees of freedom between the two models (Bentler & Bonett, 1980). The resulting difference chi-square was used to indicate whether the restrictive (orthogonal) solution was as effective in reproducing S as the more general (oblique) model. A significant difference in the chi-square indicated that correlations between factors improved the fit of the model. Such nested comparisons were only made within the eight, six and three factor models. When the best-fitting oblique model was obtained, certain parameters were then estimated according to the modification indices generated by the program. In assessing the model improvement associated with these relaxations, the chi-square differences were also examined.

Table 8.1: Characteristics of the Eight, Six, Three and One Factor Models

Model	Total Parameters	X^2	df	Adjusted Goodness-of Fit (AGFI)	X^2/ df	Root Mean Square Residual
Eight-factor Orthogonal Solution	58	2671.71*	503	.602	5.31	.243
Eight-Factor Oblique Solution	94	1002.94*	467	.846	2.15	.052
Six-Factor Orthogonal Solution	60	2381.82*	501	.683	4.75	.245
Six-Factor Oblique Solution	81	1040.50*	480	.845	2.17	.053
Three-Factor Orthogonal Solution	63	1593.78*	498	.782	3.20	.156
Three-Factor Oblique Solution	69	1272.44*	492	.808	2.58	.057
One Factor Solution	66	1385.06*	495	.795	2.79	.060

* $p < .01$

Table 8.2: Standardized Factor Loadings for the Eight-factor Oblique Solution

	Eight-Factor Model								Item Variance
	F1	F2	F3	F4	F5	F6	F7	F8	Explained
Q1	.542	0	0	0	0	0	0	0	.294
Q3	0	0	.514	0	0	0	0	0	.264
Q5	.617	0	0	0	0	0	0	0	.381
Q7	0	0	-.019	0	0	0	0	0	.000
Q10	0	.517	0	0	0	0	0	0	.268
Q11	0	.408	0	0	0	0	0	0	.166
Q15	0	0	0	0	0	0	0	.768	.590
Q16	0	0	0	0	0	0	.637	0	.406
Q17	.602	0	0	0	0	0	0	0	.362
Q18	0	0	0	0	0	.396	0	0	.156
Q19	0	0	.512	0	0	0	0	0	.262
Q21	0	0	0	0	0	0	.625	0	.390
Q24	.458	0	0	0	0	0	0	0	.210
Q27	0	.599	0	0	0	0	0	0	.359
Q28	.600	0	0	0	0	0	0	0	.360
Q29	0	0	.303	0	0	0	0	0	.092
Q30	0	0	0	.679	0	0	0	0	.461
Q33	0	.488	0	0	0	0	0	0	.238
Q34	0	0	0	.652	0	0	0	0	.425
Q36	0	0	0	.517	0	0	0	0	.267
Q37	0	0	0	.526	0	0	0	0	.277
Q38	0	.546	0	0	0	0	0	0	.298
Q40	0	0	0	0	0	.511	0	0	.261
Q43	0	0	0	0	.558	0	0	0	.312
Q44	0	0	.662	0	0	0	0	0	.438
Q45	.764	0	0	0	0	0	0	0	.584
Q46	.760	0	0	0	0	0	0	0	.578
Q47	.750	0	0	0	0	0	0	0	.562
Q48	0	0	.384	0	0	0	0	0	.148
Q50	0	0	0	0	0	0	0	.720	.518
Q52	0	0	0	0	.502	0	0	0	.252
Q57	0	.740	0	0	0	0	0	0	.548
Q58	0	0	0	0	0	.488	0	0	.238

Table 8.3: Factor Intercorrelations for the Eight, Six and Three Factor Solutions

Eight Factor Solution

Factor	1	2	3	4	5	6	7	8
1	---							
2	.766	---						
3	.720	.764	---					
4	.770	.749	.708	---				
5	.944	.842	.991	.828	---			
6	.946	1.000	.749	.768	.927	---		
7	.685	.732	.554	.518	.798	.906	---	
8	.613	.633	.397	.343	.529	.830	.637	---

Six Factor Solution

Factor	1	2	3	4	5	6
1	---					
2	.808	---				
3	.799	.796	---			
4	.770	.750	.755	---		
5	.686	.776	.642	.524	---	
6	.612	.678	.437	.341	.635	---

Three Factor Solution

Factor	1	2	3
1	---		
2	.744	---	
3	.617	.633	---

RESULTS

The Eight Factor Model

The eight factor orthogonal model was analyzed first, since it was the model that was expected, based on the previous research using EFA. The overall estimates of model fit are presented in Table 8.1. The chi-square goodness-of-fit statistic for the model with df=503 was 2671.71, with $p < .001$. While this value could have been inflated due to the large n, the AGFI of .60 and the X^2/df value of 5.31 indicated a lack of correspondence between $\hat{\Sigma}$ and S. The oblique (correlated factors) 8 factor model yielded a reduction in the chi-square value that was significantly improved over the orthogonal solution ($X^2 = 1668.77$ with df=36, $p < .001$).

The X^2/df value for the oblique solution was 2.15 and the AGFI was .846, indicating that nearly 85% of the item variances and covariances were explained by the model. The X^2/df ratio of 2.15 also indicated a good correspondence between $\hat{\Sigma}$ and S.

Standardized factor loadings for the eight factor oblique model are presented in Table 8.2. All of the loadings were greater than .30, except the leading of Question 7 on Factor 3 (Tolerance of Risk, Ambiguity and Complexity in Learning). The loadings were all associated with statistically significant t-values, except for the loading of Question 7 on Factor 3.

The correlations between factors in the eight factor oblique solution are presented in Table 8.3. In reviewing this matrix the high correlations between factors was evident. The correlation between Factor 6 (Initiative in Learning) and Factor 1 (Self Concept as an Effective Independent Learner) was 1.0. An examination of the items which loaded on Factor 6, suggested they may in fact be measuring one's self concept:

Question 40 (I can make myself do what I think I should)

Question 58 (Learners are leaders)

Question 18 (If there is something I have decided to learn, I can find time for it, no matter how busy I am)

Likewise, the correlation between Factor 5 (View of Learning as a Lifelong, Beneficial Process) and Factor 3 (Tolerance of Risk, Ambiguity, and Complexity in Learning) was .99. An examination of the items which loaded on Factor 5, suggested they could also be viewed as representing Factor 3. The questions were:

Question 43 (I enjoy discussing Ideas)

Question 52 (Old dogs can learn new tricks)

Given the high correlations between these factors, the model was respecified as a six factor model. Questions 18, 40 and 58 were specified to load on Factor 2, while Questions 43 and 52 were specified to load on Factor 3. The previously specified Factor 5 and 6 were thus eliminated, although Factors 7 and 8 in the eight factor model were labeled Factor 5 and Factor 6, respectively in the six factor model.

<u>The Six Factor Model</u>

The overall estimates of model fit are presented in Table 8.1. The respecified six factor orthogonal model produced a chi-square goodness-of-fit statistic of 2381.82 with df=501 ($p < .001$). The AGFI of .68 and the X^2/df value of 4.75 indicated a lack of correspondence between $\hat{\Sigma}$ and S. The oblique six factor model yielded a reduction in the chi-square value that was significantly improved over the orthogonal solution ($X^2 = 1341.32$ with df=21, $p < .001$). The X^2/df value for the oblique solution was 2.17.

Table 8.4: Standardized Factor Loadings for the Six-factor Oblique Solution

	Six-Factor Model						Item Variance
	F1	F2	F3	F4	F5	F6	Explained
Q1	.540	0	0	0	0	0	.291
Q3	0	0	.490	0	0	0	.240
Q5	.618	0	0	0	0	0	.381
Q7	0	0	-.049	0	0	0	.002
Q10	0	.520	0	0	0	0	.270
Q11	0	.383	0	0	0	0	.146
Q15	0	0	0	0	0	.773	.598
Q16	0	0	0	0	.627	0	.393
Q17	.606	0	0	0	0	0	.367
Q18	0	.437	0	0	0	0	.191
Q19	0	0	.485	0	0	0	.235
Q21	0	0	0	0	.635	0	.403
Q24	.460	0	0	0	0	0	.212
Q27	0	.587	0	0	0	0	.344
Q28	.602	0	0	0	0	0	.363
Q29	0	0	.272	0	0	0	.074
Q30	0	0	0	.679	0	0	.461
Q33	0	.484	0	0	0	0	.234
Q34	0	0	0	.653	0	0	.426
Q36	0	0	0	.517	0	0	.267
Q37	0	0	0	.525	0	0	.276
Q38	0	.528	0	0	0	0	.278
Q40	0	.550	0	0	0	0	.302
Q43	0	0	.621	0	0	0	.385
Q44	0	0	.638	0	0	0	.407
Q45	.763	0	0	0	0	0	.582
Q46	.760	0	0	0	0	0	.578
Q47	.747	0	0	0	0	0	.558
Q48	0	0	.376	0	0	0	.142
Q50	0	0	0	0	0	.715	.511
Q52	0	0	.514	0	0	0	.264
Q57	0	.731	0	0	0	0	.535
Q58	0	.503	0	0	0	0	.253

Nearly all of loadings were greater than .30 and many were higher than .70. After examining the questions that loaded highest on the six factors, those factors were renamed, where appropriate, based on the nature of the questions which loaded most strongly. The new labels and the questions supporting the rationale are presented below:

Factor 1: Love of Learning (No Change)

Item 45 (I have a strong desire to learn new things)

Item 46 (The more I learn, the more exciting the world becomes)

Item 47 (Learning is fun)

Item 5 (I love to learn)

Factor 2: Self-Confidence As a Learner

Item 57 (I am an effective learner in the classroom and on my own)

Item 27 (I am capable of learning for myself almost anything I might need to know)

Item 40 (I can make myself do what I think I should)

Item 38 (I'm better than most people are at trying to find out the things I need to know)

Factor 3: Openness to A Challenge

Item 44 (I don't like challenging learning situations)

Item 43 (I enjoy discussing ideas)

Item 52 (Old dogs can learn new tricks)

Item 3 (When I see something I don't understand, I stay away from it)

Factor 4: Inquisitive Nature

Item 30 (I have a lot of curiosity about things)

Item 34 (I like to try new things, even if I am not sure how they will turn out)

Item 37 (I like to think about the future)

Item 36 (I am good at thinking of unusual ways to do things)

Factor 5: Self-Understanding (no change)

Item 21 (I know when I need to learn more about something)

Item 16 (I can tell whether I'm learning something well or not)

Factor 6: Acceptance of Responsibility for Learning (no change)

Item 15 (No one but me is truly responsible for what I learn)

Item 50 (I am responsible for my learning--no one else is)

The correlations between factors in the six factor oblique solution are presented in Table 8.3. These correlations were quite high and ranged from .341 to .808. In particular, Factors One - Four appeared to be highly related. In an attempt to develop a more parsimonious set of factors which could account for the observed variances and covariances among the items, The items loading on

Factors One - Four were combined into one large factor and a three factor model was respecified.

The Three Factor Model

The overall estimates of model fit are presented in Table 8.1. The respecified three factor orthogonal model produced a chi-square goodness-of-fit statistic of 1593.78 with df=498 (p <.001). The AGFI of .782 and the X^2/df value of 3.25 indicated that this orthogonal model was more effective than the previous orthogonal models. The model did not, however, provide a good fit between $\hat{\Sigma}$ and S. An oblique three factor model yielded an improved chi-square value that was statistically significant (X^2= 321.34 with df=6, p < .001). The X^2/df value for the oblique solution was 2.58 and the AGFI was .808. While better than the orthogonal three factor solution, the oblique solution was not as effective in reproducing S as the six factor oblique solution. The factor loadings for the three factor oblique solution are presented in Table 8.5. The correlations between the factors are presented in Table 8.3.

A One Factor Model

A one factor model was estimated to determine if one higher order factor might be more effective in reproducing the observed variance/covariance matrix. The overall estimates of model fit are presented in Table 8.1. The one factor model produced a chi-square goodness-of-fit statistic of 1385.06 with df=495 (p <.001). The AGFI of .795 and the X^2/df value of 2.79 indicated that the one factor model was not as effective as the previous oblique models in reproducing the sample matrix.

Table 8.5: Standardized Factor Loadings for the Three-Factor Oblique Solution

	Three-Factor Model			Item Variance Explained
	Factor 1	Factor 2	Factor 3	
Q1	.512	0	0	.262
Q3	.437	0	0	.191
Q5	.586	0	0	.343
Q7	-.093	0	0	.009
Q10	.488	0	0	.238
Q11	.319	0	0	.102
Q15	0	0	.782	.612
Q16	0	.620	0	.385
Q17	.585	0	0	.343
Q18	.411	0	0	.169
Q19	.442	0	0	.195
Q21	0	.642	0	.412
Q24	.449	0	0	.202
Q27	.536	0	0	.287
Q28	.624	0	0	.389
Q29	.203	0	0	.041
Q30	.562	0	0	.316
Q33	.433	0	0	.187
Q34	.561	0	0	.315
Q36	.386	0	0	.149
Q37	.468	0	0	.219
Q38	.488	0	0	.238
Q40	.512	0	0	.262
Q43	.538	0	0	.289
Q44	.534	0	0	.286
Q45	.732	0	0	.536
Q46	.707	0	0	.500
Q47	.701	0	0	.491
Q48	.315	0	0	.099
Q50	0	0	.707	.500
Q52	.516	0	0	.266
Q57	.679	0	0	.461
Q58	.496	0	0	.246

Modification of the Six Factor Model

The results of the initial model testing indicated that the oblique eight and six factor models were very similar in terms of explaining the variances/covariances among the 33 items. Given the desirability of a parsimonious model, the six factor model was selected as best representing the structure of the observed variance/covariance matrix. To further adjust this "best fitting" model so that a factorial complexity greater than one could exist, the parameters in the six factor oblique model with a poor fit were iteratively relaxed to achieve a better fitting model. These iterative relaxations were based on the modification indices which are computed as part of the LISREL VII analysis (Joreskog & Sorbom, 1988). The first six iterations resulted in significant improvements in the model. These iterative changes, as assessed by the differences in goodness-of-fit tests, are presented in Table 8.6. These results have been presented along with a description of 1) the initial factor on which the item loaded and 2) the second loading when the factor complexity is raised to two, based on the modification indices. At step 1, Item 52, "Old dogs can learn new tricks", which originally loaded on Factor 3 (Openness to Challenge), also loaded on Factor 1 (Love of Learning). In step 2, Item 28, "I really enjoy tracking down the answer to a question," which originally loaded on Factor 1 (Love of Learning) also loaded on Factor 2 (Self-Confidence in Learning Ability). Item 11, "I can learn things on my own better than most people", which originally loaded on Factor 2 (Self Confidence in Learning Ability), loaded on Factor 1 (Love of Learning) after relaxation number 3. At step 4, Item 21, "I know when I need to learn more about something," which originally loaded on Factor 5 (Self-Understanding), also loaded on Factor 4 (Inquisitive Nature). Finally at step 5, Item 50, "I am responsible for my own learning--no one else is", which was hypothesized to load on Factor 6 (Acceptance of Responsibility for Learning), also loaded on Factor 5 (Self-Understanding).

Table 8.6: Table of Iterative Model Relaxations Beginning With the Six Factor Oblique Solution (Factor Complexity of One)

Step	Chi Square	df	Delta**	Delta Percent	Adjusted GFI	Question/ Factor	New Factor
0	1040.50	480	-----	----	.845	----	----
1	1012.33	479	28.17*	2.7%	.848	Q52-F3	F1
2	985.53	478	26.80*	2.6%	.852	Q28-F1	F2
3	965.60	477	20.03*	2.0%	.855	Q11-F2	F1
4	948.91	476	16.59*	1.7%	.857	Q21-F5	F4
5	935.17	475	13.74*	1.4%	.858	Q50-F6	F5

** Delta represents the decrease in the chi-square test statistic for nested models when the item is allowed to load on the new factor. The delta percent figure is divided by the original chi-square prior to a given step in the model.

* $p < .001$

The modification indices suggested which additional parameters to estimate in obtaining a better model fit. These new loadings appeared to make good "theoretical sense" and support the argument that in this "trimmed" version of the original SDLRS, some items do measure more than one factor. This final specification provided a final AGFI of .859. In other words, the model implied accounted for 86% of the variances and covariances in S. Since the incremental gain in percentage of explained variances was small, the specification search (Joreskog & Sorbom, 1988) was halted after 5 iterations.

DISCUSSION

In previous studies, the structure underlying the SDLRS has been derived through the application of exploratory factor analytic methods. These results have suggested that an eight factor model with uncorrelated factors best represents the measurement structure underlying the SDLRS. In this study, more recently developed confirmatory factor analytic methods were used in an effort to get a better understanding of the model underlying the SDLRS using a sample of public school teachers and administrators. The adequacy of the original eight factor model was compared to a similar solution with correlated factors. The results may help researchers gain a better understanding of the self-directed learning construct and may provide insight into how the SDLRS should be modified in the future.

The first conclusion drawn from this study was that an orthogonal solution to the SDLRS measurement model is clearly inadequate. For each of the specifications, a significant reduction in goodness-of-fit chi-square values occurred when the orthogonality restriction was loosened and the factors were allowed to covary. The factors are highly related. This high degree of relationship between factors would make it very difficult to isolate specific factor scores that could be used in subsequent analyses. In fact, the one factor model provided a better fit to the data than the orthogonal models. When using the SDLRS in future research, the overall SDLRS will provide a more interpretable measure than the highly intercorrelated factor scores.

A second conclusion centers around whether the factor structure underlying responses to the SDLRS corresponds to the structures identified in previous studies. These results indicate that a six factor model is as effective as the original eight factor model in describing the theoretical nature of the self-directed learning readiness construct. Three of the factors were essentially unchanged from the original eight factor model, (Love of Learning, Self-Understanding & Acceptance of Responsibility for Learning). Three other factors were conceptualized in a slightly different manner (Self-Confidence and Learning Ability, Openness to Challenges and Inquisitive Nature). The findings indicate that six dimensions characterize the structures underlying responses to these 33 items, that these six factors are highly correlated and that they are subsumed by a more general single dimension which represents the second order SDLRS structure. The results of the six factor model appeared to offer a better fit, while the one factor (higher order) model involved some loss in accuracy in predicting S from $\hat{\Sigma}$.

In summary, the original measurement model underlying the SDLRS appears to be valid with modification. The parameter estimates were all highly significant, with the exception of Item 7. The factors are, however, highly correlated and a more parsimonious six factor model was found to represent the data as well as the eight factor model. Parallel items might be developed that more clearly characterize these six dimensions. A more general, second order factor appears to represent the SDLRS construct quite well, suggesting that overall SDLRS scores would be more interpretable than the highly related factor scores. Additional studies of a confirmatory nature are needed to determine if these same models hold up when using the entire 58 item scale or when studying groups with different characteristics.

REFERENCES

Bollen, K.A. (1989). Structural equations with latent variables. New York: John Wiley.

Bentler, P.M. & Bonett, D.G. (1980). Significance tests and goodness of fit in the analysis of covariance structures. Psychological Bulletin, 88, 588-606.

Brockett, R.G. (1983). Self-directed learning and the hard to reach adult. Lifelong Learning: The Adult Years. 6(8), 16-18.

Brockett, R.G. (1985). Methodological and substantive issues in the measurement of self-directed learning readiness. Adult Education Quarterly, 36, 15-24.

Brookfield, S. (1984). Self-directed adult learning: A critical paradigm. Adult Education Quarterly, 35, 59-71.

Carmines, E.G. (1986). The analysis of covariance structure models. In W.D. Berry & M.S. Lewis-Beck (Eds.), New Tools for Social Scientists (pp. 23-55). Beverly Hills: Sage.

Carmines, E.G. & McIver, J.P. (1981). Analyzing models with unobserved variables: Analysis of covariance structures. In G.W. Bohrnstedt & E.F. Borgotta (Eds.), Social Measurement: Current Issues. Beverly Hills: Sage.

Crook, J. (1985). A validation study of a self-directed learning readiness scale. Journal of Nursing Education, 24, 274-279.

Gorsuch, R.L. (1983). Factor Analysis (2nd ed.) Hillsdale, N.J.: Lawrence Erlbaum.

Guglielmino, L.M. (1978). Development of the self-directed learning readiness scale (Doctoral Dissertation, University of Georgia, 1977). Dissertation Abstracts International, 38, 6467A.

Hassan A.M. (1981). An investigation of the learning projects among adults of high and low readiness for self-direction in learning. (Doctoral dissertation, Iowa State University, 1981). Dissertation Abstracts International, 40, 3701A.

Hayduk, L.A. (1987). Structural equation modeling with LISREL: Essentials and advances. Baltimore: Johns Hopkins University Press.

Joreskog, K.G. & Sorbom, D. (1984). LISREL VI: Analysis of linear structural relationships by maximum likelihood, instrumental variables and least squares methods. Uppsala, Sweden: University of Uppsala.

Joreskog, K.G. & Sorbom, D. (1988a). LISREL VII: A guide to the program and applications. Chicago: SPSS.

Joreskog, K.G. & Sorbom, D. (1988b). PRELIS: A program for multivariate data screening and data summarization. Mooresville, IN: Scientific Software.

Knowles, M.S. (1975). Self-directed learning: A guide for learners and teachers. Chicago: Follett.

Long, H.B. & Agyekum, S.K. (1984). Multi-trait-multi-method validation of Guglielmino's self-directed learning readiness scale. Proceedings of the 25th Annual Adult Education Research Conference (194-198). Raleigh, North Carolina.

Long, J.S. (1983). Confirmatory factor analysis: A preface to LISREL. Sage University Paper Series on Quantitative Applications in the Social Sciences, 07-033. Beverly Hills: Sage.

Oddi, L.G. (1987). Perspectives on self-directed learning. Adult Education Quarterly, 38, 21-31.

Peters, J.M. & Gordon, S. (1974). Adult learning projects: A study of adult learning in urban and rural Tennessee. Knoxville: University of Tennessee (ERIC Document Reproduction Service No. 102 431).

Sabbaghion, Z.S. (1979). Adult self-directedness and self concept. An exploration of relationships (Doctoral dissertation, Iowa State University, 1979). Dissertation Abstracts International, 40, 3701A.

Savoie, M.M. (1979). Continuing education for nurses: Predictors of success in courses requiring a degree of learner self-direction (Doctoral dissertation, University of Toronto, 1979). Dissertation Abstracts International, 40, 6114A.

Smith, R.M. (1982). Learning how to learn. Chicago: Follett.

Torrance, E.P. & Mourad, S. (1978a). Some creativity and style of learning and thinking correlates of Guglielmino's self-directed learning readiness scale. Psychological Reports, 43, 1167-1171.

Torrance, E.P. & Mourad, S. (1978b). Self-directed learning readiness skills of gifted students and their relationship to thinking creatively about the future. The Gifted Child Quarterly, 22, 180-186.

Tough, A. (1971). The adults' learning projects: A fresh approach to theory and practice in adult learning. Research in Education Series No. 1. Toronto: Ontario Institute for Studies in Education.

Tough, A. (1978). Major research efforts: Recent research and future directions. Adult Education, 28, 250-263.

Tough, A. (1982). Intentional changes. Chicago: Follett.

Chapter Nine

THE CONCEPT OF DISTANCE IN SELF-DIRECTED LEARNING

Gbolagade Adekanmbi

A careful examination of the area of self-directed learning in adult education shows the learner engaging on learning on his own. On a continuum, the idea of the learner being self-directed may range from a total reliance on self concerning the choice of the learning objectives, content, evaluation procedures, etc., to a reliance on an institutionally-planned and formally worked-out programme of learning. Wherever the self-directed learner thus falls on this continuum, a noticeable feature has been the existence of some form of distance which reduces the extent to which he can reach his goals.

The aim of this paper is to identify this distance and indeed, varieties of it, and to examine their characteristics and the possible learning problems associated with them. In the process, modalities for bridging the distance will be examined.

SOME CONSIDERATIONS

Various writers in the growing field of adult education have often attempted to chart a course different from the ones in practice in the field. The thematic stance of the works of the Brazilian writer, Paulo Freire (1970) has been to the effect that the banking concept of education should be discontinued; that literacy teaching is not mere alphabetization and that no form of education can afford to be neutral. Thus, in teaching literacy to adult illiterates, the facilitator has to close some traditional gap between himself and the learner through the choice of an appropriate content, appropriate teaching methods and the establishment of a horizontal dialogue as opposed to a vertically-directed one.

In like manner, we have observed that Ivan Illich's call for a deschooled society, Everett Reimer's charge that the School is Dead (Reimer, 1971) and Malcolm Knowles' glide "from pedagogy to andragogy" (Knowles, 1980) are attempts aimed at identifying looming gaps in existing pedagogical practices, and a call for the dismantling of the pedagogical status quo.

A look at Cynthia Brown's (1983) Confessions of an Autodidact in which she explained her deliberate journey towards savouring the best that self-directed learning could offer shows that numerous holes and gaps were seen to exist between what she thought she was up to and what she later experienced in her search for self-directed learning. A few of her comments lifted within various contexts were:

> I had no idea;
> It did not occur to us;
> I thought they were facts
> On the contrary; etc.

At the Twelfth World Conference of the International Council for Distance Education (ICDE) held in Canada, Smith (1982) talked about "A Case of Two Serpents" in his attempt at putting the distance learner first. In between what he called the "Serpent of Academic Shoddiness" and the "Serpent of the Garden Path" he identified some gap to be filled between total student autonomy and total institutional control in charting a course of success for the self-directed learner who is doing it at a distance. He had in fact also observed Weddemeyer's metaphorical allusion to the issue of "learning at the back door" which, as he noted, implied that there are indeed some learners doing their own thing "in the front door". He then added that "people of quality use the front door ... lesser folks carry out their task at the back door".

Thus, these front-door, back-door distinctions on adult self-directed learning, these confessions and allusions; these calls for deschooling society; these differences between expectations and actual practices and these attempts at some pedagogical re-examination of the learning function in adult learning all converge at some point in the discussion: that there may indeed be some form of distance in adult self-directed learning.

But first let us examine some issues in self-directed learning.

The Subjects of Self-directed Learning

Writing on method in adult education, Lindeman (1961), among others, made the following observation:

> ...Its method is founded upon the assumption that real education must not have its roots in external authorities but rather in personal experiences with reality. (Weddemeyer, 1986, p. 11)

The implication here is that when learning takes place in adult education, the adult learner as self has a greater role to play than any other individual. Lindeman had in fact added at some other point that self-directed learning is a process of personal transformation. Weddemeyer (1986) may therefore have been re-echoing this message when he observed that:

> Learning takes place "in the learner" not in a school, and is the result of a learner ability which is not necessarily dependent upon a fixed series of face-to-face interactions. (Brookfield, 1984, p. 15)

While Brookfield (1984) sees self-directed learning as self teaching, Caffarella and Caffarella (1984) have catalogued a list of synonyms other writers have used to describe the concept. They identified Knowles with the view that adults want to be independent learners; Penland with his description as self-initiated learning; and Tough seeing it as self-planned learning. (p.32)

The tendency to place self-directed learning in the category of "non-traditional" learning has received a bashing from Weddemeyer (1986) who opined that:

> Non-traditional learning cannot any longer be dismissed as some behavioral aberration to `real' learning ... For most participants non-traditional learning is not even an alternative way of learning, it is the only way open to then that is reasonably compatible with their needs and life situations. (Weddemeyer, 1985, p. 85)

The view is already gaining wide acceptance in most developing countries where the falling value of their currencies, the relative fall in their export earning and the attendant reduction in their per capita income are forcing many learners to hold on to their jobs tightly and to search for opportunities of learning through extra-murals, sandwich programs in the universities, external degree programs and other easier routes.

However, the formal institutions that plan these innovative programs as extensions of their normal schedules do not seem to have considered the fact that they now have a totally different set of students on their hands. Even in some institutions that are autonomously created to cater for the self-directed learners, there is still a lot of fall-out from the traditional practices of the past. This "chip off the old block" mentality thus has implications for not applying the appropriate strategies for organizing teaching and learning functions, thus making the creation of holes, gaps and indeed distances inevitable. Of these gaps, Weddemeyer (1986) had again observed of self-directed learners:

> Traditional conditions from institutions around their conditions for learning are appallingly misleading, because of the narrow and restrictive conceptions about teaching and learning which they perpetuate. (Weddemeyer, 1986, p. 85)

In view of the assumptions that self-directed learning, if well managed, will appropriately take care of those who have received incomplete education, and will act as some kind of response to technological growth by promoting vocational education, the distances so created along the line, as education proceeds from the learner, must be examined and bridged.

Varieties of Distance in Self-Directed Learning

The word distance in any endeavor presupposes a measure of space between two or more things, objects, persons, media, thought, etc. It connotes the presence of a vacuum that only some form of mediation, a kind of third party can help link so that the two or more things, objects, persons or ideas do not remain perpetually estranged. We can therefore talk of distance in abstract or in concrete terms. Examples of distance could then be physical, psychological or social. In the same manner, concepts like spatial and temporal distance find various levels of usage.

In considering the issue of self-directed learning, we shall limit ourselves to the examination of the physical distance, social distance, temporal distance, pedagogical distance and public distance.

Physical Distance. This variety of distance is quite typical of various forms of self-directed learning. It is characterized by the physical separation of the learner from he institution organizing teaching and learning. The learner therefore studies in a location, especially the home, without seeing the teachers or other learners for a long time. He relies solely on either the institutionally agreed mode of communicating with him or a mutually agreed mode if he is given some preference in the choice of mode.

The reality of the situation, however, is that the learner is not given this opportunity.

Some of the opportunities a self-directed learner misses as a result of physical distance are day to day interactions with the teacher, face-to-face teaching and the opportunity to participate in group activities, which the possibility of meeting other students would have created.

There are however examples of situations of physical distance that are different from the ones just described. In an extra-mural setting for example, the problem of physical distance may not relate to the absence of a face-to-face component of teaching, but to the kilometers the self-directed learner has to travel before receiving education or getting information about some aspects of his learning. It may indeed refer to the distance covered before getting to a library to complement his learning activities. All these have implications for the quality of instruction the learners eventually receives and what impact self-directed learning will eventually have on their job prospects or other life expectations.

Another distinct variety of physical distance is that implied in the writings of Brown and Bryne (1981) in which they suggested that humans tend to establish their personal territory. Such personal space is believed to expand with age. Therefore, when we consider the issue of territoriality and again look at the arrangement of seats and the general classroom settings in face-to-face component of adult self-directed learning, one begins to wonder whether we have indeed been creating adequate personal space for the adult learners. This is because most extra-mural class settings, in the evenings, especially in developing countries are the same traditional classroom settings for children in the morning.

Social Distance. The Modern Dictionary of Sociology (Theordoson and Theordoson, 1969, p. 388) describes social distance as "a feeling or actual social separation between individuals or groups". Furthermore, it noted that the greater the social distance between the groups of different status or culture, the less sympathy, understanding and interaction there is between them.

Although this phenomenon could occur in learning situations involving children, the apparent low level of their development of self-concept and self-esteem makes the issue of social distance a conceptualization of a second order. The children's classification of themselves as wealthy and brilliant and in fact as being of a better racial stock is only done in apparent reference to their dependence on their parents' descriptive sets and stereotypes.

In adult self-directed learning, the presence of social distance either between the learner and teacher or between learner and learner or between learner and the others, especially where they see one another often, is more real than apparent. These feelings may indeed be submerged in their consciousness and applied in various learning situations even when they do not talk. An anecdotal reference may suffice here as we return to our autodidact, Cynthia Brown (1983):

> My pre-Lovett studies had given me tremendous confidence in my intellectual faculties. This feeling lasted until I arrived at Vaughan College for the first seminar ... However, there was an alarmingly high number of graduates - in history, philosophy and psychology - four of them history teachers, plus two primary-trained teachers. I was dazzled by this array of academic achievement, and my confidence evaporated. (p. 228)

Brown added that at the end of six weeks, with the awareness that whoever had reasons to opt out of the course could do so, and have a refund, she was "tempted to take the money and run". This then is a practical demonstration of an aspect of social distance at work.

While social distance could be a student-student type, there is also the existence of a teacher-student form of social distance. This is clearly manifested in face-to-face components of self-directed learning. When teachers show evidences of haughtiness; of lack of mutual cooperation; when they exhibit high-handedness, an uncooperative attitude, or assume themselves to be repositories of knowledge, they are then exhibiting this trait, and must be called to order. Fear engendered by such attitudes may lead the self-directed learner to withdraw from the programme.

In an extreme situation of autonomous self-directed learning, where the student relies only on course texts to learn, social distance may take the following forms:

(1) the use of content material far removed from the social reality of the adult learner;
(2) the use of language which exhibits traits of vertical dialogue as opposed to horizontal ones;
(3) lack of adequate knowledge about the social characteristics of learners; and
(4) possible exhibition of titles like professor, doctor and other academic laurels in materials prepared.

The effects of the social assault on adult self-directed learners are multiple. The learners may look around unsuccessfully for more enlivening material to read. They may spend a longer time on the text trying to understand the concepts or principles being developed or even become angry at the entire programme.

Temporal Distance. Temporal distance occurs as a result of some form of time-lag in the learning activity. The difference in the time that it takes a course text to be prepared and the time when the learner actually uses it is an example of this phenomenon. In a teaching activity that has the face-to-face component as its main approach, temporal distance is more related to the rate at which information given in class does not match the rate of the growth of knowledge. This obsolescence in knowledge needs to be reduced.

In research carried out by Rekkadel in 1973 as reported by Barker, L.J. et al (1986) in their Cross-Cultural multi-institutional study, the term "turn-around time" gained appreciable recognition. It was defined as:

> the time from the moment the student mails in the homework assignment for a study unit until it is received by the student with the tutor's corrections and comments. (p. 18)

The general view of the study carried out by Rekkadel is that there is the possibility of lowering drop-out rate if turn-around-time is reduced considerably. The implication of the temporal distance nature of the question of turn-around-time is quite obvious.

In another study, Lampikoski (1978), observed the interval between checks in the process and progress of the studies which may in fact, stretch up to two weeks was an important structural factor affecting learning. This delay, according to Lampikoski, may result in a drop in motivation on the part of the learners. They may even eventually abandon the studies.

The issue of temporal distance could in fact take on a philosophical dimension when the initial goals of a self-directed learner change during the process of an uncompleted program. This kind of development may indeed pose problems for both the learner and the institutional provider of learning.

<u>Pedagogical Distance</u>. Of all the distance varieties, perhaps the pedagogical distance stands out as having the greatest implication for self-directed learning. This is because this variety presupposes the existence of distances in the choice of objectives, the content chosen, the media and methods being used and even the evaluative procedures adopted in carrying out learning. Thus it relates to all gaps involved in

the actual carrying out of the learning activity, the distance created between a facilitation of learning and the lack of it.

Most learning objectives are usually pre-planned. In an apparent criticism of Knowles' andragogical postulations and prescriptions that adult learners be allowed to take part in the planning, execution, and evaluation of learning activities, Pratt (1984) noted that not all adults possess the requirements for the task. He, in fact, added that most learning programmes for adult learners have been pre-planned by organizations carrying them out and they have been successful. The point he failed to add though was whether the success recorded had been a reflection of the training given or the ones the adults would have preferred to have, but to which they were not asked to make an input. Obviously, there may be occasions of deviations between learners' own needs and the institutional-set objectives (Long, 1983). This deviation is therefore a distance worth bridging to make learning more useful for the learner.

The choice of content is mostly always done by curriculum experts. Ettore Gelpi (1979), in a critique of traditional educational processes, observed that the gap between school churned-out knowledge and the educational content lying fallow in industry is wide. This tendency to regard schools as knowledge corporations, thus, has implication for the creation of distance.

Somehow, national ideologies and philosophies have a way of entrenching this myopic view of educational content which is then accepted hook, line and sinker by institutional providers of self-directed learning. The objectives set out may become an aggregate of assumed objectives for the learners.

In choosing the media and methods for instruction, some distance is also observed. Whereas, it is possible for an individual to have a preferred learning style, the institutional provider chooses a style that best suits it economically and politically. James (1984) quoting French and Cherry noted that:

> an individual preferred learning style is that style or mode through which he or she learns best. (pp. 88-89)

He then went on to identify various learning styles while later emphasizing perceptual style. The dimensions of this style are then seen as:

Print-oriented	-	learner depends on reading and writing
Aural	-	listener does not say much
Interactive	-	learner learns through discussions
Visual	-	learner must have many visual stimuli
Haptic	-	learner has to touch everything and everyone
Kinesthetic	-	learner has to move about all the time
Olfactory	-	learner learns through smell or taste.

While James observed that there were measurable variations in terms of how adults use these dimensions in learning, the visual element was found to be dominant. Yet, this visual element may in fact have been emphasized by the rate at which they read materials on their own. The import of this is that the level of accessibility of correspondence texts for learners must be examined. However, the present trend of preparing correspondence texts the same way reference materials are done, or emphasizing their use for self-directed learners may create an inappropriate distance for the learner.

Distance in evaluation procedures do occur when evaluation is regarded purely as a teacher activity. Again where they is so much emphasis on a summative type of evaluation, some distance is again being created. The earlier identified temporal distance of the Rekkadel study "turn-around-time" type can also come in here.

Public Distance. The publics identified here are governments, institutions and publishers. Thus, when any of these sets of organized entities pursue policies that tend to undermine the importance of the self-directed learning function, they are seen to be creating some form of public distance.

Governments regulate educational policies and decide through their budgets and development plans, the future of various educational programmes. A general trend in these practices has shown that governments have always placed much emphasis on the formal school system. Self directed learners have in most cases been left to stew in their own juice. The paradox however is that in most developing countries with Nigeria as an example, the so-called non-traditional area of education, is veering towards the normal scheme of things. Governments' continued maintenance of their stance in spite of this new development may be due to what has been described as the need to maintain traditional empires.

Another dimension of the distance is that created by the institutional authorities that support self-directed learning. Where an institutional provider is of the integrated type (that is, combines the traditional with other external learning or extra-mural programmes), the tendency is for the authorities to regard the programmes as (with apologies to Weddemeyer) issues at the back door of policy making. It is therefore not uncommon to have situations where the institutional authorities expect the separate units to be self-financing. This idea of leaving them in the lurch may indeed have been a replication of what government does to this same baby of the institution.

The distance created by publishers is also seen in their enormous concentration of efforts on the building of book lists that are in the formal education category. They indeed mostly harbor the erroneous impression that all school texts are for learners attending the formal school system who can easily ask the teacher to dwell more on some concepts or strange aberrant phraseologies. Even when they are aware of a class of learners outside, who have to combine work with study and the inconveniences these entail, the lure of lucre makes it absolutely difficult for them to have a change of heart. However, if they would re-examine the self-directed learners out there who are willing to buy the books their attitudes and practices might change. Talk of invoking the god of non-traditional inertia!

The discussion so far raises a fundamental issue of the need to bridge the varieties of distance in order to make learning more effective, ensure a proper motivation of the learners and promote egalitarianism in the society. It is our submission, though, that the task of bridging the distance does not rest only with either the government or the institutional provider; the buck, in some cases, also stops at the desk of the learners themselves.

RECOMMENDATIONS

Bridging the Physical Distance

In a distance education programme of a purely correspondence form, there is ample need for institutional providers to set up adequately manned study centers with the added advantage of tutorial support. Where the telephone system is highly developed, telephone support services could be introduced that will serve the purposes of counselling, giving administrative details and hinting at needed academic solutions. Random references could also be given to aid students' identification of sources of needed information. Newspapers, magazines and weeklies can also be used extensively to reduce the problem of getting information across the learners at a distance.

In face-to-face interactions of the extra-mural classes, one way of reducing the physical distance cited by learners who have to travel long distances to get to the schools is for institutional providers to decentralize the settings. Government could also enact policies that will ensure judicious spread of such schools in various localities.

The provision of library facilities within the reach of learners may require the establishment of rapport between public and private libraries on the one hand, and institutions which promote self-directed learning on the other.

On the issue of territoriality, adult education classrooms need to be designed more in tune with the self concept and self-esteem of the learners. This will allow for a freer use of space.

A Bridge Across Social Distance

The bridging of social distance in self-directed learning can be directly encouraged in situations where there is face-to-face interaction. Teachers can, especially before beginning classes, help to allay the fears of people like Cynthia Brown. When directly done, information can be given to the students showing the relationship between adults various immediate work experiences and the learning tasks they are about to engage in. The use of task analysis in starting teaching and learning in programmed instruction is quite needed here.

What the above implies is that there are learners' prerequisites which, if not considered, may hinder learning. The introduction of a learning climate which is free from all forms of anxiety and fear as a result of the social distance of a learner-learner type or that of a teacher-learner type can then be bridged.

In correspondence-based learning, the bridging here can indeed be carried out through the medium of print. An informal style of writing, a de-emphasizing of the qualifications of the writer and a generally flowing language form can reduce the question of distance. Illustrations that make use of names of learners within the context of positive attributes of their work-place and social setting can also present a more relaxed atmosphere.

The use of informal approaches like encouraging the writing of personal letters, asking learners about members of the family and the situation at the work-place and making this a two-way affair may help tremendously to reduce a lot of tension. In addition, the course writer or tutor also needs an up-to-date information on the socio-cultural practices of the learners within their social milieu so as to reduce incidences of mis-information. Editors also need to be aware of these various nuances and mark writers down when they go off course.

Bridging the Temporal Distance

Course writers can bridge the temporal distance by matching the wits of their course content with the daily explosion of knowledge in the world. They may also need to identify and make known to the learners, journals, newspapers and magazines which are easy to come by, by the learners and which are noted for creating columns that can make up for the absence of some current information in the course texts. This will reduce incidences of obsolescence in knowledge transmitted.

Where the institutional provider makes provision for feed-back in form of making students assignments and returning same, attempts must be made to ensure a high turn-around-time to sustain motivation.

Reducing the Pedagogical Distance

In bridging the pedagogical distance in self-directed learning, a look at Skinner's behavior control model as applied to correspondence education may provide some succor. Here, teaching is defined as the arrangement of contingencies of reinforcement under which students learn (Baath, 1979). In this regard, a teacher is expected to do the following:

> - define learning objectives in terms of terminal behavior;
> - identify in the learners effective reinforcers;
> - note and observe the initial behavior of learners;
> - elicit responses from the learners;
> - immediately reinforce good performance;
> - evaluate performance at the end of a teaching unit. (p. 15)

The suggestion here is that this approach has implications for the use of a course text designed along the lines of the advantages derivable from programmed instruction. A self-contained learning material of this nature thus allows for the replication of a normal classroom experience in written form.

Another model which specifically emphasizes the possible adaptive use of the course text is Rothkopf's model for written instruction. Rothkopf (1976) had observed that:

> learner performance is the result of both the nature of the nominal stimulus, that is the attributes of the text and the processing operation of the reader. (p. 15)

Thus Rothkopf goes on to emphasize three attributes of the text; <u>content</u> whose characteristics are completeness, accuracy, goal guidance; <u>representation</u>, which refers to the choice of words, use of instructional similes, metaphors or referential phrases; and, <u>form</u> which notes the grammatical structure of sentences and the use of syntactic periods.

The emphasis of Rothkopf has implications for the provision of adequate course texts by course writers and the maximal use of the opportunities that print can offer. Print, according to Gordon (1975) has some underlying capabilities which a writer can effectively use. These are the fact that:

(1) print is a separate and distinct language in itself which consists of a vocabulary and a way of using it;
(2) it can convey a meaning of its own;
(3) it can be orchestrated as people can be persuaded to read it slowly, rapidly, etc.
(4) its texture and color can show mood, credibility, acceptability and a degree of seriousness. (p. 38)

Thus in making use of the power of print to its fullest advantage, publishers may need to be more adaptive, course developers and production teams more flexible and subject matter specialists must be ready to shake off their cloak of traditional inertia.

To fully appreciate and enjoy the new distance reading materials, prepared for the self-directed learner, the learner himself has some roles to play. He needs to master study-reading techniques that would reduce the distance between him and the material being read. A number of reading methods have been identified among which is the SQ3R (Fry, 1963).

Unoh (1979) in an examination of this method observed that the letters SQ3R stand for Survey, Question, Read, Recite and Revise. A practical application for self-directed learners is that whatever material they want to read, they first lightly skim through it, reading the sub-headings, titles, and the table of contents to get a general scope of its content and scope. When reacting to the second step, they, on the basis of the earlier survey raise questions concerning the subject or course. They then proceed to read the material thoroughly and attempt to see how many questions have been answered and to what extent they relate to their own assumptions. The fourth step (Recite) then sees the learner reciting mentally, and writing down various key aspects of the topic they have mastered. In the final step, they review the entire topic by checking the main text again to see where he had erred.

While the self-directed learner may in fact find the above reading strategy useful for all kinds of materials, Unoh's (1979) prescriptions for taking down notes while reading will also be of immense benefit to him. He could do the following progressively:

> (1) make notes on the margin of a text or in a jotter;
> (2) make notes paragraph by paragraph as reading continues;
> (3) record the main points or idea and relevant supporting facts and figures with the aid of the text;
> (4) record the main points and relevant supporting facts and figures without the aid of the text after reading. (p. 47)

By bringing himself into the subject of bridging pedagogical distance through a mastery of good methods of reading and taking notes, the self-directed learner can also brace himself up to the issue of evaluation of learning material. Thus for the pedagogical distance to be adequately bridged, the process of evaluation should be in-built into the course material prepared for learners, and should be made a vital aspect of all teaching and learning programs directed at the self-directed learner. Programed instruction components allow for adequate sequencing of evaluative items as the core of the programme itself is basically evaluatory as learning progresses.

It is observed that the emphasis on the bridging of pedagogical distance has focussed extensively on the correspondence based system of instruction. This is without prejudice to other systems but most self-directed learners rely on the medium of print to carry out their learning activities. In developing countries, economic reasons and level of technological know-how dictate learners' preference for this relatively cheap medium of instruction.

Of Public Distance and the Self-Directed Learner

In bridging the public distance created by government, various governments need to awaken to the reality of the ever-growing number of self-directed learners in their countries. Adult education organizations and other institutional providers also need to influence government policies at various levels to get this message across. Governments cannot continue to maintain a traditional lukewarm attitude with the changing landscape of educational realities.

Institutions that provide opportunities for study for self-directed learners must make attempts at integrating their "learners at the back door" with those in mainstream. They may also need to create an awareness of the quality inherent in the system so that even lecturers and course writers they employ do not regard the learners as second rate citizens.

In the case of the publishing companies, a revolution in book publishing is highly required. Self-contained books that already incorporate images of the classroom situation, which allow for step-by-step reading of items, formative evaluation along the line, and a clear definition of objectives at the beginning of units of texts need to be emphasized in their task at list building. Perhaps they also need to be reminded that there is abundant market outside for their products as the world, at least, citizens in most developing countries in the world find it increasingly difficult to attend school on a full-time basis. But they can afford to pay for books that bear some relevance to the times and that are capable of meeting their needs as self-directed learners.

CONCLUSION

So far, we have considered the question of the concept of distance in self-directed learning. An over-view of the discussions shows that there are indeed varieties of distance in self-directed learning which, even though some of them may be found to exist in formal school situations, are, for the self-directed learners, a real pain in the neck. Their characteristics and effects show that they really need to be bridged.

While attempts at bridging them rest with the institutional provider of self-directed learning in terms of the choice of appropriate content and delivery methods, the learner is seen to have a lot to do to reduce the hazard. Governments, too, have to become aware of their responsibilities by recognizing the ever-increasing army of self-directed learners and the growing irrelevance of acquiring knowledge through a strict adherence to a formal system of education. Publishers have also been guilty of contributing to distance. They need to develop a new orientation towards book publishing.

On a final note, bridging the distance in self-directed learning may benefit more from an integrated approach to solving the problem, where the distance varieties are not regarded as pockets of problems being chased across a field, or the institutions and persons concerned with reducing them working at extreme opposites. It is only a concerted effort that can result in building of solid bridges across the chasm of distance in self-directed learning.

REFERENCES

Baath, J.A. (1979). Correspondence education in the light of a number of contemporary teaching models. Malomo: Liber Hermonds.

Barker, L.J. et al. (1986). Student persistence in distance education: A cross cultural multi-institution on perspective. In ICDE Bulleting, 12, September.

Brookfield, S. (1984). Self directed learning: A critique of research and theory. In Proceedings of the Twenty fifth Annual Adult Education Research Conference, Raleigh, N.C., April 5-7.

Brown, Cynthia (1983). Confessions of an autodidact. In Adult Education, 56, No. 3, December.

Brown, R.A. and Bryne, D. (1981). Social psychology. Boston: Allyn and Bacon Inc.

Caffarella, R.S. and Cafarella, E.P. (1984). The learning contract as a tool for developing readiness and competences in self-directed learning. In Proceedings ... Annual Adult Education Research Conference, Raleigh, N.C., April 5-7.

Freire, Paul (1970). Pedagogy of the oppressed. New York: Seabury Press.

Fry, E. (1963). Teaching faster reading: A manual. Cambridge: Cambridge University Press.

Gelpi, E. (1979). A future for life-long education. University of Manchester Monograph.

Gordon, D. R. (1975). Print as a visual medium. In Asheim and Fenwick (Eds.), Differentiating the Media. Chicago: The University of Chicago Press.

James, W. B. (1984). Assessment of adult learning styles. In Proceedings ... Annual Adult Education Research Conference, Raleigh, N.C.

Knowles, M. (1980). The modern practice of adult education: From pedagogy to andragogy. Chicago: Follet Publishing Company.

Lampikoski, K. (1978). Integrating study guidance in distance education. In Convergence, Vol. XI, Nos. 3-4.

Lindeman, E. C. (1961). The meaning of adult education. Montreal: Harvest House.

Long, H. (1983). Adult learning: Research and practice. New York: Cambridge Book Co.

Pratt, D. (1984). Andragogical assumptions: Some counter-intuitive logic. In Proceedings ... Annual Adult Education Research Conference; Raleigh, N.C., April 5-7.

Reimer, E. (1971). School is dead: An essay on alternatives in education. Harmondsworth, Middlesex: Penguin.

Rothkopf, E.Z. (1976). "Writing to teach and reading to learn: A perspective in the psychology of written instruction". In Gage N.L. (Ed.) (1976) The Psychology of Teaching Methods. The Seventy-fifth Year book of the National Society for the Study of Education Part I. Chicago, Ill.: The University of Chicago Press.

Smith, K. (1982). Putting the student first: Some personal perspectives of a "Tale of Two Serpents". In ICDE Conference Report and Handbook.

Theordoson, G. A. and Theordoson, A. G. (1969). A modern dictionary of sociology. New York: Thomas Y. Crowell Company.

Unoh, S.O. (1979). Reading to remember. Ibadan: University Press Limited.

Weddemeyer, C. (1981). Learning at the back door: Reflections on non-traditional learning in the life-span. Madison: University of Wisconsin Press.

Chapter Ten

ACTION SCIENCE AS A PARADIGM FOR A CRITICAL THEORY OF SELF-DIRECTED LEARNING

Mark Dorsey, Roger Manning & Tom Shindell

The thesis of this chapter is that a critical theory of adult self-directed learning offers rich opportunities for us, as facilitators of self-directed learning, to improve our practice and to broaden the research paradigm of our field. We assert that action science (Argyris, Putnam, and Smith, 1985) presents us with an excellent paradigm for a critical theory of self-directed learning. By engaging in a critically reflective process of inquiry, such as action science, we can identify our own a priori assumptions and beliefs which limit our learning as facilitators of self-directed learning.

Educators often produce unintended results which mitigate against students' successes as self-directed learners. As action science can help achieve greater congruence between intended and actual results in facilitating self-directed learning so, too, can it serve the learners in achieving their goals. This research explores the hypotheses that: Self-directed learners' use of action science will lead them to incorporate critical theory into their practice, resulting in increased ownership of their learning experiences and outcomes accompanied by increased critical reflection. We assume that a critical

---

The authors gratefully acknowledge the guidance of Oscar Mink in the formulation of the hypotheses and the structuring of the research design and of Karen Watkins and Bob Putnam in their critiques of drafts of this article.

theory enables self-directed learners to examine the unquestioned assumptions and the values upon which they act. Having studied the action science process, the self-directed learners examined here reported increased ownership of their learning experiences and outcomes as well as increased critical reflection. This paper will report our examination of these hypotheses.

A critical theory of self-directed learning asks that "three interrelated but distinct functions of adult learning" (Mezirow, 1985, p.17) be engaged. According to Mezirow these are:

> instrumental learning--task-oriented problem solving that is relevant for controlling the environment or other people; dialogic learning, by which we attempt to understand what others mean in communicating with us; and self-reflective learning, by which we come to understand ourselves. (p.18)

"Action scientists engage with participants in a collaborative process of critical inquiry into problems of social practice in a learning context" (Argyris et al., 1985, p.237). Action science utilizes rules and procedures derived from the scientific method which engage the learners' instrumental learning in the problem solving process. An example of such a rule would be reliance on hard data, "that is, data whose validity can be checked by different observers" (Argyris et al., 1985, p.12). Dialogic learning is engaged through collaborative critical inquiry within these "communities of inquiry in communities of social practice" (Argyris et al., 1985, p.12). To illustrate, this would involve the group critique and dialogue around an individual's case study drawn from a self-identified problem in that individual's practice. Self-reflective learning is engaged when "the agent is stimulated to reflect when the tacit hypothesis or pragmatic explanations embedded in action are disconfirmed" (Argyris et al., 1985, p.51). An illustration of this learning component would be individual insight into unexamined assumptions which produce self-identified errors in practice.[1]

Applying action science as a critical theory of self-directed learning, we seek to enact communities of inquiry first, among ourselves as facilitators of self-directed learning and second, among our students as self-directed learners. As facilitators we inquire into and reflect upon our practice; or, put differently, we reflect upon the gaps between what we say and what we do. This familiar gap is the gap between theory and practice and is the problem area staked out by action science. Action science provides us with an organized, guided approach (the instrumental) through group critique (the dialogic) to discovering the barriers between our theory and practice (the self-reflective). These are the barriers which prevent us from doing what we say we should do as facilitators of self-directed learning; the barriers which prevent us from practicing what we preach.

A primary benefit for us, as self-directed learners reflecting on our practice, is that we can become more competent and effective as facilitators. As our critical reflection on our current practice yields new perspectives, strategies, and techniques, self-directed learners utilizing us as facilitators may experience an enriched process which could yield greater learning potential. Additionally, we can apply these critical reflection skills in our ongoing dialogues with learners. We can offer self-directed learners alternative view points, frames of reference, and perspectives which challenge their self-limiting, self-sealing a priori assumptions and beliefs, e.g., a facilitator who

---

1 Authors' Note. Action science often seems to resemble "group therapy" to newcomers. Action science differs in that it focuses on problems drawn from practice and relies on scientific methodology to redesign more competent practice. Since our personal views on the world shape our practice, insights into these limiting views can at times be personally painful. In any learning setting, personal growth often produces some degree of turbulence in learners. That this phenomenon occurs does not equate action science with group therapy.

successfully advocates to learners that they can achieve superior research results through collaborative effort rather than individual effort.

A critical challenge to the taken-for-granted, unexamined belief systems of self-directed learners can free them to explore and integrate knowledge which is enlightening and emancipatory.

> We can provide them with alternative perspectives for understanding how social practices and institutions can be modified so as to create a society in which adults can be enfranchised to participate fully as self-directed learners in the quest for meaning in their lives. (Mezirow, 1985,p.29)

Examining the concept of a critical theory provides an important framework for considering action science as a paradigm for a critical theory of self-directed learning. To this end, let us compare critical theory and action science-as-a-critical theory.

A critical theory "is a reflective theory which gives agents a kind of knowledge inherently productive of enlightenment and emancipation" (Geuss, 1981, p.2). For Geuss, enlightenment enables "...agents to determine what their true interests are...[and emancipation frees]...agents from a kind of coercion which is at least partly self-imposed, from self-frustration of conscious human action" (p.2). The reflective process which produces enlightenment and emancipation is dialectical thinking. Paul (1984) defines dialectical thinking as "thinking critically and reciprocally within opposing points of view" (p.10). Such critical inquiry requires the establishment of a community of practice "that must become the venue for not only advocating reflective inquiry but must also become a laboratory where such practices are modeled, experienced, and reflected upon" (Ross and Hannay, 1986, p.11).

According to Argyris et al. (1985), action science is a critical theory of "social practice, broadly defined, and it is interested in producing knowledge in service of such practice" (p.232). Argyris et al. further explain that

> the aim is in part to make known what is known so well that we no longer know it - the uncovering of tacit knowledge so that it might be critiqued. And in part the aim is to make known what is unknown - the discovery of alternatives so that they too might be critiqued. The process of critical inquiry in action science is a form of public reflection and experimentation that follows rules that can themselves be used in action contexts in order to ensure the validity and usefulness of the inquiry. (p.237)

The philosophical foundations of action science are informed by the following dialectic.

> A critical social science includes aspects of the empirical-analytic sciences (mainstream account) and the historical-hermeneutic sciences (counterview), but goes beyond them to criticize what is from the perspective of what might be. Justification of the normative stance of critical theory is based on internal criticism of the practices of the community to which it is addressed. A critical social science engages human agents in self-reflection in order to save the world (Argyris et al., 1985, p.6).

We assume the reader's familiarity with the values, principles, and practices of the scientific method employed by the empirical-analytic sciences. Hermeneutics denotatively refers to "the science and methodology of interpretation, especially the Bible" (The American Heritage Dictionary, 1985). Human interactionists use the term hermeneutics in an enlarged sense as the science of understanding meaning found in everyday speech and actions. It is a science which applies the epistemology and discipline of textual interpretation to understanding meaning in any human expression.

The dialectic process is used in action science to critique "what is from the perspective of what might be" (Argyris et al., 1985, p.6). In action science group-work, when presenting a problematic case drawn from practice, e.g., work or school, the case originator presents the problems as he or she understands them (theses). The other action science group members collaboratively offer alternative theories (antitheses) as to what the originator's problems might be. Through following the rules and principles of action science which govern public inquiry, higher order explanations for and resolutions to the problems-as- originally-framed should result (synthesis). This thesis- antithesis-synthesis process is the central characteristic of dialectical thinking. "Dialectical thinkers engage in a continual process of making judgments about aspects of their lives, identifying the general rules implicit in these judgments, modifying the original judgments in light of the appropriateness of these general rules, and so on" (Brookfield, 1988, p.13). Action science provides a community of inquiry through which the dialectic process occurs.

A computer search of education research publications produced no listings related to action science. The computer search then focused on critical theory which yielded seventy citations of which sixteen were obtained and reviewed. None of the authors attempted empirical research to confirm or disconfirm hypotheses generated from a critical theory approach to education or learning. The authors fall into two broad groups. The larger group attempts to reinform education theory through application or explication of critical theory. The smaller group attempts to legitimize other approaches to education theory through rejection of critical theory as a viable theoretical approach.

Of the authors attempting to utilize critical theory to advance education theory and practice, several take an integrationist approach (Belt and Schniedewind, 1987;

Bretz and Persin, 1987; Collins, 1986; May and Zimpher, 1986; Noblit and Eaker, 1987; Soltis, 1984; Yeakey, 1987). These authors tend to see critical theory not as theory of a discretely higher order (as does Geuss [1981]), but one of an array of theoretical perspectives which can inform education theory and practice. For these authors, the incorporation of the dialogic or dialectical technique of critical theory could increase educators' and students' awareness of real life problems facing students and educational systems.

Another group of authors goes further in utilizing critical theory to critique education theory and practice (Gilder, 1987; Giroux, 1987; Ross and Hannay, 1986; Shamai, 1987; Sigmon, 1984; Young, 1986; Wexler, 1981). These authors value critical theory as a higher order, different-in-kind theoretical approach for education theory and practice. Here, critical theory subsumes other theoretical approaches as fragmented attempts to explain that which is. However, there is diversity within this camp. For example, Giroux and Wexler rely on a Marxist critique while Ross and Hannay draw on Dewey.

Two authors find critical theory inappropriate, if not dangerous, for education theory and practice. Lakomski (1987) examines several aspects of Habermas' theory, e.g.,ideal speech situation, communicative competence, and explores their applicability to education administration and teaching. According to Lakomski, critical theory has no usefulness for education administration or any other discipline since "ideal speech situations," "equality of power and status," and "truth in speech" do not and cannot exist. Willower (1985) ventures an explication of critical theory. He dismisses critical theory as Marxist ideology and as such, uncritical and non-reflective.

The authors of this paper found most helpful those articles which explore critical theory as a theoretical basis for educational practice which enhances critical thinking in learners. We hypothesized that the dialectic process of action science enhances critical thinking and increases self-directedness. The results of our investigations into these hypotheses follow.

RESEARCH

Setting

The research was conducted with fifteen graduate students enrolled in the Adult Education and Human Resource Development programs at the University of Texas at Austin. Fourteen of the students were employed full-time. All fifteen had been studying action science for eight months. This represents a 50% sample size of graduate students who were enrolled in action science at U.T. at that time. Two professors oversee the action science program. Facilitation of bi-weekly action science groups is provided by other graduate students who are ahead in the course sequence. Four to seven participants form a self-directed learning group with two facilitators present as participants and resources. These groups, as learning communities, utilize action science principles and techniques of critical inquiry and reflection to work cases. Members present these self-selected case studies which illustrate self-evaluated problems in their practice. As described earlier, each case is analyzed through the action science group process.

Design

The authors sought to inquire among their fellow learners as to their perceptions of the role, if any, action science had played in increasing self-directedness. The authors hypothesized that action science's emphasis on personal causality and critical reflection would increase learners' consciousness of self-directedness. To the extent that learners evaluate their learning or practice outcomes as successful (positive) and resulting from their own learning efforts (self-directedness), an increase in their sense of personal empowerment should follow.

The authors designed and administered a brief survey to explore the following hypotheses. (1) The study of action science will lead learners to experience increased ownership of learning (practice) outcomes. (2) The study of action science will lead learners to engage in increased critical reflection when confronting learning (practice) problems. Since action science has been defined previously as a critical theory of social practice, the authors hold that problems encountered in the workplace by these graduate students constitute learning situations. Therefore, the practice (workplace problem) outcomes are in fact learning outcomes.

Method

The written survey was designed to elicit self-evaluations of performance from the learners. Participation in all aspects of the research was voluntary. Immediately prior to administering the survey, the learners were asked to participate in research examining the action science process. The learners were asked to select both a positive and negative critical incident drawn from their practice to evaluate. The learners were given twenty minutes to write responses on an eleven-question instrument.

Following Krippendorf (1980) regarding data reduction, responses to three questions (Tables 10.1-3) were chosen for analysis. These responses seemed to yield the most relevant information for determining increased ownership of learning outcomes and increased critical reflection. Responses to several other questions were consistently either so brief or general, e.g., C.Your role?-"facilitator", E.Results?-"good", that few illustrations were produced which might confirm or disconfirm the hypotheses. This is viewed as a research design problem; that is, the brief survey instrument may lead respondents to communicate the essence of a situation in a very few words and at a high level of abstraction.

The researchers' inferences (interpretations) about the data were informed by: 1) their learning experiences with action science, 2) their knowledge of the theory base of action science and theories of self-directed learning, 3) their role as representative interpreters, and 4) additional contextual data from the surveys.

Problems

Examining the threats to the validity of content analysis (Weber, 1985), the researchers concluded that the research design is essentially descriptive in nature and not intended to yield prediction validity. The research design is problematic in terms of hypothesis validity. "Testing hypotheses about increases would require data that would permit a comparison, either before and after some practice with action science, or between two groups, one of which had no exposure to action science" (Robert Putnam, personal communication, August 7, 1989). The researchers believe that important qualitative data regarding the learners' perceptions of the relationship between the study of action science and increased self-directedness and critical reflection was communicated through the surveys.

The establishment of semantic validity was deemed central to the project of understanding the learners' responses. To ensure development of a consistent interpretation system, any discrepancies in interpretation among the three researchers were resolved by consensus. This triangulation process was consistently applied to all the reduced data. Subsequent to the original interpretation process, Bob Putnam, co-author of Action Science (1985), critiqued the initial research analysis. The researchers have attempted to incorporate his critique in a revised analysis which is hoped to contain higher semantic validity. The researchers assume full responsibility for any errors produced in the revised analysis.

Analysis

The responses to F, G, and H were interpreted as to the primary causality to which the respondents seemed to attribute the outcomes (see Tables 10.1-3). Possible attribution categories were reduced to Self, Group, and Other. While there is some personal causality implicit in a respondent's participation in a group, several respondents explicitly attributed success or failure to their Group. This is felt to be a different kind of causality attribution than a highly personal ("I"-worded) attribution. When responses were interpreted as having placed most of the causative agency to other than self (other people, processes, or situations), they were coded as Other. In some instances individual respondents offered responses which included attributions at more than one level. These were divided as separate attribution responses in order to retain the richness of the data. Therefore, the number of responses will not always equal the number of respondents. To illustrate the coding system, the following examples are offered.

Self attribution. Interpreters looked for descriptions of action or action strategy for which the respondent took primary responsibility. Example: Reason for success? "(I) Was able to clearly define role and establish ability to perform."

Group attribution. Interpreters looked for descriptions of action or action strategy which attributed primary responsibility to a group. Example: Reason for success? "Teamwork between all involved."

"Other" attribution. Interpreters looked for descriptions of action or action strategy which attributed primary responsibility to another person, a process, or situation. Example: Reason for success? "Sheer luck!"

Results

Table 10.1: Question F."Reasons for success/lack of success."

	self	group	other	total
positive outcome	14 (38%)	14 (38%)	9 (24%)	37 (100%)
negative outcome	22 (61%)	4 (11%)	10 (28%)	36 (100%)
subtotals	36 (49%)	18 (25%)	19 (26%)	73 (100%)

Table 10.2: Question G."Things you would change if you could begin again."

	self	group	other	total
positive outcome	11 (52%)	0 (0%)	10 (48%)	21 (100%)
negative outcome	15 (60%)	2 (8%)	8 (32%)	25 (100%)
subtotals	26 (57%)	2 (4%)	18 (39%)	46 (100%)

Table 10.3: Question H."What influence, if any, did action science have in the outcome?"

	self	group	other	total
positive outcome	16 (62%)	5 (19%)	5 (19%)	26 (100%)
negative outcome	9 (47%)	2 (11%)	8 (42%)	19 (100%)
subtotals	25 (56%)	7 (15%)	13 (29%)	45 (100%)

DISCUSSION

In reviewing the responses to F (Reasons for success/lack of success), respondents attributed their positive outcomes with equal frequency to Self and Group. For negative outcomes, respondents increased by 23% their attributions to Self for errors in practice, e.g., "(My) Lack of preparation." The authors speculate that the increase in specific self-critiques represents critical reflection on personal performance following negative outcomes. There is correspondingly a 27% reduction in Group causality attributions between positive and negative outcomes. We suggest that these students hold a high value on collaborative effort to which they tend to attribute successes, while they tend to seek more personal explanations for negative outcomes.

<u>Question G (Things you would change if you could begin again)</u> tended to elicit action strategies in the responses. The responses indicate a significant increase in attributions towards Other. One group of these responses represent action strategies in which the respondents would primarily act to change another person, process, or situation, e.g.,

"The notification process." These could represent either competent or incompetent strategies, but do seem to indicate some critical reflection has occured. Another group of five responses seem not to represent an action strategy, but a wish, e.g., "Not be in a group with (name)." Since there is no action strategy cited, there is little reason to posit critical reflection has occured. Self attributions for positive outcomes rose from 38% to 52% between F and G. These Self attributions (for both positive and negative outcomes) represent action strategies which target changing the respondent rather than the Other, e.g., "(I would) ask questions before reaching a conclusion." These responses seem to represent both increased ownership of outcomes and critical reflection.

Question H (re: influence of action science on outcome) produced an interesting disparity in attributions made for positive and negative outcomes. Respondents who made Self attibutions for the positive outcomes tended to cite specific personal insights or action strategies which contributed to their success, e.g., "I realized the importance of giving the male EE (sic) directly observable data so he could clearly see what behaviors he exhibited that alienated females." However, for the negative outcomes the respondents decreased the volume of responses in the Self category. That is, the respondents did not produce as many individualized explanations as to the influence of action science on their negative outcomes. Also, for the negative outcomes, the respondents reduced by three the number of Group attributions and increased by three the Other attributions.

Since there is no control group against which these results can be compared, no cause-effect relationship can be empirically established between the study of action science and increases in ownership of outcomes and critical reflection. However, a good deal of interesting data was provided by the respondents in which they imply strong to moderate perceptions of such a causal link, e.g., "Prior to action science, it (the error/problem) would have continued to be the H.R.D. manager's fault." In response to question H-positive outcomes, twelve of the fifteen respondents cited twenty-one specific actions or action strategies (Self and Other) which they interpreted in terms of action science. Interestingly, the remaining three respondents indicated strong hostility to action science throughout the survey in such statements as "I feel I was sacrificed and crucified (as a participant in an action science group)."

That the percentage of responses clustered under Self constitutes a majority of the causal attributions is a hopeful indicator of movement towards greater ownership for learning outcomes and increased critical reflection.

CONCLUSION

We have suggested that a critical theory of self-directed learning can enhance practitioner/learner competence through increased ownership of learning outcomes and increased critical reflection. It has been maintained that action science provides a useful paradigm for a critical theory of self-directed learning.

The limitations of this study do not provide conclusive proof that action science provides the perfect model for self-directed learning nor was that the intention. The learners' self-evaluations in their own words do indicate the learning potential which action science has to offer self-directed learners. The authors plan to continue these investigations through follow-up interviews with the participants in which we can seek deeper understandings of these self-directed learners.

Facilitators of adult self-directed learners are encouraged to explore action science for the potential benefits it has to offer both for self-directed learners and for those who facilitate their endeavors. It is hoped that theoreticians may inquire into the foundations and principles of action science so that self-directed learning theory may be advanced through the resulting dialectic.

REFERENCES

The American Heritage Dictionary. (1985). Second College Edition. Houghton Mifflin: Boston.

Argyris, C., Putnam, R., and Smith, D.M. (1985). Action Science. San Francisco: Jossey-Bass.

Beyer, L.E. (1986). Critical theory and the art of teach. Journal of Curriculum and Supervision. 1(3), 221-232.

Bowers, C.A. (1986). The dialectic of nihilism and the state: Implications for the emancipatory theory of education. Education Theory. 36(3), 225-232.

Bretz, M.L. and Persin, M. (1987). The application of critical theory to literature at the introductory level: A working model for teacher preparation. The Modern Language Journal. 71(2), 165-170.

Brookfield, S. (1985). Self-directed learning: A critical review of research. In S. Brookfield, (Ed.), New directions for continuing education: Vol. 25 Self-directed learning: From theory to practice (pp. 5-16). San Francisco: Jossey-Bass.

Brookfield, S.D. (1987). Understanding and facilitating adult learning. San Francisco: Jossey-Bass.

Collins, M. (1986, October). Philosophy and the role of the adult educator. Paper presented at the Annual Meeting of the American Association for Adult and Continuing Education, Hollywood, FL.

Geuss, R. (1981). The idea of a critical theory: Habermas and the frankfurt school. Cambridge: Cambridge University Press.

Gilder, E. (1987, November). Towards a critical paradigm for change: Habermas' "Ideal Speech Situation" as a meta-model of development communication. Paper presented at the Annual Meeting of the Speech Communication Association, Boston, MA.

Giroux, H..A. (1987). Citizenship, public philosophy, and the struggle for democracy. Education Theory. 37(2), 103-120.

Giroux, H.A. (1985). Towards a critical theory of education: Beyond Marxism with guarantees--a response to Daniel Liston. Educational Theory. 35(3), 313-319.

Krippendorf, K. (1980). Content analysis: An introduction to its methodology. The Sage CommText Series, 5.

Lakomski, G. (1987). Critical theory and educational administration. The Journal of Educational Administration. 25(1), 85-100.

Liston, D.P. (1985). Marxism and schooling: A failed or limited tradition? A response to Henry Giroux. Educational Theory. 35(3), 307-312.

May, W.T. & Zimpher, M.L. (1986). An examination of three theoretical perspectives on supervision: Perceptions of preservice field supervision. Journal of Curriculum and Supervision. 7(2), 83-99.

Mezirow, J. (1985). A critical theory of self-directed learning. In S. Brookfield (Ed.), New directions for continuing education: Vol. 25. Self-directed learning: From theory to practice. San Francisco: Jossey-Bass.

Noblit, G.W. (1987, April). Evaluation designs as political strategies. Paper presented at the Annual Meeting of the American Educational Research Association, Washington, D.C.

Paul, R. (1984). Critical thinking: Fundamental to education for a free society. Educational Leadership, 42(1), 4-14.

Ross, E.W. (1986, April). Practicing critical theory in social studies. Paper presented at the Annual Meeting of the American Educational Research Association, San Francisco, CA.

Shami, S. (1987). Critical theory of education and ethnicity: The case study of the Toronto Jewish Community. Journal of Education. 169(2), 89-114.

Sigmon, S.B. (1984). A contrast in schooling: the natural education of Emile v.s. Giroux's radical education. Irvington, NH: Irvington Public Schools. (ERIC Document Reproduction Service N. ED28569)

Watkins, P. (1986). From managerialism to communicative competence: Control and consensus in educational administration. The Journal of Educational Administration. 25(1), 86-106.

Weber, P.R. (1985). Basic content analysis. In Sullivan, J.L. & Miemi, R.G. (Eds.), Sage Quantitative Applications in the Social Sciences, 49, 18-21.

Wexler, P. (1981). Body and soul: Sources of social change and strategies of education. British Journal of Sociology of Education. 2(3), 166-180.

Willower, D.J. (1985). Marxian critical theory and educational administration: A criticism. Annual Meeting of the American Educational Research Association.

Yeakey, C.C. (1987). Critical thought and administrative theory: Conceptual approaches to the study of decision making. Planning and Changing. 18(1), 23-32.

Young, R.E. (1988). Critical teaching and learning. Education Theory. 38(1), 47-59.

Chapter Eleven

THE WRIGHT BROTHERS AS SELF-DIRECTED LEARNERS: THE ROLE AND RELATION OF GOAL SETTING, FEEDBACK AND MOTIVATION DURING THE PROCESS OF THEIR SELF-DIRECTED LEARNING PROJECT

Lorraine A. Cavaliere

In a letter to a noted American engineer, Octave Chanute, dated May 13, 1900, Wilbur Wright stated, "For some years I have been afflicted with the belief that flight is possible to man." (McFarland, 1972, p. 15). It was with this spirit and belief that the Wright brothers planned, developed and completed one of the most vivid examples of a self-planned, self-directed adult learning project as defined by Tough (1979), who conceptualized this behavior as a "major, highly deliberate effort to gain certain knowledge and skill" (p. 1).

The purpose of this chapter is to provide an analysis of the impact of goal setting, feedback and motivation during the self-directed learning processes employed by the Wright Brothers between 1875 and 1903, that enabled them to develop a heavier-than-air machine capable of sustained flight for the first time in the history of mankind. The descriptions of these factors and variables relative to the learning process are based upon the findings of research conducted by this author. The research focused on the resource and communication networks which developed during the process of the Wrights' inventive learning project. Drawing on the literature of self-directed learning theory and social network theory, their learning behaviors and strategies were charted using historical and biographical data bases from which a learning process model was developed to describe this adult learning project. The research traced the process of one self-directed learning project through a content analysis of historical documents using a naturalistic approach. Since naturalistic inquiry (Guba & Lincoln, 1978) was used to generate the findings, the analysis of this data attempts to explain and interpret behavior and suggest applications to existing theory.

On December 17, 1903, at the moment the Wrights achieved powered, sustained, controlled flight from level ground in their Flyer I at Kill Devil Hills in North Carolina, the future of communications, transportation, education and world affairs would begin to change significantly. And these changes were effected by the independent, self-planned learning project of two adults from Ohio, whose everyday business was the building and selling of bicycles. How did this happen and what did they do to accomplish such a feat?

THE WRIGHT'S SELF-DIRECTED LEARNING PROJECT

Born in 1867, Wilbur was the third child of Milton and Katharine Wright. Orville was the fourth of five children, born four years after Wilbur in 1871. There was a family history of a pioneering spirit, original thinking and mechanical aptitude, and the brothers grew up in a home that encouraged the pursuit of intellectual curiosity. Their formal schooling ended with the completion of high school, although they never formally graduated. They began a serious pursuit of their dream to fly in 1899 at the ages of 32 and 28. They were fully matured adults with family responsibilities (although neither married) and both were charged with a full-time business to manage. Their life circumstances were ordinary and modest, yet they had the desire and found the time to fulfill their dreams. Clearly defined goals, concentration, perseverance and the ability to reformulate concepts were the behavioral threads woven by these craftsmen into a fabric of success. These family and personality traits of curiosity, problem solving ability, persistence and innovativeness align with the characteristics of successful adult learners identified by Row (1953), Gross (1982) and Houle (1984).

The Wright brothers, working as a team, were compatible in purpose, thought and action. They worked on this self-directed learning project as if they were a single entity; their individual strengths complemented and enhanced each other's efforts. The behaviors exhibited by the Wrights in their learning project were repetitive forming series, groups and stages of action. These learning behaviors were nonlinear, demonstrating increased proficiency as the learners moved through their project. The productive outcomes of their collaborative teamwork and synergy were driven by the cyclical forces of goal setting, feedback and motivation.

The definitive variables which characterize the concept of a learning project in the literature (Knowles, 1975; Tough, 1979; Brookfield, 1981, 1984a, 1986) held true for the Wrights' learning efforts in that: (1) it was a highly deliberate effort to gain knowledge and skill, (2) it included affective changes as well as the development of cognitive and psychomotor skills, (3) the goals, learning decisions, location and use of resources, rate of progress and method of evaluation were determined by the learner(s), and (4) there was no affiliation or assistance from a formal education system or institution. The Wrights were very deliberate and systematic in articulating and employing strategies to reach their goal of manned-flight. The final project goal to invent the airplane had been clearly documented by the brothers in their letters and diary entries. Their learning project took place exclusively outside of any institutional setting, without direct institutional support (e.g., information, money, technical resources, etc.). This context for learning concurs with the findings of Penland (1977) whose survey found that the most favored locations for learning were the home and the work place -- which in the Wrights' case were one and the same -- and with Houle (1961, 1984), Tough (1979), Gross (1982) and Brookfield (1984a,b) whose research indicates that arenas outside of institutional settings prove to be fertile ground for self-directed adult learning projects to unfold.

Triggering Mechanism To Engage In Self-Directed Learning

The Wrights began their self-planned learning project to solve the problem of manned-flight. This problem solving orientation to self-planned learning was verified by Knowles (1973) and Penland (1977). The triggering mechanism for their launch into the project was the sudden death of someone they admired and read about, the famous German gliding enthusiast, Otto Lilienthal, who died in 1896 during gliding experiments. It was at this time that the Wrights began an intensive search for existing written materials on the current progress toward the solution of the problem of flight. The impact of the triggering phenomenon concurs with Spear and Mocker (1984) and Brookfield (1986) who contend that a decision to engage in a learning project, which has a specific goal, is usually preceded by some change in a life circumstance or calamitous circumstance which would induce exploration and problem solving. The death of Lilienthal was the first motivational factor in the process of the Wrights' self-directed learning project and it was this event which triggers the development of their ultimate goal: to invent a successful airplane.

CONTEXTUAL FORCES

Although this learning project occurred outside an institutional framework, it did not progress in isolation. As the biographical background and pattern of contacts indicate, the brothers were in constant contact with each other. In addition, they kept regular contact with the opinion leader of the informal information network of the time, Octave Chanute, who channeled information to and from an international aeronautical network. They continued to work within the context of a family and a business. The use of external resources, both human and material, as well as the conduct of the self-directed learning project within the context of information networks has been verified by the work of Tough (1967, 1979), Farquharson (1975), Luikart (1977) and Brookfield (1980, 1981).

The pattern of external contacts made by the Wright brothers indicate the most frequently contacted and utilized resource was one person, Octave Chanute; and only 17 contacts were initiated during the four year duration of the communication network action set which formed during their learning project. Their primary reason for making contact was to obtain information. The Wright brothers use of a person and printed material as the frequent external resources confirms the findings of Coolican (1974, 1975), Hiemstra (1976) and Penland (1977).

The communication and network patterns of the Wrights were tracked, as a separate and distinct layer of the content analysis. What emerged was an action set which formed directly as a result of the Wrights' attempt to acquire information. The Wrights had formed a very small network for the purpose of solving the problem of manned-flight. Of the eight people who composed the network, only three individuals were influential in the progress of the learning project. Such small numbers of assistants were identified in previous studies by Tough (1979) and Cross (1981), but their findings reported no less than four as the minimum number of helpers.

The findings relative to the action set formed by the Wrights concur with existing findings, in that their network was formed for a specific purpose, to gain information relative to their problem solving efforts to fly. The network functioned for as long as the Wrights needed information. As soon as the problems were solved, they disconnected from their ties and their respective links to the overall network dissolved. Involvement in the network provided the Wright brothers with information, support, and a barometric reading as to where their progress stood relative to their peer group. The importance of the network in which the Wrights interacted is an example of the importance of voluntary organizations and informal learning networks as enabling bodies for learning. This is supported by the findings of Luikart (1977), Brookfield (1981), Beder, Darkenwald and Valentine (1983).

The information needed to solve the mystery of flight was not obtained from external resources. The three critical puzzle pieces of control, airfoil design and power source were solved solely through the ingenuity of the Wrights. External information sources merely provided starting points and frames of reference from which they could compare and contrast their own experimental results. The solutions to these problems came after a series of specific behaviors were employed by the Wrights. These were the actions coded as learning behaviors and basic cognitive processes (Figure 11.1). This supports the conceptual construct of the organizing circumstance presented by Spear and Mocker (1984) which contends that the learning project is structured from limited alternatives within the learner's environment. Technology had advanced to a point where the cognitive and material resources provided excellent sociological timing for this event to occur. As such, it represents another example of the organizing circumstance (Spear & Mocker, 1984) or being in the right place at the right time. Had the Wrights tried 50 years sooner, the technological advances in materials and engineering as well as the consolidation of existing information would not have been available.

GOAL SETTING

The Wrights, acting as problem solvers in the process of their learning project, exhibited repetitive core categories of learning behaviors not dissimilar to those cited by Henry (1960), Tough (1979), Johnstone and Rivera (1965), Knowles (1975), Brookfield (1986) and Oddi (1987). These behaviors of modeling, concept construction, reading, observing, discussion, contemplating, planning, experimenting, using trial and error, practicing, and

Figure 11.1: Relationship of Learning Behaviors, Basic Cognitive Processes, Stages and Corollaries of Critical Incidents.

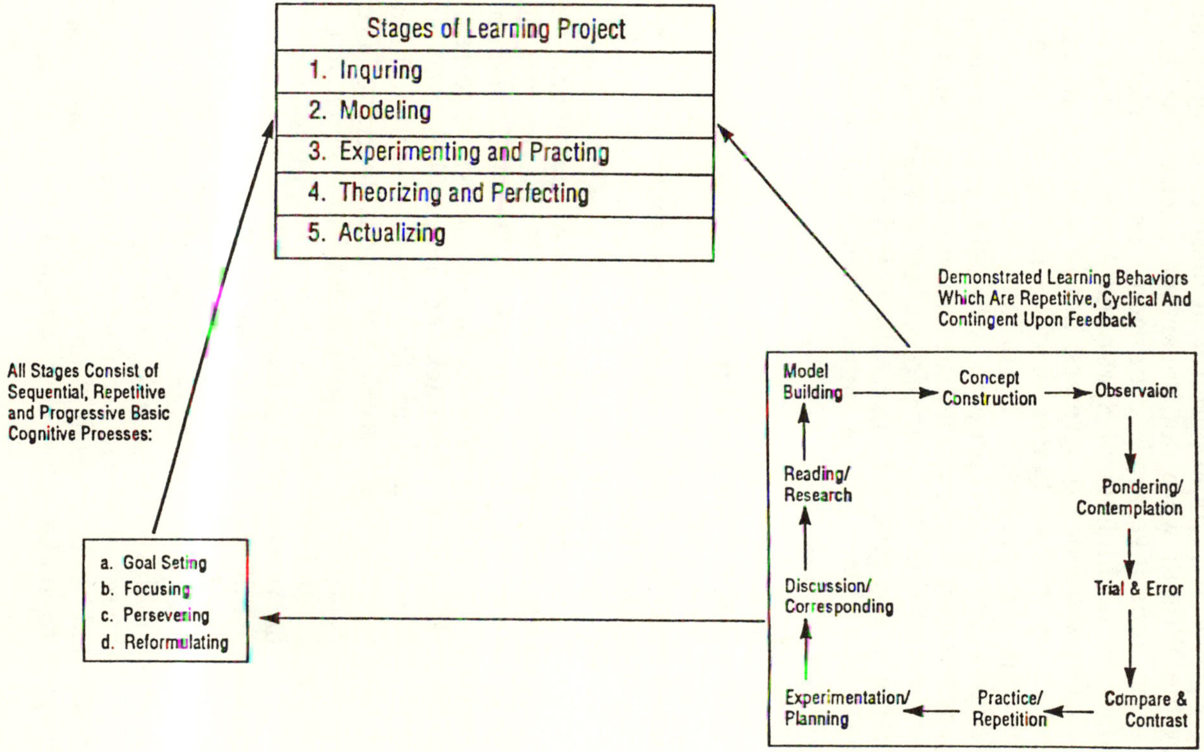

comparing and contrasting were continuous and cyclical throughout the learning project (Figure 11.1).

The sequential patterns of these behaviors exhibited by the Wrights were not linear and unchanging, but were rather repetitive and contingent on feedback. This supports the findings of Spear and Mocker (1984) that the learning sequence progresses, not in a linear manner, but rather as circumstances evolve in logical progression through the project. Fortuitous circumstances in the Wrights' life space, coupled with skill, craftsmanship and perseverance, seemed to determine the direction and progress of their learning project, rather than clear-cut pre-planning and goal setting. Although their long range goal was very clear, the planning which took place in the learning project was contingent on circumstances and feedback.

FEEDBACK AS MOTIVATION

Based upon the analysis of this case study, the contextual framework for the learning project appears to control much of the decision making employed by the adult learner. The sequence of learning strategies is contingent upon information and resources received by the learner during the course of the learning project. Thus information and resources act as feedback to the learner(s). The research findings identified feedback as motivation for action. Feedback was critical to the Wrights' decision-making processes and the success of their learning project. Feedback provided the parameters from which decisions were made and subsequent behaviors employed.

The power of feedback to drive or motivate the learner manifested itself in the findings in a variety of forms. Feedback came to the Wrights in the form of information garnered from external contacts, from the results of their own experiments and from each other.

The result of each contact provided feedback which constituted a contextual framework, the basis for the Wrights to make their next set of behavioral decisions.

Whenever their need for information became greater than their personal resources, the Wrights contacted external resources to acquire the needed information. However, the information usually proved incorrect, insufficient or irrelevant. The result, whether positive or negative, did not seem to enhance or deter their progress. What it did do, however, was provide a form of feedback which constituted parameters of existing knowledge. In this way, the results of the contacts made by the Wrights acted in the manner of a feedback mechanism, providing contextual parameters from which they modified and regulated their subsequent actions.

External information sources merely provided starting points and frames of reference from which they could compare and contrast their own experimental results. Experimental results acted as a potent form of feedback to the Wrights efforts to refine and perfect their airplane model. The acquisition of the experimental data was a result of their careful observations, measurements and notetaking of each and every trial flight with models in the wind tunnel to full-scale models at Kitty Hawk. This feedback impacted on the choice of learning behaviors more directly than on the basic cognitive processes employed.

By 1903 the Wrights realized, based upon the external and internal feedback they had been receiving from their contacts and their own experiments, respectively, their work had progressed farther than others in the field. The information provided comparisons with content and completed the feedback loop. As the holders of the information power base, this awareness seems to be the triggering mechanism or motivation for action. And, thus, the learning cycle begins again (Figure 11.2).

The directional flow of information is dependent upon who holds the information power base, the most recent and unique bits of information. Those who need information and become aware of who has it, initiate the request for information. Information is pulled through the network by those in want or need of the data, rather than being pushed by those who have it. This power position relative to movement within a resource network seems to be a potent ingredient to understanding what motivates the learner and what moves information through a system. These interpretations compare favorably with the research of Whitten and Wolfe (1974), who focused on the processes and forces moving people and information within networks. The power of involvement in the formal network as a motivator to spur learning has been cited by Brookfield (1984a) as a resource used by successful independent learners.

Figure 11.2: Conceptual Model

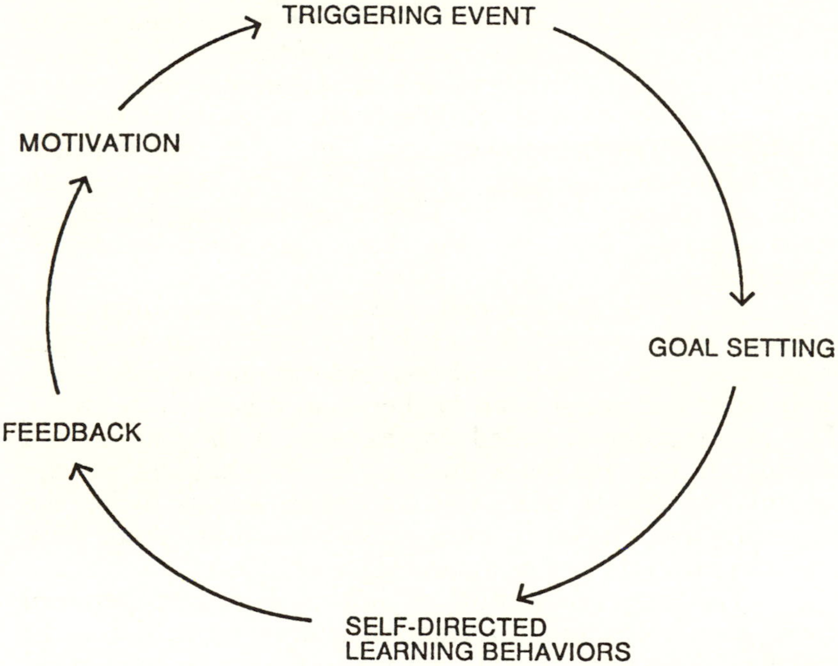

THE POWER OF PARTNERSHIP

The power of a partnership to provide feedback and motivation in facilitating the learning process was a dynamic force at work during the progress of the Wright Brothers project. The Wrights worked as a team, complementing their unique strengths and weaknesses. They worked, experimented, discussed, pondered, argued and succeeded together. As partners, they served as mirrors, sources of reflection from whom feedback was received to reformulate ideas and broaden perspectives. As partners, they served as helpers through verbal exchanges and mental probes in making judgments while adjusting ideas and advancing their learning processes. The power and dynamics of this ability to work collaboratively could spawn a variety of research themes.

CONCLUSIONS

Interpretations of the findings suggest the behaviors employed by the Wrights in their learning project were repetitive forming series, groups and stages of action. These sequential patterns of behaviors were not linear and unchanging, but were rather cyclical and contingent on the feedback they received. Although their long range goal to invent the airplane was clear, the planning and goal setting which took place in the learning project was contingent on contextual circumstances and feedback. Feedback provided one form of motivation for their continued efforts to successfully complete the learning project. Their involvement in the formal information network acted as a motivator to spur their actions as well.

The research findings demonstrate that self-directed learning does not occur in isolation and defined goals can be accomplished through practice and perseverance contingent upon feedback and motivation.

REFERENCES

Beder, H., Darkenwald, G.G., & Valentine, T. (1983). Self-planned professional learning among public school adult education directors: A social network analysis. Proceedings of the Twenty-Fourth Annual Adult Education Research Conference, 7-12.

Brookfield, S.D. (1980). Independent adult learning. Leicester: University of Leicester, Ph.D. Thesis (unpublished).

Brookfield, S.D. (1981). The adult learning iceberg: A critical review of the work of Allen Tough. Adult Education (UK), 54, 110-118.

Brookfield, S.D. (1984a). Adult learners, adult education and the community. New York: Teachers College Press, Columbia University.

Brookfield, S.D. (1984b, Winter). Self-directed learning: A critical paradigm. Adult Education Quarterly, 35 (2), 59-71.

Brookfield, S.D. (1986). Understanding and facilitating adult learning. San Francisco: Jossey-Bass.

Coolican, P.M. (1974). Self-planned learning: Implications for the future of adult education. Syracuse, New York: Educational Policy Research Center, Syracuse University Research Corporation.

Coolican, P.M. (1975). Self-planned learning: Implications for the future of adult education. An addendum to the 1974 paper. Washington, D.C.: Division of Adult Education, U.S. Office of Education.

Crane, D. (1972). Invisible colleges: Diffusion of knowledge in scientific communities. Chicago: The University of Chicago Press.

Cronin, B. (1982, September). Invisible colleges and information transfer: A review and commentary with particular reference to the social sciences. Progress in Documentation, 38 (3), 212-236.

Cross, K. P. (1981). Adults as learners. San Francisco: Jossey-Bass.

Crouch, T.D. (1971). The giant leap: A chronology of Ohio aerospace events and personalities, 1815-1969. Columbus, Ohio.

Crouch, T.D. (1981). A dream of wings: Americans and the airplane, 1875-1905. New York: W. W. Norton and Company, Inc.

Farquharson, A. (1975). Peers as helpers: Personal change in members of self-help groups in metropolitan Toronto. Unpublished doctoral dissertation, University of Toronto.

Fisher, C. S., et al. (1977). Networks and places: Social relations in the urban setting. New York: The Free Press.

Gibbs-Smith, C. H. (1960). The aeroplane: An historical survey of its origins and development. London: Her Majesty's Stationery Office.

Gibbs-Smith, C. H. (1966). The invention of the aeroplane, 1809-1909. London: Her Majesty's Stationery Office.

Glaser, B. G., & Strauss, A. L. (1967). The discovery of grounded theory: Strategies for qualitative research. New York: Aldine Publishing Company.

Granovetter, M. S. (1973). The strength of weak ties. American Journal of Sociology, 1360-1380.

Gross, R. (1982). The independent scholar's handbook. Reading, MA: Addison-Wesley.

Guba, E. G. (1978). Toward a methodology of naturalistic inquiry in educational evaluation. Monograph series, No. 8. Low Angeles: Center for the Study of Evaluation, University of California.

Guba, E. G., & Lincoln, Y. S. (1981). Effective evaluation. San Francisco: Jossey-Bass Publishers.

Henry, J. (1960). A cross-cultural outline of education. Current Anthropology, 1, 267-305.

Hiemstra, R. (1976). The older adult's learning projects. Educational Gerontology, 1, 331-341.

Holsti, O. R. (1969). Content analysis for the social sciences and humanities. Reading, MA: Addison-Wesley.

Houle, C. O. (1961). The inquiring mind. Wisconsin: The University of Wisconsin Press.

Houle, C. O. (1984). Patterns of learning. San Francisco: Jossey-Bass Publishers.

Johnstone, J. W. C. & Rivera, R. J. (1965). Volunteers for learning: A study of the educational pursuits of American adults. Chicago: Aldine Publishing.

Kerlinger, F. N. (1979). Behavioral research: A conceptual approach. New York: Holt, Rinehart and Winston.

Knowles, M. (1973). The adult learner: A neglected species. Houston: Gulf Publishing Company.

Knowles, M. S. (1975). Self-directed learning: A guide for learners and teachers. Chicago: Association Press.

Krippendorff, K. (1980). Content analysis. California: SAGE Publications.

Kuhn, T. S. (1970, 1962). The structure of scientific revolutions. Chicago: The University of Chicago.

Long, H. B. (1983). Adult learning research and practice. New York: Cambridge.

Long, H. B., & Hiemstra, R., et al. (1980). Changing approaches to studying adult education. San Francisco: Jossey-Bass Publishers

Luikart, C. (1977). Social networks and self-planned adult learning. North Carolina: University of North Carolina.

McFarland, M. W. (Ed.) (1972). The papers of Wilbur and Orville Wright: 1899-1905. (Vol. I). New York: Arno Press.

Mezirow, J. (1985). A critical theory of self-directed learning: From theory to practice. New Directions for Continuing Education. San Francisco: Jossey-Bass.

Mitchell, J. C. (1969). The concept and use of social networks. In J. Clyde Mitchell (Ed.), Social networks in urban situations. Manchester, England: Manchester University Press.

Oddi, L. F. (1987). Perspectives on self-directed learning. Adult education Quarterly, 38 (1), 21-31.

Penland, P. R. (1977). Self-planned learning in America. Pittsburgh: Book Center, University of Pittsburgh.

Price, D. J. de. S., (1965). Networks of scientific papers. Science, 149, 510-515.

Roe, A. (1953). The making of a scientist. New York: Dodd, Mead.

Rogers, E. V. (1962). Diffusion of innovations. New York: The Free Press.

Rogers, E. M., & Kincaid, D. L. (1981). Communication networks. New York: The Free Press.

Ruben, B. D. (1984). Communication and human behavior. New York: MacMillan.

Ruben, B. D. & Weimann, J. M. (1979, Spring). The diffusion of scientific information in the communication discipline: Conceptualization and propositions. Communication Quarterly, 47-53.

Spear, G. E., & Mocker, D. W. (1984, Fall). The organizing circumstances: Environmental determinants in self-directed learning. Adult Education Quarterly, 35 (1), 1-10.

Tough, A. M. (1966). The assistance obtained by adult self-teachers. Adult Education, 17, 30-37.

Tough, A. M. (1967). Learning without a teacher: A study of tasks and assistance during adult self-teaching projects (Educational Research Series 3). Toronto: Ontario Institute for Studies in Education, .

Tough, A. M. (1968). Why adults learn: A study of the major reasons for beginning and continuing a learning project. Toronto: Ontario Institute for Studies in Education.

Tough, A. M. (1978). Major learning efforts: Recent research and future directors. Adult Education, 28, 250-263.

Tough, A. (1979). The adult's learning projects: A fresh approach to theory and practice in adult learning. (Research in education series no. 1). Toronto: Ontario Institute for studies in Education.

Tough, A. (1982). Intentional changes: A fresh approach to helping people change. Chicago: Follett.

Whitten, N. E., Jr., & Wolfe, A. W. (1974). Network analyses. In J. J. Honigmann (Ed.), Handbook of Social and Cultural Anthropology. Chicago: Rand McNally.

Wright, O. (1953). How we invented the airplane. Harper's Magazine.

Chapter Twelve

SELF DIRECTED LEARNERS: WOMEN CLIMBING THE CORPORATE LADDER

Joanne Lambert & Jeanie Rountree-Wyly

In the 1980s women steadily overcame barriers and assumed leadership roles in fields that were traditionally male. A decade ago, according to the U.S. News and World Report (Nov. 29, 1982), the nation's space program allowed no women astronauts. Now there are eight women astronauts. Ten years ago even the largest U.S. banks could count on one finger of one hand their number of female Vice-Presidents. Now some giant banks have more than 100 women as Vice-Presidents and even one or two as Senior Vice-Presidents.

In 1972, women in companies with 100 or more employees held only 1 in 8 management jobs. Now they hold 1 out of 5. Ten years ago 13 women served in the House of Representatives. There are now 21 who serve, which sets an all time record. Just over 300 women sat in state legislatures in 1972. The present figure exceeds 900.

Women who comprise 51.3 percent of the U.S. population still only represent 5 percent of executives in the top 50 corporations, 10 percent of astronauts, 12 percent of state legislators, and two percent of U.S. Senators (U.S. News and World Report, Nov. 29, 1982).

Who are the women climbing the corporate ladder? How do they get to the top? What makes them different from the women who don't make it to the top? Are they just lucky? Or in the right place at the right time? And if they are, how do they succeed at the top after they get there?

How have they acquired the knowledge needed in order to compete and survive in their respective careers? Are they self-directed learners?

Oddi (1987), in addressing learning perspectives, notes the ambiguity in the concept of self-directed learning and some confusion about a uniform definition. Therefore, a study of self-directed learning from a behavioristic point of view, provides consideration of the learner's relationship toward and reaction to environmental pressures as motivator or triggering mechanism for making choices.

Recent studies by Gibbons, Bailey, Comeau, Schmuck, Seymour, and Wallace (1980), in analyzing biographies of famous experts, identified self-education which began in youth and carried through to adulthood. Long's (1988) biographical analysis sheds further light on men of self-direction in learning. Other biographical surveys have included men and women of fame who have exhibited self-direction in learning.

Brookfield (1984) criticized the focus of research in self-directed learning as being directed mainly toward middle class adults, and a more recent review of literature by Caffarella and O'Donnell (1987) listed verification studies of other categories of learners. Included in this review were general population, Cooperative Extension participants, nurses, engineers, adults in community colleges, farmers, undereducated adults in rural Vermont, older adults, adults in the professions, black adults, prospective parents, clergymen, and adult basic education students (p. 200). A need for additional research was suggested "using as subjects people from different social classes, ethnic groups and cultural backgrounds" (p. 209). Women in the corporate world, upwardly mobile, exhibit many of the characteristics of the self-directed learner, and would seem to be worthy of study.

An exploration of women who have displayed self-directed traits of learning may provide some insight to assist educators in motivating and accommodating others. For the survey at hand, a representative sample was selected from business, industry, and service institutions. One woman, through training and retraining herself for each level within her field, became the most powerful woman in the film industry, holding a position formerly reserved only for a man. Another inherited her corporate position at the death of her husband, and educated herself to fill his shoes. From the field of education emerges a fourth-grade dropout who in adulthood teaches herself to speak English and ultimately rises to the upper level of university administration. The unlikely field of religion provides the fourth woman who achieves power and position through self-directed learning, and does so despite lack of a college degree.

Houle (1961) through interviews classified self-directed learners in terms of goal-oriented, activity-oriented, and learning-oriented. He addressed the value of histories and biographies as a source for study of the continuing learner. He recognized the limitations of this source, however, since some authors because of their own viewpoints and perspectives tend to include learning information, while other authors ignore such details altogether.

Study of self-direction in learning for contemporary women in the corporate world can be accomplished through articles in journals, newspapers and other current magazines and tabloids. There is a tendency to include more information concerning personal learning preferences and pursuits in these publications than in biographies because of the newsworthiness of such items to the modern reader. Therefore, news articles in magazines, journals, and newspapers provides the major source of information for the study.

Using these resources, exclusive of biographies, a study of self-directed learning techniques among four women who are successfully climbing the corporate ladder provide models for consideration of similarities and differences.

SHERRY LANSING-FILM PRODUCTION INDUSTRY

The first example is Sherry Lee Lansing, who was born in Chicago, Illinois, on July 31, 1944. Sherry Lee Lansing is the daughter of Margo Heiman, a Jewish woman who fled to the United States from Nazi Germany. Upon her father's early death, her mother worked as a realtor to support herself, Sherry, and another daughter, Andrea. She later married Norton Lansing, a furniture manufacturer, and had two more children, Richard Lansing and Judy Lansing.

A self-directed learner early in life, Sherry graduated from the University of Chicago Laboratory High School, a special school for gifted children, in 1962. Four years later she earned a B.S. degree from the department of theatre at Northwestern University. Sherry received all A's in college, but "Not because," she quoted, "I'm bright, but because I worked hard and studied all the time."

Sherry Lansing went to Los Angeles and taught mathematics at Watts High School for three years after graduation from college. She then turned to a career in modeling. Sherry appeared in television commercials in 1969-1970 for the Max Factor Company and Alberto Culver Company. Between modeling assignments she was able to take on a few small acting roles in "Loving" and "Rio Lobo," a John Wayne movie. '

"I was a terrible actress. I found it so difficult and painful to do," admitted Lansing. She looked around the movie set, was fascinated by the production process, and wondered what all the technicians and others were doing. To find out, she enrolled in film classes at the University of California at Los Angeles and the University of Southern California. Once again Sherry Lansing was involved in self directed learning by participating in classes which would teach her about the film industry and in going to over seven movies a week to learn about the role of production.

Miss Lansing, through her film "Loving," which had Raymond Wagner as its executive producer, began reading scripts in 1970 at $5.00 an hour for his small production company, Wagner International. Within two years she was working with writers, developing seven plays as an executive story editor.

In 1975 she accepted a job as executive story editor, which at the time was the ultimate non-acting job a woman could attain at a major studio. She advanced to Vice-President of Creative Affairs, the second highest ranking production post of her first Vice-Presidency title, in March of 1977.

Ready for even more direct involvement with production, in November 1977 she switched to Columbia Pictures studio, where Daniel Madrick, her mentor, had taken over the helm of production. He lured her to that company with a job overseeing projects from the very beginning. First she was named Vice-President for Production in September of 1978. She stepped up to Senior Vice-President of the studio quickly. Sherry Lansing stated, "A woman couldn't make a mistake without everyone wondering how she got the job." Realizing her professional advancement, she nonetheless believed that a woman never would be the president of a major movie company.

When her contract at Columbia expired in November 1979, Lansing spent several weeks considering other opportunities, such as the possibility of producing her own movies or becoming an anthropologist to satisfy her love of travel. But in January of 1980 she instantly became known as the most powerful woman in the film industry when she became President of Twentieth Century Fox. Her three year contract stipulated an annual salary of $300,000 plus bonuses.

Sherry Lansing, a self directed learner, graduated from high school and college with high honors, went on to teach mathematics, modeled, acted, and became a producer with relatively no experience or education for the film industry. She took courses and attended as many as seven movies a week to learn about the movie industry. Through self-directed learning she was able to climb the corporate ladder to the top level in the movie industry, which was President of Twentieth Century Fox.

MARGIE SCHOTT-BUSINESS CORPORATIONS

Another self-directed learner is Margie Schott, born Margaret Unnewehr in 1928, the second of Edward and Charlotte Unnewehr's five daughters. Her grandfather was the world's premier cigar box manufacturer and her father made a fortune in lumber, so that made her a rich third-generation Cincinnati German Catholic. Marge's father would not allow his daughters to eat with him until they were old enough to behave. He also wouldn't allow them to be sick because he didn't believe in doctors.

Little Marge became the son her father never had, which is why her nickname is "Butch." Marge's father motivated her to pursue self directed learning by encouraging her to stay home and attend the University of Cincinnati. He said she could go to work for him, and he would buy her a white Packard Clipper. So she did -- and he did! Marge was the only one of five daughters who worked for her father. However, this only lasted a short time, as Marge decided to marry Charles J. Schott in 1952. He was heir to an industrial fortune, he was German, he was Catholic, and he was Cincinnati society. Charlie bought Marge a 72-acre estate in Cincinnati, known as Indian Hills. At this point Marge was content to throw fabulous parties and raise money for charity.

Marge's first blow in life was when she found out she couldn't have children. This may explain her love for animals. Marge bought a Saint Bernard while in Switzerland and ended up with 14 because it was pregnant. Her husband bought her an elephant which they donated to the zoo. But Marge did pursue learning. One year she made picture frames, covering them in leather to match the furniture in her husband's office. Then it was bees, because she wanted honey. Next she bought cattle to pursue another adventure. Then suddenly in 1968 her husband died. Boom! No warning! 42 years old, dropped dead of a heart attack (St. Athoplos, 1985). She was left with a car dealership, a shopping center, a brick company, a concrete products company and a landfill company. Marge Schott was 39 at this time. She immediately became Chairman of the Board of a car dealership which never made money. The management of Schott Buick tried to force her out. So she fired all the department heads and moved everyone else in the company up one notch. Marge was on her own. Once again she was immediately pushed into self-directed learning along with a lot of bluffing.

In less than three years stocks jumped 40% at Schott Buick and Marge opened a second dealership called Marge's Chevrolet (Van Biema, 1985).

In 1980 Schott bought into another venture, the Cincinnati Reds baseball club. In 1981 she became a limited but far from silent partner in the ball club. At this time, the Reds were owned by the Williams brothers. The team was going down the tubes, and by 1983 attendance had reached an all time low.

Then came Marge Schott, a born promoter. By mid 1984, the Williamses had decided to sell the team, which had lost an estimated 25 million dollars since 1981. Marge then bought the team for 13 million dollars. When asked why she bought the team that had lost so much money she responded, "You reach a time in your life when you either do something you feel is extremely important--step up to the plate and take a shot--or you'll never do it" (St. Athoplos, 1985).

The Reds have been very successful in her tenure, winning more games from 1985 through 1987 than has any team in their division. The franchise has become profitable after losing 25 million in the three preceding years. The baseball team is now among the financial elite, thanks to Marge Schott.

Marge Schott, a self directed learner, began at a young age by learning how to run every piece of machinery in her father's company. Then she took a short rest from learning after marriage. However, all of a sudden, she was thrown into self-directed learning at the age of 39. She once again depended on self-initiated learning in order to direct a major GM corporation. She had to become a financial wizard in a short amount of time. Her success speaks for itself, as she not only learned one dealership, but opened another corporation and ultimately bought the Cincinnati Reds baseball team. Marge Schott, a self-directed learner, though thrown into this situation, has proven that through self education you can achieve what never seemed possible.

GUADALUPE QUINTANILLA-HIGHER EDUCATION

Self-direction in learning is exhibited in academia through observing the success of Dr. Guadalupe Quintanilla, Assistant Vice President for Academic Affairs at the University of Houston, who came with her family from San Luis, Mexico, to Brownsville, Texas, when she was eleven years old.

Enrolling in school in her new hometown, "Lupe" was administered an IQ test to determine appropriate level of placement. The little girl scored 67, was immediately labeled mentally retarded and was demoted from fourth to first grade. She sat in the back of the first grade classroom cutting out paper dolls, coloring, and helping the teacher by escorting the younger children to the bathroom. Lupe begged her parents to allow her to drop out of school. They consented, reluctantly, and she spent her days at home reading in Spanish to her blind grandfather.

By the age of 15 Lupe married and started a family, eventually bearing two sons and a daughter. When her first son entered school, he was branded a "slow learner," just as his mother had been, and the same thing eventually occurred with the next two children as they entered the public school system. Lupe cried, believing that she was the cause of all the problems. She worried that they had inherited their characteristics from her.

Lupe finally approached the school principal with her concern about her children, because she observed that they seemed fairly intelligent around her at home. The principal explained the problem. They spoke Spanish at home and were unable to adequately communicate in

English at school. He suggested that she should speak to them in English at home.

Guadalupe, now age 29, determined that she must learn to speak English in order to save her children from the humiliation and separation she herself had experienced. So she began her search for help. At this time, no adult education programs were available in the school or community, so she went to the local hospital, the telephone company, the high school, and the junior college for assistance. All she asked was to be permitted to sit in the back of the classroom during educational or training sessions to hear people speaking English. She felt that she could learn by listening if given the opportunity to hear proper use of the language beyond the conversational street talk. But none of the agencies contacted would grant her request. Guadalupe finally persuaded the registrar at the junior college to admit her as a special student on an individual basis for a one semester trial. The registrar agreed to waive the required GED test for admission in this one instance. Guadalupe had by now taught herself to speak a fair amount of English for communication purposes, and felt some degree of confidence that she could pass the language portion of the test, but knew that she had absolutely no chance to pass the math portion.

After getting her children off to school, riding the bus to college, returning home to care for her family, then regularly studying until 2:00 or 3:00 a.m., Guadalupe completed the semester. She put in many extra hours making up for all the years she had missed in formal schooling, and made the dean's honor roll at the end of the semester.

Always teaching herself outside the classroom to make up for educational and cultural deficiencies, this self-directed learner pursued her education through both formal and informal means of learning.

Motivated now to continue her education, Guadalupe learned to drive a car when she transferred to the university 140 miles away. She left home at 4:00 a.m. each morning for the round trip, and earned her bachelor's degree in biology three years after her first step into the classroom. She later completed a master's degree in Spanish literature and a doctorate in education, cutting a career path toward teaching and educational administration that ultimately led her into her present position.

From mentally retarded fourth grade dropout, this self-directed learner continues her career up the ladder, at the same time taking pride in the successes of her children, two of whom are attorneys, and one a doctor.

BARBARA CLEMENTINE HARRIS-RELIGION

For another self-directed learner, Barbara Clementine Harris, the religious hierarchy of the Episcopal Church is the equivalent of the corporate ladder. As the first woman bishop of the Episcopal Church, Barbara arrived at her current position through self-directed learning, combined with enthusiasm, dedication and motivation. Her ordination, in fact, represents much more than just a milestone for women in the Church.

Born into a traditional black family in Philadelphia, Barbara's early life involved the usual public school education, coupled with a strong attachment to the Episcopal Church. She was a brilliant student who found an abundance of time available to devote to her church and civil rights activities. Through self-education and involvement in racial and gay rights issues in the church, Barbara worked her way into a position as a writer for The Witness, a monthly journal published by a politically and theologically radical left-wing group of the Church. She worked her way up through the structure of the publication, becoming editor and eventually publisher.

During this period she was taking time off from her job as head of public relations at Sun Oil Company in Philadelphia, where she had also worked her way up through self-taught methods of meeting and marketing techniques for the corporation.

Joining efforts of the Church to register black voters in the South, Barbara even traveled to Mississippi and

Alabama in support of that mission. She marched behind Rev. Dr. Martin Luther King in the Selma to Montgomery demonstration, and campaigned vigorously for rights of her race. Throughout all of these activities, Barbara was married and divorced. She fought viciously for women's rights in the Church, using the voice of The Witness to publicize her cause.

Barbara was continuously educating herself in politics, government, and theological issues in order to carry on her crusade. Her formal studies included correspondence courses and tutoring prepared her for the necessary qualifications for ordinations and consecrations in the Church.

In what was termed by some churchmen an "illegal" ordination ceremony in 1974, eleven women became the first female priests of the Episcopal Church. While Barbara literally led the procession at this event, she was not one of the eleven. However, she continued her pursuit of her ideals, and a few years later abandoned her executive position with Sun Oil Company in order to devote her full energies toward her theological goals. She was ordained as priest after passing ordination examinations, spent several years in the early 1980s as chaplain at Philadelphia County prisons, and served a small parish at Morristown, Pennsylvania. A greater audience was reached, however, through her advocacy of racial justice and prisoners' rights, and through her opposition to the racial segregation system of South Africa.

On February 11, 1989, with Barbara Harris's consecration as bishop in the Episcopal Church, another milestone was reached for this self-directed learner.

The unlikely consecration of a female bishop involves more than a gender issue. While this action is in itself a contradiction of the traditional Episcopal Church belief in apostolic succession, major objections focus on the specific qualifications set forth for the position. Barbara Harris is the only bishop who not only lacks a seminary degree, she is also the only bishop ever ordained without an undergraduate degree of any kind. And while bishops have divorced while holding the office, none have previously been chosen after a divorce.

Barbara Harris is a self-directed learner who through self education and pursuit of her goals is breaking barriers and climbing the corporate ladder of the theological hierarchy.

CONCLUSIONS

Corporate ladders are being scaled daily by female self-directed learners. These are but a few of the examples of the types of women who through self-direction are changing their lives. And as more women discover the means of upward mobility through the power of self education, they will realize, in Brookfield's (1984) words, "the power to alter their individual and social environment and to create their own reality."

The four women explored in this study illustrate changing values among business, industry, and service institutions. Positions formerly reserved only for men are being filled more than adequately by women who have prepared themselves for their roles. These women are representative of the many others who seek education and training through both formal and informal means in order to achieve their goals. Even as they are role models for other women, setting patterns and examples to follow, they are also a challenge for educators and leaders in academia, who have the opportunity to serve this new clientele.

Educational providers should further explore the training needs of women who have the desire to progress in the corporate world, giving particular attention to any tendencies toward self-directedness in learning. Similarities and differences among these women should be compared to determine whether common characteristics emerge to assist agencies and institutions in serving this population.

Consideration for future research on career women who pursue higher levels in the corporate world might include the following: What are the preferences for style of learning among women climbing the corporate ladder? Do they generally prefer formal courses leading toward degree or certificate programs? Or do they tend toward informal learning through noncredit programs or advanced reading materials? Do these women train themselves deliberately for the next step up the ladder, or do they achieve the next level through promotion, then train themselves to perform as needed? Finally, are there patterns of motivation for learning that successful women hold in common? Further study through examination of biographies, newspaper and journal articles, should be supplemented with personal interviews of women in the corporate world to provide a more thorough base for analysis of commonalties.

REFERENCES

Associated Press. (1989, January 17). Episcopal church close to adding woman bishop. The Daily Oklahoman, 14.

Barron, J. (1988, September 25). Episcopal diocese chooses first woman to be a bishop. The New York Times, 1.

Briggs, David. (1989, February 12). Woman bishop. The Dallas Morning News, 6.

Brookfield, S. (1984). Self-directed learning: A critical paradigm. Adult Education Quarterly, 35(2), 59-69.

Caffarella, R. S. & O'Donnell, J. M. (1987). Self-directed adult learning: A critical paradigm revisited. Adult Education Quarterly, 37, 199-211.

Capouya, J. (1988, July). Queen of the riverfront. Sport, 28-37.

Demaret, K. (1983, October 10). With a presidential appointment, an erstwhile 'slow learner' proves she lacked only English--not brains. People Weekly, 69, 70.

Gibbons, M., Bailey, A., Comeau, P., Schmuck, J., Seymour, S., & Wallace, D. (1980). Toward a theory of self-directed learning: A study of experts without formal training. Journal of Humanistic Psychology, 20(2), 41-56.

Gordon, M. (1988, October). Back with a splash. Savvy, 46-49.

Houle, C. O. (1961). The inquiring mind. Madison: University of Wisconsin Press.

Kramer, R. (1979, August). Screen queens. Working Women, 35-37.

Langway, L., Dentzer, S., Malamud, P., Foote, D., Copeland, J. (1981, September 14). Women and the executive suite. Newsweek, 65-69.

Nuwer, H. (1986, June-July). Marge Schott: Queen of diamonds. Modern Maturity, 40-43.

Oddi, J. F. (1987). Perspectives on self-directed learning. Adult Education Quarterly, 38, 21-31.

Picasso, P. (1984, October). Making it big at thirty. Harper's Bazaar, 207.

Sheila, M., Kasindorf, M., Friendly, D. (1980, January 14). In ladd's place: A lass. Newsweek, 69-70.

Smith, M. (1989, February 2). Lupe's story; From dropout to doctorate. Dallas Times Herald, 21.

St. Athoplos, D. (1985, July 15). Marge has them eating out of her hand. Sports Illustrated, 42-54.

Staff. (1988, October 3). Elected, Barbara C. Harris. Time, 83.

Staff. (1988, October 10). Episcopal church moves into mainstream with election of first female to bishop post. Jet, 9.

Staff. (1982, November 29). U. S. News & World Report, 50.

Steinfels, P. (1989, February 12). Woman is consecrated as Episcopal bishop. The New York Times, 1, 6.

Steinfels, P. (1988, September 26). Advocate of equality. The New York Times, 8, 12.

Steinfels, P. (1988, November 26). Many in church oppose naming woman bishop. The New York Times, 6, 7.

Thompson, K. D. (1988, December). The woman who's bishop. Black Enter-prise, 20.

Van Biema, D. (1985, July 22). A millionairess named Marge proves a Schott in the arm for the dogged Cincinnati Reds. People Weekly, 99-100.

Wohwill, J. F. (April, 2970). The emerging discipline of environmental psychology. American Psychologist, 25, 303-312.

Chapter Thirteen

THE DRIVE TO LEARN: SELF-DIRECTED LEARNING IN A FORMAL INSTITUTIONAL SETTING

Angela Sgroi

So far, most discussions of self-directed learning in the adult education literature have considered only that learning undertaken by individuals in specific learning projects, exclusive of the formal institutional setting and of formal instruction. This chapter presents a different view of self-directed learning. It differs from much of the literature in three ways: it views self-directed learning as a manifestation of an internal process of control by the learner; it describes self-direction in learning which is developmental and lifelong and not a discrete project; and it looks closely at the learning process itself (called for by Caffarella and O'Donnell, 1987), including the interaction between the teacher and the learner. Based upon findings from field research of the learning engaged in by adults who study modern dance, this chapter describes the self-directed aspect of that learning--learning which takes place within a formal institutional setting.

The original intent of the study was to explore the quality and process of learning by adults who seriously studied the art form of modern dance as an avocation. Grounded theory was employed as the methodology for data collection and analysis. Specific field research techniques used for data collection were participant-observation of dance classes and in-depth interviews of adult dance students.

One of the unexpected but consistent discoveries of the study, the self-direction of the learners, emerged as a major element in the teaching-learning interaction. This was especially surprising in a learning tradition and environment which is teacher-directed. For that reason, this research provided a unique perspective for considering self-direction in adult learning.

SELF-DIRECTED LEARNING IN MODERN DANCE

After observing and listening to the adult learners in this study, it became very apparent that these were people who are in control of their learning. They decide what it is they need or want to learn and they go about decisively selecting the place, the time, and the teacher; deciding what they will or will not learn; and, even, deciding to temporarily relinquish control to someone else. How is control of one's own learning exerted in a formal instructional setting? The particular setting for the classes described here is actually only one part of a culture which dictates the behaviors of both teachers and learners.

The Setting and Culture of Learning Dance

The setting and culture of the dance class is one that expects obedience from its students. It begins at the door of the dance studio. The place for dancing, with its layout, equipment and posted materials, defines the kind of behavior expected and signals a change in role for those entering the place. The dressing room, in particular, and changing into the dance costume, are aspects of the setting which help define the behavior and role of the person who enters as "dance student."

One dancer's remarks on the importance of going to a class in a dance studio reflects the change in role triggered by the setting.

> There's something about coming into a studio where there's this nice open space and you are not surrounded by your everday things. It makes it more special. It makes you feel like you are doing something.

The structure and action of the dance class, derived from the ballet training tradition (Terry, 1971), are cultural elements which further influence the course the learning will take. All of the action of the classes follows the same process. The teacher demonstrates the movement and the students imitate the movement. In most classes there is no time spent on creative activity such as improvisation or composition. The focus is on control and articulation of movement.

Despite a learning environment, derived through tradition, which is completely teacher-directed, the adult learners expressed and exhibited complete control of their own learning. This control began with the choice of dance as a subject of study, the decision to overcome the barriers to learning, setting expectations of the teacher, and the decision to engage in the learning (including the degree and level of participation).

<u>The Decisions</u>

> Actions, they say, speak louder than words, louder and truer. When people dance, they dance naked in their spirits. (Barnes, 1969)

The dance students are aware of this, and it seems to be one of the things that draws them to dance. They say things like: "When other people do [dance] combinations,...I get a feeling for...what makes them so special." "It's a completely different form of expression."

<u>To choose modern dance</u>. The first decision, then, is the choice to actively study dance. They report choosing dance for a variety of reasons. It provides a medium through

which ideas and feelings inside of a person can be communicated. The art form has an emotional and intellectual impact, the aesthetic, which these dancers find compelling. It is something they love to do which they can give to themselves. One dancer reports: "[Dance] for me is very calming....And it is just for me. I can go inside and move and for me it's very peaceful." Modern dance is something which "fits," they say. It fits their bodies and their spirits. They choose to actively learn to dance because they want to learn the magic--how thoughts and feelings are translated into a poetry of movement.

<u>To overcome barriers</u>. Another decision, for most, is the decision to overcome (often formidable) barriers to participation. Some were physical. One woman had suffered a broken back; many dealt with the physical limitations of aging; and one dancer could not hear the rhythm or the melody of music. All of the dancers had to make time to dance in their extremely busy lives. All had full-time, usually professional jobs, and most had primary home and family responsibilities.

Physical barriers were not the only ones to be overcome. Decisions had to be made concerning psychological barriers, as well. Most common was the feeling of insecurity and even fear in doing something that they were not very good at, or were too old for. A fifty-year-old dancer remarked:

> I'm convinced that I'm too old to be here with kids. I'm much too fat to be running around in a leotard....It's not comfortable. I don't feel capable. I have to convince myself that it's OK for me to do this.

She never misses a class.

<u>To choose the teacher</u>. The students of modern dance expressed clear expectations for their teachers. They demonstrated control of their learning in this area, also, by

their decisions to participate or not to participate. Many of them reported staying with a dance class because of the teacher, taking additional classes because of the teacher, and even choosing modern dance (instead of ballet or jazz) because of the teacher. Similarly, they do not stay with a teacher they do not want. After two classes with a new teacher, one student "stormed" out in the middle of class. Less dreamatic, but equally decisive, class size dwindled in that class from an average of twelve to an average of three or four within one month's time.

Student expectations of teachers require the teachers to have full knowledge of modern dance and teaching dance; to have high expectations for their adult students; to work with the whole person; and to inspire trust. One dancer summarizes the kind of knowledge good teachers have:

> They know music. They know what they want. They can keep the class going; change the music when they feel it isn't the right energy....I like the fact that they are willing to give you corrections that are really helpful. You know I expect them to do that kind of thing.

Especially important to these adult dance students is correction and positive feedback during class. All of the teachers observed in this study were constant in their use of both and their students expected and appreciated it. Dancers reported positive evaluations of teachers who paid a great deal of attention to individual students and cared about their progress. They usually determined this by the frequency and tone of the teacher corrections to others in the class and by the accuracy of corrections made to themselves. Since one of the goals of the learning is to learn the magic of making art, a guide who knows how to create the magic as well as what it looks like when she/he sees it, is essential to the process.

Expectations of "the good teacher" extend to that teacher's high expectations of the students. As one dancer explained it, her best teachers:

> always treated the classes in a professional way. So even though we're not going to a New York stage, they still would give you the same class as they would give other people....I think it makes us a lot better dancers.

How to engage in the learning process. Perhaps the learning decisions most pertinent to a discussion of self-direction in learning are those decisions made during the actual learning process. At this point, the learner has made the decision to engage in the learning and is immersed in learning behaviors.

The adult dance students articulately and specifically reported their learning behaviors. A pattern emerged which is represented below in Figure 13.1.

The learning pattern is presented here as circular, but it is actually more like a spiral. Even a spiral, however, presents a linear picture which is only partially accurate. All of the behaviors occur all of the time. Learners continually follow the teacher, push through and evaluate their learning. The sequence suggested by the representation above is based upon the fact that while all of the learners engage in all of the behaviors most of the time, some of the behaviors logically can only follow some of the others. One cannot push through difficult movement until one submits to the guidance of the teacher, for example.

Once in class, the students of dance defer to the teacher's organization and style. Even when they relinquish control and submit to the teacher, the dance students are thinking and controlling what they learn, however. It is as if they apply a self-teaching style to that of the teacher. One of the dancers says that she not only concentrates on following what the teacher is doing in class, but, at the same time, she tries "to see myself succeeding...[and then] let it go."

Figure 13.1: Pattern of Learning Behaviors in a Development-Oriented Learning Situation

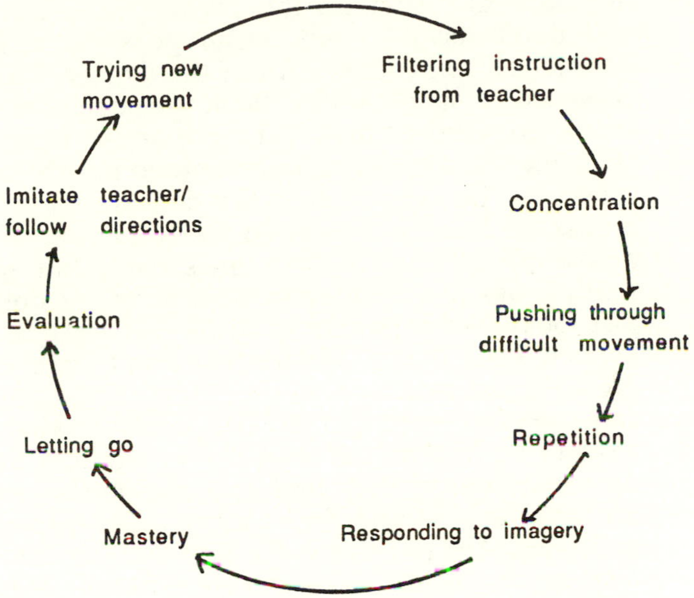

They try things, even activities they feel insecure about, like improvisations. The teachers run classes in such a way as to force the learners to continue trying throughout difficult movement phrases. This is what Jules Henry (1960) referred to as "jamming the machine." At the same time, the learners push themselves. A segment from the field notes describes this:

> It [the movement phrase] starts with a walk across the floor, arms in V-shape. It quickly moves on to a step, step, jump, jump sideways with arms in V. So far, so good. The accompaniment has a regular, strong beat which emphasizes each movement. Then Sarah [the teacher] quickly adds on and the group is suddenly doing step, step, jump to the side,

> step, step, jump and then cross over and do a sideways leap-up step to the other side, step over and leap jump. Nobody is getting this. Everybody is off the beat. They do this two or three times and still don't have it, but Sarah goes on and adds another eleven counts. All of the dancers look very confused. Sarah walks them through the entire sequence several times, but there are so many small steps that no one seems to be able to put the pattern together. She insists that the dancers try to move across the floor in twos doing the sequence. They go across about four or five times each, but no one really looks like they know what they are doing. It just looks like a jumble of arms and legs. Yet the dancers keep trying. Where they don't know what to do, they just make up steps. Most of the time one can see that each person has decided what parts have to be hit and so, even if they stumble through on some counts, they find movements they can hit on other counts and that carries them through the sequence. Usually this is the first and last count and one or two spots in between. Sarah lets them struggle through at least three more times. Finally, she stops and clarifies a few key spots. This helps tremendously. The whole sequence looks better. People are beginning to look like dancers again, and less like drunks stumbling across the floor.

After following the teacher, the learners in the above sequence engage in most of the behaviors listed in the pattern. They try the new movement. They are in deep concentration. As they are forced to take on more and more difficult steps, they push themselves through. Repetition is the primary activity used in this instance to learn the movement. Often, imagery is injected into the teacher's explanation of the movement. Music is a frequent support. Finally, some degree of mastery is attained.

How to assess the learning. The dance students discussed evaluation of their learning with the same certainty and clarity with which they discussed their other learning behaviors and decisions. Evaluation is an extremely important part of the learning process for these dancers. This can be seen by the frequency and variety with which they monitor their progress. Correction and feedback from the teacher is a must.

Some outside markers of learning progress were mentioned by some of the dancers. One, for example, (a physical education teacher) applied for, and received (with the second year's application) a Kennedy Center Fellowship in dance based upon an audition tape of her original choreography. Both the rejection of the first application with its explanation of the rejection, and the successful second application provided this learner some measures of her progress in dance. Performances in dance concerts provide other measures of attainment in dance.

Their own self-evaluation is constant and critical. Self-evaluation takes many forms. Two forms derscribed most frequently by the dancers are evaluation by comparing oneself with others, and evaluation using internal "objective" measures. It is common for dancers to compare themselves against other dancers in the class. Typical comments by dance students were: "I think one measures oneself always towards what is, who is much better than you." and "I see myself sort of in the middle upper level...you tend to rate yourself somewhere along in the group."

Without specifically pointing to outside measures, the dancers discuss their progress against some internal "objective" measure which is somehow identified by "feel." They say things like "That still feels kind of clumsy. There are parts of the class that still feel not there." Clearly, "there" is some quantity which exists only inside of the dancer, yet she implies here that it is clear to her when she attains it.

That the measure is identified by a feeling does not diminish the certainty of the evaluation. One student provided a more specific explanation. He explains that he notices feeling more confident in his movement and finds that he worries less about whether his steps are correct or not. This results in a much greater feeling of control and freedom in his dancing.

To learn dance outside of class. For all of the dance students, taking the modern dance classes was only one part of their overall, on-going learning in dance. So, in fact, the decision to participate in a class was only part of a larger personal learning pattern, even if the learner did not see it as a plan. In addition to taking dance classes, most of the dance students either attended dance concerts or watched professional dance on public television. Many read about dance in magazines or newspapers, or books about the lives of famous dancers.

A group of dance students cooperated one semester in choreographing, producing and performing their own public dance concert. They called themselves the Independent Choreographers. Since they met while attending a modern dance class, they elicited support from their teacher, especially in the compositional and performance aspects of the concert.

The value of a qualitative study of adult learning in the arts was that it provided the researcher the opportunity to see the learning as it took place within the full context of the learner's life rather than seeing only that learning carved out for study by the researcher. What became clear in this study was that students of modern dance learned dance in many different ways, at different times, for different purposes, and at different levels. When viewed from the whole-life perspective, learner control became that much more apparent.

Long (1986) identifies three basic frameworks within which the thinking about self-directed learning tends to fall: the psychological (cognitive process and degree of personal autonomy), the sociological (degree of interaction with others and the balance of power in those interactions), and the structural (learning process and the degree of autonomy of the learner. The identification of these broad frameworks supports a view of self-directed learning as a phenomenon which takes place across an individual's whole life.

Teacher-Learner Interaction

There is a give and take between the teacher and the learners which seems to enrich the experiences of both. The dance students have some insecurities about their ability to dance; they seek a teacher who knows the field and how to teach it. They are serious and committed to learning dance; they seek a teacher who has high expectations for them. They are mature individuals with varied and rich life experiences; they appreciate the teacher who treats them as a whole person. These are some aspects of the interaction between the teaching and the learning. There are others.

The teaching techniques and learning behaviors are similarly interrelated. The dancers are attracted to the movement of dance. They must move; so the teachers they stay with are those who, through careful pacing, can keep the class moving.

They are after the "magic" of dance, that is, the way that movement is projected so that the viewer can "feel" the ideas and impressions behind the movement. The use of metaphorical imagery is one technique the teacher uses to accomplish this. Thus, the viewer does not see someone leaping around the room, but a person reaching out toward the ends of the earth in some imaginary search.

Because they trust the teacher and have decided to temporarily relinquish control, they are willing to suffer the frustration and confusion of being pushed through difficult movement.

They insist upon constant correction and feedback from their teachers. It is part of a broader system of self-evalutation.

A conceptual model of interest to this discussion is one devised by Jarvis (1989) which focuses on the teacher-learner interaction as it applies to control of the learning. Figure 13.2 represents an adaptation of this model after the specific data from the study on adult dancers was applied.

Jarvis' model, which is conceptual in origin, is supported here with data derived from a grounded theory methodology. Both the model and the grounded-theory-derived data show adult learning as being completely interactive and interdependent.

On the one hand, there is the adult learner who is very much in control. If there is one thing about the learning patterns of the adults in the study, it is that they make the decisions and they are in control. On the other hand, there is an intense, loyal attachment to a (trusted) teacher to whom the learner has relinquished control. The attachment is not always made, but when it is, the influence of the teacher is very strong. In addition, traditional learning in dance sets the teacher as master and the student as follower. This tension between control and deference defines the nature of the teaching-learning interaction for adults who study modern dance.

The teacher of any dance class, therefore, begins with the support of traditon and custom. In adult amateur dance classes, the interaction takes over at that point. In order to maintain the role of master, the teacher mustdisplay most of the qualities and behavior patterns expected by the learners.

The adult learners submit to the teacher's expert guidance for several reasons: for the specialized knowledge of a visual medium, for a structured dance experience, to develop the discipline necessary to dance, for leadership in perfecting the art and the craft, and for correction from someone with an artistic sensibility. Unlike other accounts of self-directed learning, these learners place themselves under the expert guidance of the teacher, often for extended periods of time, for the reasons listed. Unlike some students of dance, these adult students seem to reserve the right to regain control as appropriate.

Figure 13.2: Teacher vs. Learner Control of Learning in Adult Dance Classes (adapted from Jarvis, 1989)

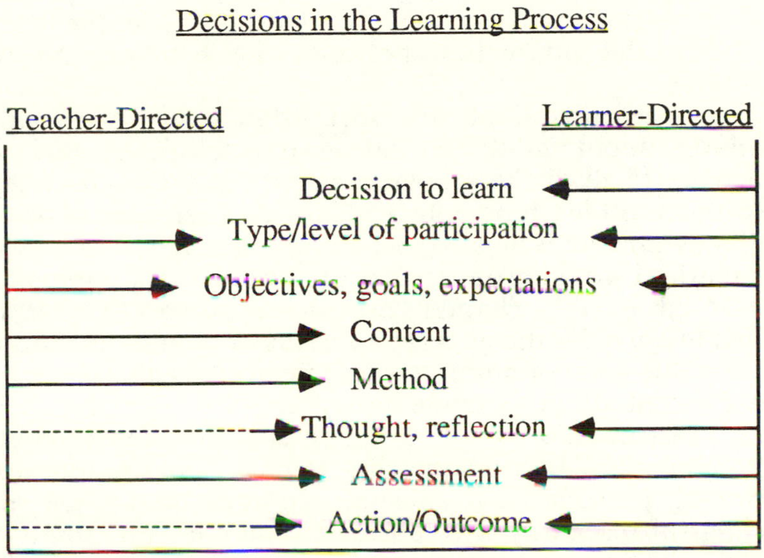

CONCLUSIONS

This chapter began by stating that the intent was to present a different view of self-directed learning than what presently exists in the prevailing literature. The view differs in three ways: it looks at self-directed learning as a manifestation of an internal process of control by the learner; it describes self-direction in learning which is developmental and on-going rather than a discrete project; and it focuses closely on the learning process itself, including the interaction between the teacher and the learner.

A discussion of this sort often leads to broader thinking about adult education--its definition and its practice. If all of the scholarly activity in the area of self-directed adult learning only leads to consideration of better methods and materials for teaching, then we have missed the mark. I would propose that the research and discussion presented in this chapter provide a perspective within which to consider the general approach to adult education.

One view of adult learning favored by this author is the concept of perspective transformation introduced by Jack Mezirow (1978). The dance students, for example, overcame many barriers in order to engage in the learning, including personal and societal attitudes about age and feelings of insecurity with the body and with the ability to move. Those barriers were further demolished as the learning progressed. This process of changing one's intellectual and cultural frames of reference constitutes perspective transformation as defined by Mezirow. This view of adult learning makes an intrinsic distinction between the learning of adults and the learning of children. It addresses a fundamental difference between the two.

For example, their cultural frames of reference tell them that they are too old to learn modern dance. Through dialogic process and reflective thought they are able to push beyond that frame and explore how an adult learns modern dance. They report advantages to dancing as an older person which their cultural frames of reference did

not address, such as the fact that they know themselves and their bodies better now; they are better and therefore, calmer learners now; they can interpret dance and music in more meaningful ways at this stage of their lives.
Building this perspective, however, will require accepting that there is a wide range of personal autonomy and control in adult learning, reconsidering the definition of adult education, careful to distinguish it from education for children.

The adults in this study, to a person, exhibited considerable autonomy and decision-making power in their learning. They were a highly educated group of experienced learners who represent one end of a continuum. Most teachers of adult education experience a wider range of learner control among their students. In fact, every teacher knows those adults who refuse to take even the smallest step in learning without direction from the teacher. They represent the other end of the continuum.

If perspective transformation provides a way to define adult learning and distinguishes it fundamentally from the learning of children, is there, similarly, a way to define adult education which provides a theoretical distinction from education for children?

If we return to that illusive task of defining adult education, I would argue that one societal factor defining "adult" is the expectation that the individual is responsible for himself or herself. This assumes that all adults are, therefore, responsibe for their own learning. This factor, when included in a definition of adult education, provides a framework for approaching any work one does related to adult learning.

By changing the way we see adult learners, we are forced to change the way we respond to them as teachers. The change is a subtle one which has to do more with assumptions and expectations than with specified teacher behaviors. For example, laws in our society are written and enforced based upon the assumption that adults <u>are</u> (not should be) responsible for their own behavior. Those adults who do not meet this expectation are then handled by the law enforcement and judicial system.

If any insight can be gained from the adults discussed in this chapter, it might be that adult educators are best advised to begin with the assumption that adults are responsible for their learning, even when that learning is dependent upon the skill, knowledge or guidance of the teacher.

This does not mean that the teacher no longer provides information, guidance or knowledge to their students. The data presented here indicates that self-directed learners can temporarily relinquish control to obtain needed guidance and knowledge from a teacher. It means only that each time that infomation, guidance and knowledge is given, the teacher must consider whether more is learned when these are given or when they are discovered. The answer will vary with every situation, with every student and with every teacher.

REFERENCES

Caffarella, R. S. & O'Donnell, J.M. (1987). Self-directed adult learning: A critical paradigm revisited. Adult Education Quarterly, 37, 199-211.

Henry, J. (1960). A cross-cultural outline of education. Current Anthropology, 1, 267-305.

Jarvis, P. (1989). Model for interaction between learner-direction and teacher-direction of learning. Paper presented at the Third North American Symposium on Adult Self-Directed Learning, University of Oklahoma, Norman, Oklahoma.

Long, H. B. (1986). Self-direction in learning: Conceptual difficulties. Lifelong Learning Forum, 3, 1-2.

Mezirow, J. (1978). Perspective transformation. Adult Education, 28, 100-110.

Spear, G. E. & Mocker, D. W. (1984). The organizing circumstance: Determinants in self-directed learning. Adult Education Quarterly, 35, 1-10.

Terry, W. (1971). The dance in America (revised ed.). New York: Harper and Row Publishers.

Chapter Fourteen

SELF-DIRECTION IN ADULT SECOND LANGUAGE LEARNING

Robert E. Nolan

The purpose of this chapter is to explore some of the paradoxes that become apparent when one applies the concept of self-directed learning to adult second language learning. The first part of the chapter will review some of the recent commentaries on self-directed learning, especially those which critique methods used to research self-directed learning. It will be demonstrated that such criticisms can be clearly exemplified as well as analyzed in the case of adult second language learning. The second part of the chapter will review the findings of a specific study of self-direction in second language learning as an example of how this area of research in self-directed learning can clarify some of the issues of the debate.

The first of these issues includes a criticism put forth by Brookfield (1986) that self-directed learning research, in general, lacks any attempt to corroborate interviewees' judgements about their own self-directed learning with external, objective criteria. Indeed, the typical researcher makes a largely unwarranted assumption that the subject interviewed was successful in the learning activity on the subject's word alone. According to Brookfield (1986), a reliance on self-reported estimates is questionable.

Secondly, recent critics have described self-directed learning research as having a too limited focus on what Brookfield (1986) calls the mechanics of formal instruction. Oddi (1987) concurred that most of the research on self-directed learning assumes that the process of self-directed learning in some way parallels the sequence of activities normally associated with formal instruction--viz., setting goals, developing strategies, choosing resources, etc. Chene (1983) elaborates on this critique of identifying self-direction with the normal steps involved in formal instruction when she points out the confusion of the concept autonomous. Autonomous can refer to a psychological state or it can refer to a particular learning methodology. Often in the literature these meanings are confused (Chene, 1983).

Spear and Mocker (1984), whose research was based on interview data obtained from 78 self-directed learners, involved in learning projects at the time of the interviews, maintained that self-directed learners depended heavily on their environments to guide their learning. This finding countered the opinion of those who analyzed self-direction in learning along the lines of self-instruction. Learners in the Spear and Mocker study did not preplan their activities. Rather, they often followed strategies supplied by the environment and often fortuitously (1984). Whereas Smith (1982) saw the process of self-direction as "deciding what, when, how, and where to learn; for setting realistic goals; for finding learning resources and choosing and implementing learning strategies" (p. 22), Spear and Mocker (1984) identified other organizing circumstances. Research conducted by the latter revealed that self-directed learning is triggered by changes in life circumstances in which the circumstances themselves become one of the learning resources. They also found that the structure of the learning, including methods used, was provided by the environment. Instead of intentional planning, these learners often expected that the means for learning would be contained within the new situation itself.

Fourthly, Brookfield (1984) criticized research in self-directed learning for its class bias. Almost all populations interviewed from Houle's (1961) study of inquiring minds to Tough's (1971) investigation into adult learning projects have been upper middle class professionals. To reinforce

Brookfield's observation, Caffarella and O'Donnell (1987) identify only three studies (Kratz, 1978; Leean and Sisco, 1981; Shackelford, 1983) of other than middle class populations.

Finally, the research reported here relates to Chene's (1983) critique regarding the social nature of learning. Self-directed learners always have to test their new knowledge against someone else according to Chene, which makes all learning, whether self-directed or not, a social act involving others. All learning is socially mediated, unless a person has already learned the material to the extent that the learner can test the new learning without the help of others. If the learning under consideration leads to competency, then autonomy is only relative (Chene, 1983).

It is the intention of this researcher to address the anomolies pointed out by researchers cited in the preceding section in his description of self-directed second language learning. In using second language as a special case of self-direction in learning, one sees that:

1) evidence is available to judge the success of the learning as the literature on self-assessment in second language proficiency supports (Jacobovitz, 1970; Painchaud and LeBlanc, 1980);
2) second language learning is not easily described in terms of the mechanics of teaching or formal learning--setting goals, determining objectives, identifying resources, etc. Self-direction in learning described here includes self-teaching in terms of autonomous methods used; but, it also includes self-direction as a psychological state--the psychological control of which Long (1988) speaks;
3) adult second language learning is, as Spear and Mocker (1984) maintained, highly dependent on the environment for structuring the learning;
4) the particular sample here described is not limited to any one social class or level of education, although level of education and ethnic origin became important variables as will be seen; and

5) adult second language learning described here includes the social dimension proposed by Chene (1983).

METHOD

The adult second language learner in this study was any person who learned a second language as a function of a particular career, occupation, or change in life style, including cross-cultural marriage. Second language was defined as any language other than the learner's native language learned as an adult for the purpose of using it in its total cultural context.

The population studied included people who had learned a second language to the extent that they were fluent or had at one time been fluent in that language. The population excluded learners who had studied the language as an academic discipline at some time prior to their adult learning experience. The following table describes the sample (Table 14.1 on the following page). All subjects involved in this study were volunteers.

Autonomy or self-direction was defined as controlling one's own second language learning by deciding what to study, how to study it, and in what order, that is, decisions about specific content, method, and sequencing. Like Spear and Mocker (1984), the researcher discovered during the course of his research that the environment itself was influencing these learner decisions according to the learner's life situation.

In line with critiques later posed by Brookfield (1986) and Chene (1983) that researchers simply assume that subjects interviewed attained competence in their areas of self-directed learning, proficiency in this study was defined as communicative competence, the ability to communicate with a native speaker in real-life situations. For this study a self evaluation instrument with a ten-point scale was used to assess learner competence. The cut-off point for communicative competence was judged to be a composite score of seven or above on a self-assessment scale (See Exhibit No. 14.1, following pages). Although proficiency measures obtained in this study through use of a self-assessment instrument are not to be equated with proficiency tests or evaluations done by native speaker observers, their use has been legitimated by the field of foreign and second languages (Jacobovitz, 1970; Painchaud and LeBlanc, 1980). In response to Brookfield's critique, a valid self-assessment instrument is more convincing than a simple assumption on the part of researchers that the learning was successful based on the word of the subjects alone.

Table 14.1: Description of the Sample

	American Born	Foreign Born
Valid cases	25	26
Mean age at the time learning began	24.9	21.9
Range	21 - 34	16 - 34
Females	11	9
Males	14	17
Years spent in the second language environment	4.7	6.7
Range	.5 - 20	1 - 20
Mean years of formal education completed	16	11
Range	BA - MA	0 - MA
Country of origin	United States	Southeast Asia 9 Latin America 12 Europe 5
Invalid cases	(0)	(7)

Exhibit 14.1: Communication Level Self-Appraisal Scale

Indicate the level at which you speak and understand the target language using the scale below to rate your communication level in each situation listed on the following page. As you go through the check list of social situations, you may want to question me about interpreting the scale or the situation. Rate yourself using the scale below from 1 to 10 for each of the situations described on the next page in which you have spoken the target language:

10---the only thing that distinguishes me from a native speaker in speed, vocabulary and accuracy is a slight or moderate accent.

9----I communicate with native speakers in this situation with complete confidence that I will understand everything and make myself understood.

8--

7----I am able to communicate well, but sometimes feel self-conscious because of my accent or from fear of making minor grammatical mistakes.

6--

5----I am able to satisfy basic communication needs in this situation, but cannot always say exactly what I want to for lack of the right word.

4--

3----I am able to communicate haltingly and frequently rely on help from my listeners.

2--

1----I am unable to communicate.

Note: Numbers without a description on the scale above should be used to indicate levels between those described.

Using the scale on the preceding page, rate your ability from 1 to 10 to communicate in the target language in each of the following situations:

_____a. socially defined situations such as weddings, funerals, birthdays, formal introductions, etc.

_____b. obtaining specific information about a purchase, a health problem, travel information, a money transaction.

_____c. idle conversation, small talk, bar conversation, etc.

_____d. serious conversation on a topic such as politics, culture, religion, the state of the economy.

_____e. informal social situations such as a dinner at the home of friends who are native speakers, dinner conversation in a family setting.

_____f. job specific situations such as describing your work to a colleague or supervisor.

_____g. reporting or narrating events that happened in the past such as historical or biographical anecdotes.

_____h. talking to a native speaker about numerical matters that might involve mathematical operations such as calculating the interest on a large sum.

_____i. conversing on the telephone.

_____j. writing a social letter to friends.

_____k. writing a business letter.

2. Did you at one time or do you now think in the target language? _____yes _____no.

3. Did you at one time or do you now speak the target language (check only one):

_____a. at all times including moments of relaxation?

_____b. at all times excluding moments of relaxation?

_____c. only outside of the home?

_____d. only while on the job?

4. Rate your pronunciation on a scale of 1 to 10 with 10 indicating near native ability. _____

An open-ended protocol was developed after the one used by Tough (1971). However, questions were tailored to the language learning process rather than to the learning process in general. Subjects were asked how they went about learning a second language following the protocol. Interviews were tape recorded and later transcribed verbatim. It was the transcripts which provided the principal data of analysis as is illustrated in Figure 14.1.

INDEXING	---------	Categorizing events, conditions and attitudes deemed important to the researcher.
UNDERLINING TRANSCRIPTS	---------	Identifying events, conditions and attitudes important to the researcher.
AUDIO PLAYBACK	---------	Filling in omissions,correcting misinterpretations, searching for further significance expressed by the subject.
NOTE TAKING	---------	Identifying events, conditions and attitudes deemed important to the subject.
INTERVIEWING ↑	---------	Questioning according to the conceptual orientation of the researcher, probing with follow-up questions.

Figure 14.1: Levels of Data Collection and Analysis from Interviewing to Indexing

FINDINGS AND CONCLUSIONS

Learners described themselves as dependent and autonomous at nearly every stage of their learning. First, consider the evidence of dependence or the opposite of self-direction. The majority of the learners interviewed either began their learning by enrolling in formal language programs or used hired tutors. Dependency for them was described as relying on a linguist or a teacher to structure and set the curriculum for their learning. The typical learner in this sample was seen to be unable to organize his or her own learning without some guidance from a resource person.

A number of learners reported experiencing cognitive and emotional resistance in this dependency relationship with a language expert because they felt pressured, felt reduced to the state of a child, or felt hostile towards the language expert. It would be no surprise to some of the critics of SDL that the learners who reported feelings of resistance to learning in this situation of dependency were American born, college graduates. Others, most notably Southeast Asians, showed no resistance to the dependency relationship with a language expert. Among some Asians the acceptance of a dependency relationship did not preclude autonomous efforts.

If autonomy or self-direction is defined as controlling one's own learning by deciding what to learn, how to learn it and what sequence to follow, then purely autonomous learners were not found. More often than not, autonomy in the learning process complemented learner dependency on a resource person. Some learners who were engaged in formal learning where all the planning was done for them, found ways to use self-directed strategies apart from the formal setting. This finding parallels that of Wenden (1981) who interviewed 25 adult second language learners who had lived in the U.S. for two years or less and who were enrolled part time in advanced level English classes at a New York University. She identified and described isolated self-directed strategies used by adult second language learners already engaged in formal classes where a relationship of learner dependency could be presumed.

There were other kinds of learners whose learning could be described as self-directing in the beginning of their second language learning experience. These self-directed learners either attempted to learn from books or simply became immersed in a second language environment through travel, immigration or migration. Some of these learners, both educated and undereducated, began their second language learning in work situations. However, they eventually found the need to either supplement their self-directed efforts with formal language classes or have recourse to an informal tutoring arrangement. The process at play here relates to the social dimension of which Chene (1983) alluded. Until the language learner receives confirming "feedback" from a social reference group, then, he or she has not yet "learned."

Manifestations of learner autonomy, then, were largely seen as learning on one's own without the assistance of a resource person or teacher. This type of self-direction could rarely be identified in isolation, with no admixture of dependency relationships with a language expert, a formal class, or a tutor.

Those who began their learning as autonomous learners (about 20% of the sample), could be subdivided into "active" and "passive" learners. The "passive" learners did not see themselves as engaging in learning at all, but rather as working and surviving in a foreign land. These learners resemble the Spear and Mocker (1984) sample who viewed their environments as providing the structure for their learning. In this study, the "passive" group was composed of largely migrant workers who learned English informally as a function of job or survival.

The more "active" self-directed learners, on the other hand, attempted various strategies such as acquiring books, viewing television programs in the target language, or observing people closely in real life situations. On the other hand, perhaps due to the nature of the volunteer sample, all but one of the active, autonomous learners eventually engaged in formal learning by paid instructors, even after as much as eight years of attempted self-directed learning. The one exception already possessed a graduate degree in linguistics, spoke a second language and was married to a native speaker of the target language which was to be her third language.

Other learners exhibited considerable autonomy in their learning even though they were engaged in structured language programs where a dependency relationship with language experts prevailed. They seemed to have a need to control their learning and were often uncomfortable in a formal setting. They satisfied this need to control the planning and structuring of their own learning by doing self-directed activities after class hours. These activities included the hiring of nonexpert tutors who would then be expected to follow the instructions of the learner. Examples of the use of nonexpert tutors include reading aloud to native speaker volunteers and practicing newly attained language skills with children who were native speakers. One learner reported an experience of controlling his own learning within the confines of a specific curriculum. Although the curriculum was pre-determined, it was competency based thus allowing the learner to test out of a determined level whenever he was ready. This arrangement made him feel as if he were in control of his own learning, even though he did not control the sequencing or the content. The above is an example, perhaps, of psychological control in contrast to pedagogical control (Long, 1988).

The findings related to learner dependency and autonomy can be summarized in the following statements:

1) the adult second language learners in this study exhibited learning behaviors that were both dependent and autonomous;

2) U.S. born adults of high occupational status resisted learning a second language in formal learning situations which involved a relationship of dependency with the language expert; and

3) there seemed to be no relationship between progress in learning and self-direction. On the contrary, those who were the most proficient speakers engaged in traditional learning where a dependency relationship to a native speaker tutor or an expert existed.

From the data of this study it may be concluded that there is no such thing as a purely autonomous adult second language learner. Data of the 51 interviews identified a pattern of successful adult second language learning. Successful learners began as dependent learners in formal, intensive language programs or in part-time tutorial relationships with friends or relatives in which the learner had little or no choice in what learning activities to engage in. Content, method and sequencing were all predetermined by the language expert or tutor. This first stage was followed by a long period (usually longer than the formal period) of informal, situational learning that was largely self-directed.

The theory proposed to explain the learning patterns evident in the 51 interviews already exists in the literature of lingustics. According to the "Monitor Theory" (Krashen, 1977), the learner first develops an inner monitor through formal, dependent learning. Only after this period of formal learning does the learner, through self-directed strategies over a longer period of time, develop an acceptable level of performance.

POSTSCRIPT

The findings of the 51 interviews conducted in 1981 were again scrutinized in the Spring and Summer of 1985 when this researcher was given the task of training four faculty members (ages 60, 58, 40 and 29) for work in developing countries by preparing them for an internship in Costa Rica. At that time, he used the Community Language Learning (CLL) method (Curran, 1976) in an intensive 12O-hour program. Using the CLL approach, a nonexpert, Colombian tutor was employed as a resource. Learners attended scheduled CLL learning activities approximately five days a week for six hours. Both the Colombian and the experimenter served as resource persons rather than as instructors in the traditional sense. Learners sat in a circle where they conversed with each other in English. For each English utterance they were immediately given the Spanish equivalent which they repeated to the group. Facilitators always stood behind the learners. Following this method, the learners always controlled the exercises or conversation or drill.

After engaging in the CLL learning activities for 120 hours, learners then travelled to Costa Rica where they attended a traditional audiolingual institute in which they spent another 12O hours in formal learning. Of interest here is that the Curran method assumed a large degree of self-direction in the pacing, sequencing and choice of content, whereas the method used in the Costa Rican institute did not. Months after that learning experience ended, informal, unrecorded anecdotal reports given to this researcher by the learners indicated negative reactions to the Costa Rican experience which was highly structured and teacher-controlled. Learners spoke of experiencing extreme frustration with their learning efforts in the Costa Rican Institute to the point of being reduced to tears on occasion. No measures of learning rates were available for comparison.

REFERENCES

Brookfield, S. (1984). Self-directed learning: A critical paradigm. Adult Education Quarterly, 35(2), 59-71.

Brookfield, S. (1986). Understanding and facilitating adult learning. San Francisco: Jossey-Bass.

Caffarella, R. and O'Donnell (1987). Self-directed adult learning: A critical paradigm revisited. Adult Education Quarterly, 37(4), 199-211.

Chene, A. (1983). The concept of autonomy in adult education: A philosophical discussion. Adult Education Quarterly, 34(1), 38-47.

Curran, C. (1976). Counseling-learning in second languages. Apple River, IL: Apple River Press.

Houle, C. (1961). The inquiring mind. Madison: University of Wisconsin Press.

Jacobovitz, L. (1970). Foreign language learning: A psycholinguistic analysis of the issues. Rowely, MA: Newbury House.

Krashen, S. (1977). The monitor model for adult second language performance. In M. Burt, H. Dulay & M. Finocchiaro (Eds.), Viewpoints on English as a second language. New York: Regents.

Kratz, R. (1978). The effects of programs which foster self-directed learning on the drop-out rate, the length of stay, and the preference for self-directed learning of adult basic education students. (Doctoral Dissertation, State University of New York at Albany, 1978) Dissertation Abstracts International, 39, 1263A.

Leean, C. and Sisco, B. (1981). Learning projects and self-planned learning efforts among under-educated adults in rural Vermont--Final Report. Washington, D.C.: National Institute of Education.

Long, H. (November, 1988). Psychological control in self-directed learning. Paper presented at the national conference of the American Association for Adult and Continuing Education, Tulsa, Oklahoma.

Oddi, L. (1987). Perspectives in self-directed learning. Adult Education Quarterly, 38(1), 21-31.

Painchaud, G. and LeBlanc, R. (May, 1980). L'auto evaluation: les cas des langues seconds. Proceedings of the 21st Adult Education Research Conference, Vancouver, British Columbia, pp. 157-162.

Shackelford, R. (1983). Self-directed learning projects among black adults in Havana, Florida (Doctoral Dissertation, The Florida State University, 1983). Dissertation Abstracts International, 44, 647A.

Smith, R. (1982). Learning how to learn. Chicago: Follett Publishing Company.

Spear, G. & Mocker, D. (1984). The organizing circumstance: Environmental determinants in self-directed learning. Adult Education Quarterly, 35(1), 1-1O.

Tough, A. (1971). The adult's learning projects: A fresh approach to theory and practice in adult learning. (Research in Education Series, No. 1). Toronto: Ontario Institute for Studies in Education.

Wenden, A. (1981). The process of self-directed learning: A study of adult language learners. Proceedings of the 15th Annual TESOL Conference, Detroit. (ERIC Document Reproduction Service No. ED 221 O65)

Chapter Fifteen

TOWARD A THEORY OF SELF-DIRECTED LEARNING: AN APPRAISAL OF GIBBONS' PRINCIPLES & STRATEGIES

Huey B. Long & Stephen K. Agyekum

Adult educators are often inclined to proceed with research and practice with limited consideration of previous research finding that might constructively inform their work. It appears that the investigation of self-directed learning conducted by Maurice Gibbons and his colleagues (1980) provides a good example of our failure to examine a particular research product in depth. The study conducted by Gibbons, et al., frequently has been cited, but the nature of citations and absence of critical consideration has limited the potential value of the work.

There are two major elements of the study by Gibbons, et al. that should attract the attention of adult educators. The first element of the investigation is the research methodology. The second part that should be noted concerns the findings and implications. It appears that the research design procedures have attracted much more attention than the results of the study. Therefore, the purpose of this investigation was two-fold. First, we were concerned with describing the use of the research conducted by Gibbons' et al. and secondly with examining selected principles and strategies for developing self-directed learning as suggested by the authors.

In order to address our objectives the paper is divided into the following sections: (a) a brief description of Gibbons' research is provided along with a listing of the fourteen "principles" the investigators identified, (b) a summary of the results of a review of how the research by Gibbons et al. is reported in adult education literature concerning self-direction is presented, and (c) some criticism of three selected principles is shared.

According to Gibbons, et al. their research was designed to obtain some answers to the question of "what are the principles of self-education and of teaching people to be self-educated" (p. 42). In order to obtain the answer to the above question a biographical analysis was conducted of "... people who became expert in a field which did not include formal training" (p. 44). Their initial list of possible subjects whose biographies were available consisted of more than 450 individuals. Next they constructed four different groups of subjects: entertainers; inventors, explorers and creators; people of letters, science and philosophy; and administrators, organizers and builders.

Eventually the researchers examined the biographies of twenty individuals who lived in the twentieth century. They read each biography searching for anything "which could possibly have influenced ... subject's lives and their becoming expert in their fields" (p. 45). For each of the items discovered a precise one-sentence summary was recorded on a card with the book title and page number. After six of the subjects had been studied, the cards were spread upon a table and the process of category building began. All investigators participated and eventually 154 categories representing distinctive features of the subject's nature, life or time were recorded. The following eight metacategories were developed:

1. Background (e.g. family, community personal history)
2. Subject's Personal Characteristics
3. Subject's Learning Methods
4. Subject's Relationship with Others
5. Conditions Under Which the Subject Lived
6. Key Incidents in the Subject's Life

7. Motives, Causes, Reasons behind the Subject's Behavior
8. Subject's Attitudes, Opinions, and Philosophy

(Gibbons, et al., 1980, p. 45)

A definition was written for each of the 154 categories.Then a seven point rating scale that included all categories was developed. Each of the categories was subsequently rated on the scale according to its perceived influence on the subject's becoming expert in his or her field. Numerical averages of the ratings for each of the categories for the twenty subjects were then placed in rank order. Gibbons and his colleagues list 40 items judged to be the most influential. The influential items as identified by Gibbons, et al. are available in their work and will not be listed here.

Following the presentation of the findings the authors provided a list of 14 "principles" of self-education. The principles are listed below:

1. In self-education the locus of control is in the self-educator whereas in formal education the locus of control is in institutions, their representatives, or their prescriptions. *Teaching for self-education involves helping students to internalize control over their own learning.*
2. Self-education is usually a concentrated effort in one field rather than a general study of many. *Teaching for self-education involves helping students to identify and become expert at the activity or activities that may become central in their lives.*
3. Self-education is usually applied education--learning for immediate application to a task, and from the practical experience involved in executing it. *Teaching for self-education involves integrating theoretical studies with*

technical training and practical application. It means learning for specific use now rather than learning for possible use years later.

4. Self-educators are self-motivated, that is, they are committed to achievement in the field of their choice, even when faced with difficulties. *Teaching for self-education involves helping students to generate their own drive toward their own goals rather than stimulating them to pursue goals set for them by others.*

5 Self-education is usually guided by a vision of accomplishment, recognition or rewards valued highly by the individual. *Teaching for self-education involves helping students to see themselves successfully experiencing very desirable attainments. It involves learning to plan an effective way of making that vision a reality.*

6. Self-educators tend to settle on the particular field in which their interest, talents, past experiences, and opportunities are combined. *Teaching for self-education involves patterns of exploration which enable students to try out a wide range of fields of activity.*

7. Self-educators tend to settle on the unique pattern of formal, informal and casual methods by which they learn best--drawing from such possibilities as study, observation, experience, courses, training, conversation, practice, trial and error, apprenticeship. productive activity, group interaction, events, and projects. *Teaching involve helping each student to develop a personal learning style.*

8. Self-education involves the development of attributes traditionally associated with people of character: integrity, self-discipline, perseverance, industriousness, altruism, sensitivity to others, and strong guiding

principles. *Teaching for self-education should promote, model, and reward the development of personal integrity rather than the opportunistic pursuit of offered rewards, of self-discipline rather than obedience, of inner drive rather than the avoidance of punishment or the pursuit of artificial rewards, of caring rather than sustained competition and of strong internalized principles rather than externally imposed rules.*

9. Self-education involves the development of attributes usually associated with self-directed and unique, even radical people: drive, independence of thought, nonconformity, originality, and talent. *Teaching for self-education involves promoting drive rather than passivity, independence rather than dependence, originality rather than conformity, and the talents that make individuals unique rather than the tasks that make them all act the same.*

10. Self-educators use reading and other process skills to gain access to the information and guidance they need for their projects. *Teaching for self-education involves training in the process skills, such as reading and remembering, especially at the moment students urgently need to gain access to information.*

11. Self-education emerges as a theme that runs through a number of important experiences in the person's youth; later experiences maintain and develop the theme until it becomes a conscious focus of choices in the person's life. *Teaching for self-education involves helping students to identify themes emerging in their lives, to build on those they choose, and to create new themes they desire.*

12. Self-education is best cultivated in a warm, supportive, coherent environment in which people generally are active and there is a close relationship with at least one other person. *Teaching for self-education involves creating an active environment in which a student's self-directed activities are warmly supported and there are many opportunities to form close working relationship.*
13. Self-educated people seem to like others and to be liked or admired by them; they seem to be healthy in attitude, body, and mind. *Teaching for self-education involves promoting a holistic approach to learning so that students not only master some knowledge or skill, but they also develop a healthy attitude toward themselves, others, the world and their activities.*
14. In addition to cultivating expertise, the characteristics described above outline a process of education suitable for the development of a mature personality, for achieving self-actualization and for the process of learning. *Teaching for self-education involves helping each student to become an expert, a participant, and a person.*(Gibbons, et al., 1980 p. 52-55)

USAGE IN THE LITERATURE

A computer search was conducted to identify articles or books, published since 1980, on adult self-directed learning that cited or referred to Gibbons, et al. In addition to the identified works other published research dealing with adult self-directed learning were examined. A total of seventeen items were identified and reviewed to determine exactly how Gibbons' research informed the content of the identified works.

Nine of the sources identified (Brookfield, 1984, 1985b, 1986; Hiemstra, 1988; Houle, 1984; Jarvis, 1983; Knowles, 1980; Long, 1983; and Smith, 1982) failed to include a reference to Gibbons, et al. As the book written by Knowles was published in 1980 it was probably at the printers well before the Gibbons article was published. Also Jarvis, Long, and Smith's works were well underway if not also already in manuscript stage. Thus, five of the nine authors had some realistic opportunity to refer to Gibbons' research. As the work by Brookfield (1985b) was more concerned with application it is surprising that Gibbons' study was ignored in that place.

Eight articles and books containing references to Gibbons, et al. were identified and reviewed (Boyd and Fales, 1983; Brockett, 1985a, Brockett, 1985b, Brockett, 1985 c; Brockett, Hiemstra and Penland, 1982; Brookfield, 1985a, Caffarella and O'Donnell, 1987, 1988). It is clear that few different authors are involved in the above publications. Brockett was author or co-author of three items and Cafferalla and O'Donnell authored two of the works.

The nature of the references to Gibbons, et al. as reported in the above works is surprisingly similar. The comments about the Gibbons research are limited, with one exception, to the research methodology. The references by Caffarella and O'Donnell are identical in their two publications, hence nothing new about Gibbons work was contributed from one publication to another. Brockett has made most frequent reference to Gibbons, et al. In his two independently authored articles he restricts his comments to research methodology and personal characteristics associated with self-directed learning. The article co-authored by Brockett, Hiemstra and Penland (1982) contains the only identified direct reference to the results, e.g. principles, of Gibbons' work. They note the following:

> From this initial study , Gibbons, et al. laid a foundation of principles that might contribute to a theory of self-directed learning. They suggest, in part, that self-education can help individuals assume control for their learning , undertake learning for specific use in the present, promote personal integrity, and develop expertise in an area while remaining open to exploring many fields of activity. (1982, p.174)

The eight articles identified and reviewed provide no criticism of the principles recommended by Gibbons et al, make no suggestions for testing them or for ways of applying them, and fail to attempt to relate them to any kind of theoretical framework. The lack of attention shown to the fourteen principles is shocking when one reviews the comments by Brookfield (1986) and others concerning the limited knowledge that adult educators have about how to develop or stimulate adult self-directed learning behavior.

Given the above conditions. Let us purpose to correct the oversight now. The next part of this paper examines three of the fourteen principles. Time and space will not allow us to examine others, however, it appears that a general impression of the principles is provided by the review of the first three principles.

PRINCIPLES

Gibbon's first three, principles are analyzed in the following paragraphs. The initial major criticism of the principles is noted here. It appears that the researchers made no attempt to distinguish between principles and strategies. In reality each of Gibbons' principles seem to consist of two parts: the principle and a strategy. In the published work the two parts are distinguished by regular type and italics. In the following analysis we make a formal distinction between the two parts and identify them accordingly.

The following procedures were used in the analysis. First, each of the three principles and strategies were examined to determine (a) their instructive value, e.g. are they overly broad and general, or are they too narrow and specific? and (b) what kinds of hypotheses flow from the principles or strategy statement?

Principle 1
In self-education the locus of control is in the self-educator, whereas, in formal education the locus of control is in institutions, their representatives, or their prescription.

The principle as stated is somewhat unwieldy. In reality two principles are presented. The first clause in the complex sentence states that the locus of control is in the self-educator. The second notes that in formal education the locus of control is in the institution, etc. If we take the sentence clauses independently we have a more workable analytical framework.

Problems with both clauses emerge from the definition of locus of control. Is control an all or nothing phenomena? or are there degrees of control? Secondly, formal education as represented in the principle is also an all or nothing situation, e.g., total control is indicated.

In essence it appears that the principle is overly complex and too broadly stated.

Strategy 1. Teaching for self-education involves helping students to internalize control over their own learning.

The strategy given is partly consistent with the principle. It is only partly consistent because of the implication in the principle that the locus of control in formal education is in the institution. If we accept the caveat noted previously that locus of control may be partial or exist in shared amount by the learner and the institution, then the strategy loses some of its contradictory character.

Yet the strategy, as expressed, may have limited value to the teacher who wishes to "help learners internalize control over their own learning." Greater specificity of how and why the strategy may be applied is required before we can move this strategy to the level of a tactic or technique.

Hypotheses. It is possible to develop some working hypotheses, based on the first principle and strategy, that might be tested. To do so, however, we must develop some operational definitions of key terms such as the following:

* Self-educator
* Locus of control
* Institution, representatives and prescription

An example of such an array of hypotheses, without defining the terms here would be as follows:

1. There is no difference in the locus of control of the self-educator and the non self-educator.
2. Locus of control can be developed by teachers through specific kinds of activities.
3. Locus of control can be measured in some activity in formal education.
4. Degrees of institutional locus of control can be changed.
5. Interaction exists between the degrees of locus of control manifested by learners and institutions.

Principle 2
Self-education is usually a concentrated effort in one field rather than a general study of many.

The above principle communicates, but once again it is a complex statement that needs to be divided into simpler parts.

It would best be stated as follows:

1. Self-education is usually a concentrated effort in one field.
2. Self-education does not usually include a general study of many fields.

The above simplification of the principle lends it to easier and perhaps more accurate testing. Once again, however, it is necessary for the terms to be defined. Key terms that must be operationally defined are as follows:

* Self-educator
* Concentrated effort
* One field
* General study of many fields.

Strategy 2. Teaching for self-education involves helping students to identify and become expert at the activity or activities that may become central in their lives.

The above strategy is consistent with the principle. Yet, even if the philosophical issues are ignored implementation of the strategy is less than direct and clear. How does a teacher help students to identify activities that may become central in their lives? The strategy as stated suggests that such activities are "programmed into the learner's genes and that teachers roles are like that of a miner. Somehow, the idea of developing interests and even picking and choosing among many interests is implied as being less than desirable.

Hypotheses. Several hypotheses could be designed to address the above principle.

1. There is no difference in the self-education of individuals involved in concentrated efforts of study in one field and those involved in the study of many fields.
2. Personality characteristics are associated with the proclivity to concentrate learning efforts and activities.
3. Concentrated learning effort is a learned behavior.
4. Concentrated learning behavior will emerge from student choice.

Principle 3
Self-education is usually applied education- learning for immediate application to a tasks, and from the practical experience in executing it.

Once again the principle is too complex for easy use. It could be simplified as follows:

1. Self-education is applied education
2. Self-education is enhanced or motivated by immediate application.
3. Self-education benefits from the practical experience in executing the learning.

Broken down into the above simple statement we have three principles that may help us to target our practice and research once we define the terms. Terms that need to be defined for both application and research are as follows:

* Self-education
* Applied education
* Immediate application
* Practical experience
* Executing learning

Strategy 3. Teaching for self-education involves integrating theoretical studies with technical training and practical application. It means learning for specific use now rather than learning for possible use years later.

The above strategy is perhaps the clearest and most informative of the previously identified strategies. Tactics, or procedures for integrating theoretical studies with technical training and practical application are not readily apparent, however. Furthermore, there is some question of what is theoretical and what is practical. Dewey (1983) indicates that the distinction between the two depends on the knowledge base of the individual. Thus, an individualized tactic is implied if the practical and theoretical vary according to individual.

Terms once again rise up to deter us. To proceed in an analysis and investigation of principle and strategy three we must arrive at some operational definitions. Some of the troublesome terms not previously noted are as follows:

* Immediate application
* Task
* Practical experience
* Execution
* Learning
* Integrating
* Theoretical studies
* Technical training
* Specific use
* Learning for possible use later

Hypotheses. Some hypotheses generated by the third principle and strategy are as follows:

1. Given an immediate learning task self-education will occur.
2. Self-education will not occur when learning is for later use.
3. Self-education is associated with experience involved in executing it.
4. Locus of control, e.g. self-education, will be developed and strengthened by integrating theoretical studies with technical training and practical application.

CONCLUSIONS

This paper was designed to (a) determine how the work of Gibbons et.al. had been reviewed and discussed in adult self-directed learning literature; (b) and to critically analyze three of the principles identified by Gibbons and his colleagues.

To accomplish the above objectives the research report of the Gibbons investigation was summarized. Then seventeen articles, books and chapters in adult self-directed learning were reviewed. Finally, the first three principles identified by Gibbons were critically analyzed.

Based on the procedures noted, the following conclusions are noted:

1. The article by Gibbons, et al. has not greatly influenced application processes in adult self-direction in learning. The work is most frequently cited to refer to the research methodology used rather than to findings.
2. Based on the analysis of the first three principles it is concluded that the principles have limited use in their current form. Further specification and precision in stating the principles is required.
3. The principles may be useful as a point of departure in analyzing other literature on developing self-directed learning among adults.
4. The principles may also be useful in stimulating the development of research designs that permit testing of specific hypotheses suggested by Gibbons, et al.

REFERENCES

Boyd, E. and Fales, A. (1983). Reflective learning-key to learning from experience. Journal of Humanistic Psychology, 23(2), 99, 117.

Brockett, R. (1985a). The relationship between self-directed learning readiness and life satisfaction among older adults. Adult Education Quarterly, 35(4), 210-219.

Brockett, R. (1985b). Methodological and substantive issues in the measurement of self-directed learning readiness. Adult Education Quarterly, 36(1), 15-24.

Brockett, R. (1985c). A response to Brookfield's critical paradigm of self-directed adult learning. Adult Education Quarterly, 36(1), 55-59.

Brockett, R., Hiemstra, R., and Penland, P. (1982). Self-directed learning. In Chester Klevins (Ed.), Materials and methods in adult and continuing education. Los Angeles: Klevens Publications, Inc.

Brookfield, S. (1984). Adult learners, adult education and the community. New York: Teachers College Press.

Brookfield, S. (1985a). Analyzing a critical paradigm of self-directed learning-A response. Adult Education Quarterly, 36(1), 60-64.

Brookfield, S. (Ed.) (1985b). Self-directed learning: From theory to practice. New Directions for Continuing Education Series. San Francisco: Jossey-Bass.

Brookfield, S. (1986). Understanding and facilitating adult learning. San Francisco: Jossey-Bass.

Caffarella, R. and O'Donnell, J. (1987). Self-directed adult learning--A critical paradigm revisited. Adult Education Quarterly, 37(4), 199-211.

Caffarella, R. and O'Donnell, J. (1988). Research in self-directed learning: Past, present and future trends. In Huey Long and Associates. Self-directed learning: Application and Theory. Athens, Georgia: Adult Education Department, University of Georgia.

Dewey, J. (1983). How we think: A restatement of the relation of reflective thinking in the educative process. Boston: Heath (original work published in 1933).

Gibbons, M., Bailey, A., Comeau, P., Schmuck, J., Seymour, S., Wallace, D. (1980). Toward a theory of self-directed learning: A study of experts without formal training. Journal of Humanistic Psychology, 20(2), 41-56.

Hiemstra, R. (1988). Self-directed learning: Individualizing instruction. In Huey B. Long and Associates. Self-directed learning: Application and practice. Athens, Georgia: Adult Education Department.

Heimstra, R.; Essman, E.; Henry, N.; and Palumbo, D. (1987). Computer assisted analysis of qualitative gerontological research. Educational Gerontology, 13, 417-426.

Houle, C. (1984). Patterns of learning. San Francisco: Jossey-Bass.

Jarvis, P. (1983). Adult and continuing education: Theory and practice. New York: Nichols Publishing Co.

Knowles, M. (1980). The modern practice of adult education: From pedagogy to andragogy. (Revised edition). New York: Cambridge, The Adult Education Company.

Long, H. (1983). Adult learning: Research and practice. New York: Cambridge.

Smith, R. (1982). Learning how to learn: Applied theory for adults. Chicago: Follett Publishing Co.